£6.15

THE
LIGHTHOUSE
KEEPER'S
WIFE

THE LIGHTHOUSE KEEPER'S WIFE

AN AUTOBIOGRAPHY
JEANETTE APLIN

To Jonny, Lissa and Timmi.

First published April 2001

Cape Catley Ltd
Ngataringa Road,
P O Box 32–622
Devonport, Auckland
New Zealand

Email cape.catley@xtra.co.nz

Typeset in Sabon 10/13.5

Designed and typeset by Kate Greenaway, Auckland
Cover by Christine Cathie Design, Auckland
Printed by Astra Print, Wellington

ISBN: 0-908561-87-3

Contents

Author's Note

This story constructed itself more than thirty years ago. It burned itself into my brain, awaiting its time to come to life. Finally, in September 1997, I tired of waiting for inspiration to kickstart me, and attended a five-day writers' workshop in Picton, run by writer-publisher, Chris Cole Catley. The first thing she asked of us was, "Write briefly what you want to gain from this workshop." Ten heads bent, ten pens scribbled on ten clean pages. I wrote that I had this lighthouse story and that I felt if it wasn't written soon it'd be lost. "It's cluttering up my mind . . . I feel I need 'permission' to either write it or banish it . . . yet I don't want to let this story go."

When my page came back to me I saw that Chris had scrawled across the bottom. "What *is* this story?"

Eventually my turn came to explain. "Well, you see, I was once a lighthouse keeper's wife . . ."

I saw that the word 'lighthouse' immediately lit a sort of romantic flame in the minds of the other people in the class, and the questions began. "What lighthouse? Why did you live there? For how long? Did you have children? Was it scary? It must have been so-o exciting . . ."

And Chris, the wise tutor, old enough to be the mother of most of us, said, "It is interesting and so typical of women as a whole that you say you need 'permission' to write this story . . ."

During the following five days, as I produced little pieces of what might one day become my book, it was as if Chris and my supportive classmates were giving me the 'permission' that I needed. By the end of the week, I was sure the time had come.

Over the next three years, Chris became first my mentor and eventually my friend. Each time I sent her a couple of chapters she read them and asked for more. Not every first-time author is this lucky.

Later I was invited to another workshop by a group of writers who met with Chris at Lorna Manson's place, Cockle Cove. People often assume that everyone in the Marlborough Sounds must know one another but the journey between Cockle Cove in Queen Charlotte Sound and my own home on D'Urville Island would take me the best part of a day and I knew I'd be away from home for several more.

At this workshop I arrived with a burn on my leg that wept and wept from beneath its huge Opsite dressing. I felt the eyes of my classmates upon it and knew that it needed explanation. I told them I'd fallen from my trailbike soon after leaving home and my leg had been scorched by the exhaust pipe. I had fallen from my bike because I'd been in a hurry and also because it was laden with two packs, a large one on the carrier and a smaller one on my back. These had made it awkward to steer around a washout about a metre deep.

"A metre deep?" someone queried.

"Well, er, nearly a metre. It's hardly a road. Just a steep dirt track. There's no vehicle access at all to our place. I was running late to catch the boat on the other side of D'Urville Island . . . One reason I was late was that the tide was high and I had to get my gear off to get around the beach. . ."

'You swam?"

"No, I waded, keeping my packs up out of the water. I should've noticed the state of the tide earlier and taken the long route around the hillside. But I was pushed for time because of the wild boar . . ."

"Wild boar?"

"Yes, my dogs got hold of it in the bush the night before. It was bedtime, really. I was giving them one last run before going away. I hate leaving them."

"Does someone look after them for you?"

"Yes, Sue does. She lives across the bay and comes around the beach to feed and exercise them."

"But tell us about the wild boar."

"Well, I took the dogs with me to pick up my bike. It was up the hill, about a thousand feet up, where I'd left it at the beginning of the muster on the farm next door. It was the muster and the shearing that made me so busy before I left home. . ."

"But the wild boar?"

"Well, it was the last straw. On the way down the hill the dogs were running behind the bike as usual and suddenly I saw it rooting on the side of the road. It was a big black one. I yelled at them to stay in behind but it was too late. They took off—I took off after them. . ."

I stopped for breath remembering the fearsome sounds: yapping and screeching and snarling and snapping, most of it coming from the angry boar. I'd blundered after them down into the dark bush in the gully, then rushed back to my bike and zoomed round the road to the next gully and then on foot into the bush again, then over the ridge, adding my own screams to the commotion. "Wayleggo, Quin! Git in behind, Trix!" There wasn't a man in the bay, Sue's husband and mine both working away from home. . .

The writers, all strangers to me and, as far as I knew, all from Wellington, were staring at this warrior woman and waiting for the rest of the story.

"Did you get the boar?" prompted one.

"Did you kill it?"

"Me, kill a boar? No fear. I just wanted to get close enough to call the dogs off before it ripped them up. It made me late home, that's all, and I was so revved up I couldn't sleep. That's why I was so disorganised in the morning."

I was a mouse woman after all, and the talk quickly turned back to the serious business of writing.

Later I said to Chris, "My book's going to be quite long. . . I'm still only halfway through part one—and I've already written eight chapters. There's so much to write about the first year at the lighthouse. Part two'll cover the last eight years. Of course it won't be eight times as long, but. . ."

Chris seemed to have no doubts. "My dear," she said, (rather grandly, I thought), "we shall just have to consider making it two books."

Two books! Whoah! One step at a time, please, I thought. This is one book (though I am now working on another). The story unfolds from the beginning. . .

With no electricity in our D'Urville Island house I had written so far by hand and often by lamplight, later typing it out on my old portable typewriter. I'd looked at the other writers' professional-looking manuscripts with envy and wondered if it might be possible for me to have a computer in a house with no electric power.

Over the next year, Pip, my husband, hunted out any computer that he could find and cleverly learnt its tricks. Then he bought me a Brother laptop, put a solar panel on the roof of our 'office' and a large battery below it. He soldered together dozens of tiny pieces of magic to make a panel for the wall and, for the first time, there were switches in our house and I had an electric light bulb hanging over my desk.

Next time at Cockle Cove I proudly reported that I, too, had entered the computer age. True, I had no instruction book and Pip had already left for the Auckland Islands to monitor albatross so I was having to work it all out for myself—but I simply knew that my book would go ahead in leaps and bounds from now on.

And it did, thanks to Pip's unfailing belief in me, his unflagging energy and support, his even temperament. But words aren't adequate to thank *him*. One of my single friends put it in a nutshell: "But you're so lucky to have *a Pip*."

I owe thanks, too, to many others: to Mick and Susan, and Rachel and Richard who listened to 'readings'; to Bruce Thomas who worked into the night with me to convert the disc of my manuscript on his state of the art computer; to my neighbours, Sue and Terry Savage, and Gillian and Guy King for their tolerance and practical help; to my friends who are dear to me but whom I dare not name for fear of missing out one of the many who cheered me on; and to those lighthouse people who appear in this book.

Last but not least, my love goes out to Helen and Fred who survived in spite of me and because of me and were irrevocably shaped and moulded by their early years on remote islands as children of the lighthouse.

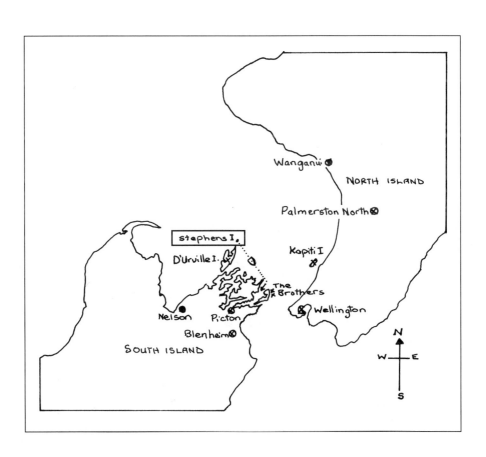

Wanganui ⊗

NORTH ISLAND

Palmerston North ⊗

Stephens I. ▪

D'Urville I.

Kapiti I.

The Brothers

Nelson ●

Picton

Wellington

Blenheim ⊗

SOUTH ISLAND

N
W — E
S

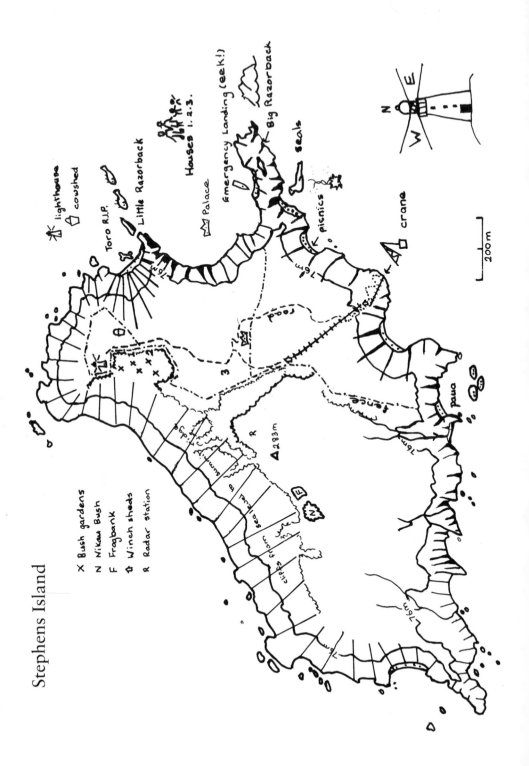

Stephens Island

X Bush gardens
N Nikau Bush
F Frogbank
⇧ Winch sheds
R Radar Station

lighthouse
cowshed
Toro R.I.P.
Little Razorback
Houses 1. 2. 3.
Palace
Emergency Landing (eek!)
Big Razorback
seals
picnics
crane
fence
paua
283m
cliffs from seal...

200m

CHAPTER 1

MARKING TIME

Pip left for the lighthouse without me. The taxi came for him, he kissed me goodbye outside my father's gate and then was driven away through the dark streets to Port Nelson. There he was to board the lighthouse tender, *Enterprise*, at midnight. We had deposited all our worldly possessions at the Mapua wharf, which was quite close to the orchards where we'd lived for the previous three years, and in the evening the *Enterprise* had called in there and everything we owned had been loaded into her hold. Now, after picking up Pip at Nelson, she would travel on through the night to Stephens Island—the place we'd soon be calling 'home'.

In the first light of the new day, while I lay in bed asleep, Pip would clamber on to a cargo net and be whirled up off the deck of the *Enterprise*, up and away above the heaving sea, and be dropped, by crane, onto the landing block at Stephens Island. This much I knew already. I'd been told about it and imagined it so many times. Now I stood at my father's gate and watched the red tail lights of the taxi until they disappeared.

As the little sister in my family I'd grown up well accustomed to being left behind. "How you used to bawl when we went off without you!" my older sisters had often reminded me, and I remembered doing that—clinging to a picket gate and howling out my lonesome outrage for all the world to hear.

Now Pip had set out on our adventure without me, and it was up to me to have our baby as quickly as possible so I could get out to Stephens Island myself. There was no point in howling at *this* gate, no matter how much like an abandoned child I felt, so I went back around the garden path and quietly let myself into the house.

I spoke into the dark gaping doorway of Dad's bedroom "He's gone.

Yes, everything's all right. Goodnight." I looked in on the little round face of our sleeping son, Fred, and then I took myself off to bed in the tiny slant-roofed room which had been mine throughout my teens.

Laboriously I arranged my hugely pregnant body among the humps and hollows of the lumpy mattress that I had slept on all through my childhood. Mum, with her penchant for saving and scrimping and making something out of nothing, had made this mattress herself. It was just a large, sacklike shape stuffed with snipped-up rags. Underneath it there was, now, a perfectly good innersprung but she'd believed the lumpy, homemade affair on top gave you warmth and "something to snuggle into".

I knew from long years of experience that no matter how carefully I made the bed in the morning, or how neatly I tried to smoothe the bedspread over it, it would always look as though a family of pigs had taken shelter beneath the covers. As a child I had burrowed happily around, making a nest, but in the four years I'd been away from home I'd grown used to sleeping on the smooth, sleek strength of our modern 'Sleepwell' with the 'Vono' base. With my belly so swollen and distorted it was hard enough, on the best of beds, to get comfortable. My arms seemed to get in the way and they felt as if they were joined to the wrong parts of my body. Some women manage to remain relatively elegant and trim throughout pregnancy but I wasn't one of these. At six months I had already looked and felt as if I'd swallowed a weaner pig, and now it had obviously grown to be a full-sized porker—a very energetic animal which frequently dug its snout and trotters into my belly.

As I tossed and wiggled beneath the blankets my mind was as reluctant to rest as my body. I felt again Pip's last affectionate kisses and the warmth of his arms and saw myself forlornly watching the tail lights of the taxi, just two little red eyes blinking out of sight where the road grew steeper.

Surely this baby couldn't be too far away. This afternoon the doctor had said, "Two weeks, at least," but he could be wrong. Maybe this one would be early. Fred had been late, (two weeks overdue and nine pounds two ounces. A good strong baby!) so this one would probably follow the same pattern. But maybe I'd had the dates wrong for Fred (I was never regular). Maybe I'd be in and out of that maternity ward in no time at all!

However much I tried to convince myself, deep in my heart I knew that this baby would also be a latecomer and that Pip would be waiting at the lighthouse, getting deeper and deeper into the new life and having all the fun without me. Even if the birth was tomorrow I'd have to stay in hospital for several days. When Fred was born I'd been 'let out' early because it was Christmas. On Christmas morning, instead of wheeling the wrapped-up babies into the ward on trolleys as usual, the nurses had pranced in carrying as many as they could hold in their arms and on each tiny head had been a red crepe paper hat with a tuft on top and all of us mothers had burst out laughing because they'd looked so cute and elfin, and were no longer just rows of hot dogs wrapped up in bread on a trolley.

Because Fred and I were both strong and healthy—and it *was* Christmas, after all – 'the sister' had allowed us to go home that afternoon, only nine days after the birth, even though two weeks was the official length of stay for new mothers and their babies. But nearly two years had passed since then and ideas were changing rapidly. This time I wouldn't be a new mother. As an old hand I might be let out even earlier, and then I could get out to Stephens Island within another week, but that would be a month away at the very least.

A month! By then I'd be used to this lumpy old bed again! But maybe Dad and I could take this awful old top mattress to the dump. Then I saw my mother patiently snipping fragments of material into tiny pieces smaller than a fingernail. When dressmaking she'd used every bit of fabric, large squares for making quilts, irregular scraps for patchwork, and the small, useless bits (which were not useless at all) were the ones she'd snipped into the equivalent of cotton waste for stuffing.

I decided I'd have to put up with the lumpy mattress and stared around me into the gloom of the little bedroom, half expecting to perceive a ghostly presence. If Mum were anywhere, now, it would surely be here in this house where she'd spent the last eight years of her life—especially that long, bad year of her final illness, but nothing moved. I saw and heard nothing extraordinary at all, and I turned for comfort to the idea that maybe she was already reincarnated inside my body, for it had happened in the right order, Mum's dying and then my pregnancy soon after. Reassuring as this idea was, however, I had to reject it because, through and through, I was Mum's daughter and she'd been a woman with her feet firmly planted on the ground, actually often up to her knees and elbows in good, rich compost—no artificial fertilisers for her!

Once or twice she had threatened to 'come back and haunt' us but that had been funny. Her password for opening the secret doors of life was 'commonsense' (closely followed by 'compost'). Yes, above all else, we must have commonsense. I'd need plenty of that when I finally got to the lighthouse. I'd be like a real pioneering woman, and—if Mum could only look down and see me, I'd make her so proud!

Nelson's sunny October days flowed easily into summer. It was a new experience for me to live with Dad without the presence of another adult. I cooked and cleaned and toddled about in the garden with Fred beside me—I with my ever-growing belly making me waddle like a mother duck.

Neighbours I'd known for years called to me over the fence or popped in for five minutes to chat. Most of them were curious and interested to hear about the lighthouse and, like ourselves, few of them had ever heard of Stephens Island even though it was one of the many blue humps actually visible on the horizon from further around the bay. Pip and I had had to delve into dusty corners of the library to find out about our new home. Now I answered people's queries like an expert although it was two weeks before I could hand out first-hand information because there was no telephone linking Stephens Island to the mainland, and maildays were only once a fortnight.

The first thing most people remarked on was my continuing presence in the street, and I'd answer as serenely as possible.

"Hullo, Mr Cook. Yes, I'm still in one piece. It can't be long now. No, the doctor says it's not twins but it might still be another week."

"Yes thank you, Mrs Hobbs, I'm feeling really well. I got a letter from Pip today and he's settled in nicely. Yes, he says the tuataras are great gadgets and there's one living at the back door that he's trying to tame."

"Hullo, Mr Morris. Yes, I heard from Pip and he arrived safely. No, he said it was a piece of cake going up on the crane but he says the

The lighthouse station from the air. Number 3 house is hidden behind the ridge. Cape Jackson is on the horizon.

Left: Working the crane.

Below: Number 3 house with The Palace beyond.

The box ready to descend on *Enterprise's* deck.

Left: Down the very steep trolley rails to the landing.

Below: North from the landing, the Big Razorback.

Perfect impression – a gecko discards its skin.

A tuatara carries off a large weta.

A male tuatara emerges from its burrow.

Top: A rare Stephens Island frog, but photographed later, in 1971.

Top right: Fairy prions, or dovies.

Left: A skink makes off with a large weta.

Above right: The tiny miracle of ground weta hatching.

motor nearly shakes off its mountings. Yes, he went up on a cargo net. No, no, they have some sort of box for the families to go up in, but really I'd rather go up on the net myself. . . oh, no, of course not, not with the babies. . ."

"Aunty Alice, we were only joking about tuatara egg omelettes! They're a protected species. Yes, they're like big lizards and there're all sorts of other interesting things out there—rare frogs, big wetas, and millions of sea birds. . . Yes, I always have liked bugs and things. They don't frighten me at all and I just can't wait to see everything."

"I can't wait. I can't wait." But I *had* to wait and find something to keep me occupied. Before long the neglected interior of Dad's house was as clean and shiny as a doctor's clinic. I was most industrious. Mum hadn't been a great housekeeper. She hadn't worried much if there were fly spots on the ceiling and clutter on the unused end of the kitchen table. It was a couple of years since she'd been her real old cheerful self, my good old Mum, so there was plenty of cleaning for me to get stuck into, purging my soul some might say, for there are some who believe that fanatical housekeeping is symbolic of deeper things such as loads of guilt and sin to be expunged. Well, I didn't have overly much on my conscience at that stage but I had time on my hands and it wasn't guilt that I tried to scour away out of that house. It was the memory of Mum's illness. I could feel the cancer that had stalked both her and her nearest neighbour (a younger woman) and had killed them both within a few weeks of each other. Its menace lurked in every backyard waiting to strike again, and I wondered how my father could so calmly carry on with his normal life.

Dad was already seventy years old and he had his routine. I fitted my life around his. Every morning he rose at six and lit the fire which he'd laid the previous evening, then he made himself a brew of tea. He heated the pot, measured in the tea leaves, poured in the freshly boiled water and he left it to draw while he toasted a thick slice of bread. Fred, still in soggy nappies and pyjamas, stood beside him peeping into the firebox and watching the bread toasting on the brass fork. He waited while Dad spread it with butter and Marmite and divided it into four, then he scrambled onto a chair so he could have a finger for himself. They ate like companions, conversing lopsidedly, Dad murmuring and Fred chirping. This ritual flashed me back to my own beginnings in a different house—the music of Dad's teaspoon stirring sugar into his early morning cup, Mum sipping her tea in the bedroom and myself standing at Dad's elbow, sniffing the toast and Marmite and waiting for my share.

I saw the bond between Fred and Dad grow stronger by the day and sometimes my over-fertile imagination conjured up a cosy but frightening picture. If something awful should happen to Pip I could live like this, here in Nelson, forever with Dad, Fred and the baby. And at that thought, I shivered as though someone walked over my grave, as if the reality of my life could now be little more than standing, each morning, beneath the revolving clothesline, pegging out the freshly washed clothes and nappies with Dad's garden flourishing around us and the modest, working-class homes of the neighbours scrambling up the hillsides on either side of Emano Street.

From the little valley it was only a mile into the heart of Nelson, and each Friday Dad delivered me to the doctor's surgery for what I hoped would be my last antenatal check-up.

I was as familiar with that surgery as I was with our own home for I had started work there as a seventeen-year-old school leaver. I had spent two years answering the telephone, shuffling record cards and keeping accounts. I'd dusted the furniture, sterilized instruments, scrubbed the wooden doorstep, cleaned the brass name plate and arranged flowers in the waiting room. I'd juggled appointments, helped old people fill in their claim forms and absorbed a fascinating array of information about the secret troubles of ordinary mortals. I'd also surreptitiously acquired most of my sex education from the book the doctor lent out, slipped into a plain brown paper bag, to couples who were 'having problems'. Now, because I'd come to trust and respect him, I had chosen my former employer, Chips Woods, to be 'my' doctor and I felt safe in the knowledge that he did his best for his patients albeit at considerable expense to his own family life.

On the fifth Friday, which simply *had* to be the last, the end of my appointment coincided with his afternoon tea break, and, after going to the back of the stately old house to say hello to his wife, I suddenly hurried back to him.

"What about a dose of castor oil?" I asked. "Would that work?"

He carefully packed his pipe with aromatic tobacco of his own blending, clenched it between strong teeth, lit it with a few puffs and a single match and inhaled. Relaxed, at last, in that first sweet swirl of smoke, he took the pipe from his mouth and said, "It can't do any harm. It's definitely full term now. . . But a baby comes when it's ready." He paused, sucking on his pipe again, and I waited for some further grave pronouncement. "You'd better hold on until after ten o'clock tomorrow night because it's my annual fishing trip to French Pass. . . " His face wore a pleased expression as he contemplated this rare event. I knew how seldom he had the opportunity to be away from his responsibilities, even for one day. It was, indeed, a once-yearly occasion. I also knew that I wouldn't care whether he was back from his fishing trip or not—or whether all the doctors in town were away on a fishing trip together—because he had given me the approval I needed and I was going to have this baby at last!

I had got this idea from the neighbours who, growing tired of merely asking after my health, had begun to offer advice. And this was it. I knew this was it!

On the way from the surgery to my father's house I called in on the friendly corner chemist to whom I once used to deliver prescriptions when going home from work. "I'll have a small bottle of castor oil, please," I said politely, straight-faced.

He laughed as he handed it over. "It won't work, you know."

I felt myself flushing and grinning foolishly. Then he said kindly, "Have you heard from that man of yours again?"

"Yes, he's getting tired of waiting for me. Every time he gives his weather report to Wellington Radio he waits for a telegram from me, and all they say is, 'Weather received and we have nothing for you.'"

"Ah, well, can't be long now," the chemist sympathised. "One and ninepence, thanks."

As I fished around in my leather purse, sorting out a shilling, a sixpence and a threepence, he said, "Remember, just drop us a quick note if you need anything sent out to that lighthouse."

Beside me at the counter was an elderly lady whom I recognised as an old patient from my days as a doctor's receptionist. "That's the stuff," she said, nodding at my bottle of castor oil and eyeing my belly. "That'll do the trick." Then she dug into a paper bag she was holding and handed Fred a sweet shaped like a plane.

"See, it's an aeroplane," I told him. Then, because it didn't look much like anything, really, I made flying motions with my hand and said, "Whooo oo oo. Whooo oo oo," and as I waddled from the shop, I felt elated, as though I were embarking on an adventure with the good wishes of friends ringing in my ears.

Fred flew the plane about in the air. "Oo oo oo," he went. He was still holding it in his hand after we'd crossed the road and started up the hill. "You can eat it, Fred," I laughed, catching his hand and nibbling a corner off one bright pink gelatinous wing to demonstrate. "It's a lolly."

"Lol," he chirped, tasting it for himself. "Lol!" he said again in surprise and stuffed the whole thing into his mouth at once. Although he'd previously had liquorice and chocolate this was his first lolly, ever, and in spite of feeling that my mother was looking disapprovingly down at us, I refrained from telling him that it would likely rot his tiny teeth right out of his head.

That night, after easing my bulk into the bath, I contemplated the little bottle apprehensively. The label was reassuringly simple. "Tasteless Castor Oil. A mild and speedy cathartic for adults and children," then the dose rate, nothing more. Well, who knows about these old wives' tales, I thought, raising the bottle and sucking out about two tablespoons of its gluggy contents—probably with more courage than accuracy.

The word 'cathartic' was new to me but, that night, I learnt its meaning. Compared with that old childhood laxative, California Syrup of Figs, which had clearly been designed for curly haired cherubs like those in its advertisements, this stuff was for hardened sinners and, by morning, I was thoroughly purged of everything—except the baby. Under the circumstances I hardly dared believe that the desperate dragging feelings in my abdomen were anything more than a reaction to the castor oil's mean assault on my intestines, so I said nothing to Dad who went, every Saturday, to the rifle range for an all-day 'shoot'. But this morning he was reluctant to leave me. Perhaps he'd been disturbed by my nocturnal activity, although he was certainly far too modest to mention such a thing.

Finally I shooed him from the house. "No, no. There's nothing to worry about. I'll be still here when you come back tonight."

The day dawdled along slowly for me. Saturday voices wafted in from the street, morning faded into noon, and the bed in the porch grew warm in the sun. I felt the need to lie down on it, and puffed my way through contractions while Fred bounced about beside me, quite delighted at having me play a new kind of game. I kept reminding myself that when he had been born I had been in and out of hospital for three days before he finally arrived and no way did I want to go through that performance again. I'd heard of women giving birth alone but there were neighbours all around if things got desperate.

I was relieved when Dad returned at six o'clock, but, determined there would be no false alarms with this confinement, I said as casually as I could, "I think we might have to get going after tea."

He had already noticed our bags at the door, a little overnight bag for myself and a suitcase ready to go with Fred to the friends who were to care for him. "I'll take you now," he said.

"No, after tea will be fine. I'm just going to boil us some eggs." So we had a light meal of toast and soft-boiled eggs which would remain in my memory forever because of the effort it cost me to act naturally. Then Dad drove me the short distance to the hospital and left immediately to deliver Fred to our friends who lived an hour's journey away.

At that time Nelson Hospital was considered to be quite innovative. It had been one of the first to allow fathers into the delivery room and Pip had been present at Fred's birth. This time, however, I was among strangers. There wasn't even anyone pacing the corridor on my behalf, but I didn't care, and I certainly didn't wait for the doctor to return from his fishing trip. By the time he bustled in, his swarthy face flushed from a day in the sun, a locum had supervised the delivery, the baby had already been whisked away to the nursery and a helpful nurse had dispatched a telegram for me. It was to be transmitted to the lighthouse at six a.m. by the New Zealand Coastal Radio Station. It began, "Happy birthday, darling. . . " because I had managed to produce our daughter on Pip's twenty-fifth birthday—a feat of which I felt inordinately proud.

CHAPTER 2

To the Lighthouse

U sually lighthouse personnel travelled to Stephens Island on
the good ship *Enterprise*. Every second Tuesday, at 4.00 a.m., she
left Picton with her cargo of mail and supplies for the island, a journey
which, on a good day, took five hours. Private visitors also generally
chose to go this way and stayed as guests of the keepers until the
Enterprise returned a fortnight later; but there was another route and
this was from French Pass township by private launch. Compared with
the free trip on the *Enterprise*, it was a costly alternative but it was the
one often chosen by maintenance staff from Nelson and by people
making quick, official visits. Because of our new baby, the Marine
Department, which was the god of the lighthouse service, had agreed
that if we could get to French Pass township by road, it would finance
our launch trip from there to Stephens Island. This journey would be
easily accomplished in one day whereas the usual one on the *Enterprise*
necessitated an overnight stay in Picton.

I stood in front of the French Pass garage, (just a workshop with
a couple of bowsers in front), and looked out onto a bright bay specked
with distant islands. I clasped the baby, now ten days old, in my arms.
Fred stood at my side and Dad, who'd driven us all the way in his tiny
van, had gone up to the house above the garage looking for someone to
sell him petrol. At last I was on the brink of the new life, knowing for
sure, now, that we'd be a real lighthouse family, and feeling that life
would never again be mundane or boring. Already, that day, the tortuous
road we'd travelled from Rai Valley had made it seem that we'd entered
a different world.

So this is where the doctor came for his fishing trip, I thought. There
wasn't much to the village; just a few houses, the garage, an old, old
shop and a big old-fashioned boarding house all tucked into a little bay

at the end of a long peninsula. I'd known of French Pass, itself, for some years, ever since the newspapers had reported a man and dinghy missing there and Mum had said, "It's a bad place, full of strong currents and whirlpools big enough to suck a small boat down—and it may never be seen again."

It was the route taken in the old days by passenger boats travelling from Nelson to Wellington and Mum had told me something about a dolphin, Pelorus Jack, which had followed the ships. She'd talked as if there had been something supernatural, almost mythical, about it but I couldn't remember, now, what she'd said.

I could hear Dad speaking to a woman as they came down a path to the garage. He was asking her about the best place to park his van and telling her proudly of our destination. Then I was horrified to hear him almost begging for a cup of tea and a place for us to rest as we waited for the launch. But the woman rose to the occasion.

"Stephens Island lighthouse!" she exclaimed, peeping at the baby's tiny face. "Away out there! You *are* brave!" And, before we knew it, we were ensconced in the comfort of her kitchen, Dad with his cup of tea and I nursing the baby.

The woman, Paula, stood ironing her family's clothes; a tall, handsome figure deftly smoothing creases from the gathers and ruffles of a cluster of bright little dresses. She made us feel welcome by asking us questions and telling us of her own transition from town to country life; how they had come to the French Pass settlement and built their house and garage six years before—just at the time the road was put through—and how isolated it had seemed, but not nearly so much as Stephens Island, itself.

"Oh, I do think you're brave," she said again. And, with sudden foreboding, I squirmed and clutched the sleeping infant closer to me and my eyes followed Fred who was toddling about quietly inspecting new territory.

If I were being brave, then there must be something to be afraid of. I had wanted adventure and excitement and I had hoped that I'd be strong and courageous, and I knew that I would rejoice in those wild, inhospitable lighthouse landscapes. For the past six months I had lived on my imagination. I'd dreamed that ships in storms and drowning sailors and ancient bones on barren beaches would all be just a part of our everyday lives. Our children would run barefoot and free with windblown hair and they'd find strange sea creatures thrown up by the tide. My head had been full of such romantic notions, but, now that the reality was close, the word 'brave' hung in the room, full of connotations of danger and risk.

Suddenly I felt irresponsible and foolhardy and wondered if we were doing the right thing. I remembered back to our interview in Wellington when we'd been instructed to pack everything we owned into strong wooden boxes. Just any old box wasn't good enough for the lighthouse service. There were regulations—and for good reasons. If we struck a rough trip we might have to claim from insurance; therefore, we must list everything in a notebook. We must buy one especially for the purpose. It would be used again and again as we shifted from station to station. All boxes must be strongly braced; they must have wooden lids well screwed down, good strong metal or rope handles on the sides and neat paintwork. Mattresses were to be folded and wrapped in plastic before being sewn into sacking covers.

Dad had spent the winter searching for good solid boxes. And Pip, who was a builder by trade, had rebuilt and braced and screwed and fitted them with handles and lids. I had given each one three coats of paint and printed 'M.J.APLIN. STEPHENS ISLAND LIGHTHOUSE' lovingly on its lid. There'd been boxes of all sizes and shapes, including a wooden crate for our chooks, and all were impressively strong.

These preparations had, quite literally, forecast stormy seas ahead. Many people had warned us direly of perils that might be waiting for us, (and particularly for the children), but we had laughed at their fears and privately called them "a bunch of old fuddy duddies!" Then, (and this was something much more threatening), during the week I had spent in the maternity ward, one of the mothers—the older one who lay in the corner regaling us with tales of her daughter's constipation and her husband's late circumcision, and who sighed theatrically and said that love was just an animal passion at any rate, and who whispered behind her hand quite a lot—said to me one day, "Perhaps I shouldn't tell you this, but you're better to know these things beforehand. There was a baby born last month, to a family over the bay at Farewell Spit, and when they got it home to the lighthouse it died!"

Other women had heard the same story but they hastened to assure me there must have been something wrong with the baby, or maybe it had been the plane ride to the Spit that had harmed it.

Of course I'd been much too sensible to show concern at the story. I'd ignored the little chill I'd felt deep down inside me. It was a tale far removed from the security of the maternity ward where all of us, dressed in our pretty bed jackets and dressing gowns, languished on our beds at the expense of the State and I'd refused to be worried.

Now, in Paula's kitchen, again ignoring that nasty little chill, I said with more honesty than she probably realised, "I'm not very brave at all!" Always I'd wanted to be fearless but had feared I was well short of the mark, and feared even the day that I'd be tested.

There was reassurance and strength in every line of Paula's body. "Well, now," she said, "It's not everybody takes a new baby out to Stephens Island."

"Where *is* Stephens Island?" I asked, peering out through the french doors of her dining-room.

"It's well out of sight," she said. "Right out past all the other islands and to the left. You'll see the boat coming across from D'Urville Island long before it gets here."

D'Urville Island was so big it looked like part of the mainland. Beyond the near point on the left, its partly wooded hills stretched many miles into the distance, and no premonition or sixth sense warned me of its future importance in my life. At that moment I was sure that the lighthouse was my destiny.

Dad, who was really quite an old-timer, loved to talk about the good old days. "D'Urville Island," he said affectionately. "I felled bush there in the twenties—over a year in the camp there. There were two gangs of us. The others were mainly Maori—mostly Elkington boys. Strong fellows, all Mormons, and they made, aw, wonderful bread. . . all in the camp oven but no salt in it—no salt!"

"Well, isn't that interesting," Paula said. "This Turi, who's coming from the island to pick you up, will be one of them."

Dad continued his reminiscing. He was a bushman from way back but he'd been on a war pension since before I was born and this all seemed to me like ancient history. I began thinking that Paula would be sick of us hanging around. Then, to make matters worse, he started telling her how keen I was on tramping and the outdoors and how, if anybody would make a go of living on a lighthouse, it would be me. Good old Dad! Always so openly proud of his daughters. How I wished he'd shut up.

But Paula was a generous-hearted woman. "I can see that you'll love it," she said to me. "And there's Turi's boat, now. You can just see it." And, after spending some time searching the distance, I, too, perceived a tiny dot growing slowly larger as it came toward us from far up the coast of D'Urville Island.

In later years I would meet lighthouse keepers' wives whose initiation into the service was by way of storm, sea sickness and chaos, but ours was a chosen day. The only ripples on the sea were those made by the thirty-five-foot launch, *Belfast*, as she came smoothly alongside the wharf. After introducing themselves to each other, Dad and Turi Elkington talked as if they were old friends. Turi was younger than Dad by about fifteen years or perhaps fewer—his smooth face bore few age lines—but he remembered the bush felling gangs and he said that Dad would be welcome to make the journey with us on the *Belfast* that day.

Our luggage, which included cartons of vegetables from Dad's garden and all the usual kind of baby paraphernalia, was quickly stashed away in the hold and I sat serenely on deck leaning against the guard rails, soothed by the sound of the motor and the quiet yarning of the two men. If I'd taken part in their conversation I might have acquired some local knowledge as we slid easily up D'Urville Island's eastern coast, but largely I was absorbed in amusing my infants and in happy contemplation of the imminent reunion of our little family.

Somewhere we made a call into a bay to deliver bulging sacks to three urchins in a broken dinghy, and, like a tourist, I watched them curiously. Straight, sun-blond hair fell about above their eyes and they looked salty and dry-skinned with strong, rough little hands sticking out from the frayed sleeves of shrunken jerseys. They spoke matter-of-factly, in country voices, man to man with Turi, and they handled their boat as casually as town boys would their bikes. I sensed that these boys were a different breed from myself and my own tidy little toddler, and, dressed as I was in pale blue skirt and white cardigan, I suddenly felt conspicuously over-civilised. I wondered if my upbringing would ever allow me or my children to look as much at ease in our new environment as these boys did in theirs.

There were few signs of habitation on D'Urville Island. We passed miles of bush and scrub-clad hills with the occasional homestead tucked into a sheltered bay. Towards the north, steep farmland was still green with the flush of spring.

There had been a smattering of islands on our right but after about two hours we completely left the shelter of land to cross Stephens Passage. There, although the sea was still calm, I rummaged in my bag for warm clothing. The afternoon was wearing on and the sun had lost its heat. Nothing indicated to me that, at other times, the water around us could be tumultuous with fierce tidal rips. Although I saw broken water and dark clusters of rocks to the west in the passage, my eyes were riveted on the crouching silhouette of our destination.

By now the men had fallen silent, and, in the carry-cot beside me, the tiny face worked, puckered and gave a strangled cry. Fred was pointing and repeating hopefully, "Dadda, Dadda," and soon we were abreast of the south-western extremity of Stephens Island—a sheer wall of rock, in deep shade, rearing up about two hundred feet from the sea. After that, we passed several inaccessible coves, each backed by vertical cliffs and tussock-topped bluffs. Everything looked high, dark, sheer and totally inhospitable, yet I felt the power of the place reaching out to me and I hadn't the slightest doubt that we were on our way home.

Our eyes were all now focused on one object, the thing we had heard so much about, the apparatus for lifting us from boat to island— the crane! It stuck up from the base of a promontory about thirty or forty feet above the tide. We came closer and closer, passing now quite a nice beach where the steep tussock came right to sea level without the usual cliffs. With the engine idling, Turi swung himself down into the hold and heaved up our gear, Dad taking it from him and stacking it on one side of the deck. I lifted the baby gently from the carry-cot and wrapped her in her delicate white shawl. I wound it around and around, swaddling her safely so that only her nose and eyes could be seen. Then I passed her to Dad while I gathered together my day-bags. Jiggling his little bundle up and down, Dad drew Fred to him and pointed up at the crane which stood on top of a concrete pillar rooted in the rock-face itself. In spite of the smooth surface of the sea, the water swelled slowly up and down the wall of barnacles below.

The boom of the crane swung around, and, suspended from it by a single thread, was a square box. Standing in this box, head and shoulders above its white walls, was a familiar, bearded figure grinning down at us. Fred watched uncertainly as the box halted ten feet or so above the water.

"Who's that there?" prompted Dad. "You know who that is." Fred stared intently.

"Gidday, Fred," called the figure cheerfully.

And, suddenly, from deep down in his tummy, Fred laughed his funny rumbling laugh. "Ha ha ha! Ha ha ha!"

By this time Turi had expertly manoeuvered the boat underneath and the box descended accurately and with hardly a thud onto the deck. Dad, quickly abandoning his grandfatherly role, was there to help as Pip deftly unclipped the metal rings from the great iron hook. The boat pulled away from the dark proximity of the rock face and, out in the sunshine again, described a slow circle.

Pip sprang from the box onto the deck, shaking hands first with Turi, then with Dad. "Good to see you, Jim," he said. "It'll be a long trip back home for you." Now that Dad had caught sight of 'our' island he'd be turning around and going back with Turi. He said he thought perhaps he'd spend the night at the old boarding house at French Pass before driving home.

Every one was beaming and I gave Dad an awkward little hug. In our family, once my sisters and I had reached the age of about five, kissing and hugging had become obsolete. It was considered to be 'sloppy stuff' and only Grandma had dared to plant unwelcome wet kisses on our cheeks. Now, feeling the roughness of Dad's woollen sports coat under my arm and the sandpaper warmth of his creased cheek against mine, I choked a little.

"Thanks, Dad. Thanks for everything. You look after yourself and we'll see you at Christmas."

He looked into my face in his direct way—he had such kindly wrinkles around his eyes, "Yes," he said. "You'll be all right here with Pip, now." Then he bent down, gentlemanlike, and said goodbye to Fred. He was such a decent man, my dad, and I was momentarily jolted by a guilt-ridden vision of how empty his life might be without us.

As the boat came, once more, beneath the boom of the crane our family climbed into the box. We crouched down inside it so that our heads were out of the way of the wire ropes and it was a peculiarly safe feeling to be packed into such a small space with my dearest family and to be able to see only ourselves and the sky above. Dad caught the dangling hook and latched it onto the rings on the wire ropes above our heads. His face looked down at us with a last goodbye. Then the sky turned above us and we rose toward it.

The safe feeling quickly evaporated. What if the cable should break? Would the box sink or would it float? Would we tumble out or go down like a stone? My ever cautious mind began working out the best strategy for extracting myself and the babies from the box if we fell and became trapped at the bottom of the ocean. But I thought I had heard that the cable and crane were regularly checked and officially certified as safe, and, realising that my imagination was simply up to its usual tricks, I made sure that my face was a mask of nonchalance because, as Pip had written in his letter, it was all "just a piece of cake".

"Up we go-o-o," I crooned to Fred. "Round and rou. . ." and there we were, already bumped gently down onto the landing.

A big, boyish fellow with hefty arms leaned over us to unhook the iron rings. He laid the wire ropes down each side of the box and we scrambled quickly out. "Thanks, Dave. This is Dave," Pip said. "But let's get up away from the block."

"Hullo, Dave," I said, looking about me. I saw the heavy hook swing away from above his head and I saw the crane standing on its pillar with its motor running and a man working the gears. I saw that it was linked to the land by nothing but a skinny bridge with pipe handrails. Behind the bridge, I saw a sturdy trolley resting at the foot of a set of railway tracks. It was empty and waiting. I saw that the so-called 'block' was a concrete pad built into a cavity in the rock. Wire rope threaded through rusty stanchions fenced off only part of the seaward side of it. I saw the sea, quite a long way down below, and it looked dark and deep. In front of me, a short flight of waterworn steps led upwards and I sensed that the block was a place of work—of men's work. It was men's territory. It was not a place for women and children to linger. I felt Pip propelling me towards the narrow steps, and, still tightly clutching the baby, I fairly scampered up them out of harm's way with Pip and Fred following closely behind.

So here I was. It was November 1966. I was twenty-three years old and all primed up for the Grace Darling lifestyle. I'd landed, at last, on the remote and rocky island. There hadn't been a raging sea and I hadn't had to be brave and I hadn't even caught a glimpse of the lighthouse. So far, it hadn't been anything like the stereotyped pictures many of us carry in our heads of a tower welded onto a rock with tempestuous waves breaking against the door. In fact, the lighthouse was totally out of sight. It was situated miles away on the far side of the island and, like the houses, themselves, it was six hundred feet above sea level.

Of course I had known what to expect and I knew that, in New Zealand, people didn't actually live inside lighthouses. There would be no round rooms and curved furniture for us. I was perfectly aware that we'd be living in a normal house and that Grace Darling, the English heroine whose portrait had hung in my grandma's bach, (presiding, like the image of Christ, over our holidays at 'the bay'), had belonged to a different place and earlier, tougher times.

I knew that our family wouldn't be alone in the lighthouse life, for New Zealand lightstations were allotted staff according to their remoteness and difficulty of access, all of which was presumed to affect the workload of the keepers. Stephens Island was, therefore, a 'three-man' light because it was considered to be one of the most difficult to run. Pip's official title here was 'second assistant'; Dave, whom I'd just met, was 'first assistant' and the man driving the crane would be the 'principal keeper'. Although it was called a three-man station, each man, of course, had dependents—always a wife and usually children—and, although we had been looking forward to a life of freedom, I knew we'd also be part of a tiny, tight community within which each of us would have to function as harmoniously as possible. Not only that, we would also be subject to the hundreds of rules and regulations laid down by the Marine Department.

I had understood all this and not found it a worry. Now, in the process of landing, I had felt the reality of it. The men were working as a team. At this very moment, Dave and the principal keeper were busy sending down a canvas sling, in which to winch up our belongings. There was smooth co-ordination and a feeling of discipline. Now, in the rocky alcove at the top of the steps, I met a small, expectant cluster of people—the wives and children of the other two keepers. This meant that the entire population was there, at the landing, to welcome me. With Pip grinning and introducing us all to each other, I was like a little fish that had been lost in the wide ocean, finally swimming back into the safety of the shoal. The lone heroine image vanished from the back of my mind and I felt the allegiance of the group even as I was introduced to each individual—two wives and four children. I was already one of them and I could tell that I was being accepted by them without question.

I even felt quite comfortable in my pale blue skirt, for the other women and children were very tidy. Cis, the wife of the principal keeper, was radiant in a flame-coloured shift. Her serious-faced son, Anthony, stood beside her, his stubble of dark hair a mere painted sweep over his scalp. Cis was a Maori, dark-featured and wavy-haired. With easy courtesy she reached out a shapely arm to Fred and was soon hearing the unintelligible, staccato tale of our day's journey. Dave's wife, Peggy, had three children sheltering in the folds of her cotton skirt. She was pale-skinned and slender and welcomed me with a few matter-of-fact phrases. Then she ran one hand self-consciously through her rampant red hair, saying, "It's time it had a cut."

Several people had warned me that I mustn't 'let myself go to seed' out on the lighthouses (as if I would) and I knew, now, that with women like Peggy and Cis for neighbours, there'd be no danger of my standards slipping.

Next, everyone turned their attention to the baby. Looking proudly into her eyes for the first time, Pip said, "Hullo, Helen. She looks just like Fred. I s'pose all babies look the same," whereupon three female voices chorused sternly, "No, they don't!"

"But she does look the same as Fred did," I added. "At the hospital there wasn't any doubt about who she belonged to, even though they forgot to give her a name bracelet."

"Well, she's a pretty good birthday present," Pip said, plucking at the shawl. "Has she got arms and legs? Here, you check her out, Peggy. I'd better go back and help Dave with the gear."

Peggy lowered Helen down so that the four silent children could make her acquaintance.

Anthony, who was about ten years old, said politely, "She's very little," and Geoffrey, Alison and Dean smiled but said nothing.

Looking down at the sea, I suddenly saw the *Belfast* motoring away into the distance with Dad waving from the stern. I waved frantically in reply and, at the same time, there was unexpected silence as the sound of the crane's motor died. Then its driver bounded across the narrow bridge and up the steps, with one hand already outstretched.

"Arne," he said. "And you and the little ones are well?" His speech was slow and foreign with a pleasantly harsh accent, and, knowing that he was principal keeper, and that, on station, his word was law, I appraised his rough-hewn face hopefully. Like his wife, he was about forty years old and rather dignified. There was something about him, a sort of rugged dependability that made it seem that he was akin to the rocky cliffs themselves. With some relief, I felt that he was a man I could trust.

Pip and Dave, who had been stacking my gear onto the trolley, now joined us and the last leg of my journey was about to begin.

Arne went ahead, followed by Anthony. Arne, with his long angular legs, loped up the steep zigzag path which was carved out of the rock. His son's bare brown legs churned in his wake. The rest of us gathered ourselves together and everyone said, in spite of my protests, that I definitely was not allowed to carry the baby. Dave strode off with her tucked like a little bundle of rags under one huge arm, leaving us all to follow.

"Hey, slow down, Dave!" Peggy finally yelled. He waited, passed Helen to Cis and hoisted his small son, Dean, onto his shoulders. Pip did the same with Fred and we made better progress.

Everyone kept asking me if I was okay as if I'd been ill, and I said of course I was all right, brusquely brushing off their kindness. I hadn't been for a good walk in weeks and I found I was enjoying myself. It was two hundred vertical feet up to the level area below the first winch shed, and, having arrived before us, Arne was up in the shed with the motor running and the trolley crawling up the steep incline below.

"That's called the Lister shed," I was told, "because it's got a Lister engine. The trolley's turned there, on that turntable, and pushed along to this one. Then it goes right up to the Ruston shed at the top."

"And the Ruston's got a Ruston engine," Dave said.

I'd never have guessed! All engines were the same to me. I squinted upward, far up, to where I could see a little bit of a building in the distance.

Thank goodness we're forbidden to ride on this thing, I thought. Then I pulled Fred along to watch the trolley as it crept up onto the first turntable.

He was entranced by anything with wheels and, holding my hand tightly, he gave an intelligent commentary. "Wuk. Wuk. Der, Mumma. Wuk. Wuk."

The other children also stood quietly with their mothers, (they certainly weren't an unruly bunch), and we watched Dave and Pip push the trolley along to the second turntable, line it up with the rails above, and secure it to the wire cable, ready to be hauled up to the Ruston shed when they'd finally got up to that height themselves. After this we climbed up the track past the Lister shed until we came to a rough sort of road.

Pip said, "The taxi's waiting just around the corner past Charing Cross." Charing Cross was up ahead of us, a cutting in the rock where the rails passed overhead and someone had scrawled its name on one of the supports, *Charing Cross*. I tried to think where the real cross existed—was it in London? Or Sydney? And then I saw that there really was a taxi, parked on the other side, where the road was less steep. It was a little yellow crawler tractor with a large wooden trailer on behind.

Helen had been passed around from one to the other and, now, she was quietly, but more and more definitely, telling us that it was more than four hours since she'd been fed at French Pass. Cis, who obviously loved babies and small children, crooned, "Ooh, little one, you'll be up in your new home in no time at all," then she began to sing to her.

Peggy, Dave, Pip and the children climbed into the trailer. I followed and sat beside Pip who had Fred between his outstretched legs. Cis passed Helen to me and climbed in herself. Arne, sitting on the tractor, warmed up the engine and cranked it into gear.

"Sit down properly, Geoffrey. Put your legs out in front of you, Alison." The parents were stern. We sat with our backs against the high sides of the trailer, our feet meeting in the middle, then the little crawler began rattling and clanking up the earth road.

The dewy chill of late afternoon already lay in the gully and the air smelled strangely like dirt and damp birdcages. Across from us the steep slope, almost bare of grass, was pitted with hundreds of black holes about the size of rabbit burrows.

"Tuataras?" I asked Pip.

"Some," he said, "but mostly birds."

"What sort?" I asked.

"Dovies. They're sea birds. They come in at night."

"I can't wait to see one," I said.

Someone answered, "You'll see them, all right. Wait until tonight." The others laughed. It had almost sounded like a threat.

The road climbed around the hillside, through a gentler, greener landscape now, and sheep with lambs afoot grazed in the basin below us.

Our own sheep, I thought. One-third of them were ours. There was a system on light-stations which governed the ownership of farm animals. The outgoing keeper sold his animals to the incoming keeper for five pounds per cow and ten shillings per sheep—regardless of market prices elsewhere in the country. Officially this station carried one hundred sheep and one milking cow per keeper—regardless of actual numbers. So Pip and I were now the proud owners of a flock of sheep and a cow. We were farmers! I thought happily of the wooden butter churn and the cream separator we'd managed to purchase from a neighbour before leaving the orchard district.

When I was young, Dad had milked a cow and churned the cream into butter in just such a wooden churn and I was thrilled to be returning to such a rustic lifestyle. It seemed that Stephens Island, and the lighthouse service in general, had everything I could wish for. It was exciting and rugged, yet it was peaceful and countrified, and, of course, it had the sea. It sprawled out below us like a clean, white blanket, fading into a fine-weather haze over the North Island, and I was quite sure I could never want anything different or better than this—never in the rest of my life.

I stopped musing because we were passing huge water tanks and a white barracks-type building.

Pip said, "The Palace!" He'd written of The Palace and, though he'd said it was used mainly for storage, I'd ridiculously expected it to look rather more like its name—grander. It was an old navy building; a relic from the war. A useful legacy, no doubt.

Above this, a level road wound around the island from skyline to skyline. Our own house was tucked out of sight just around the corner, and the Ruston winch shed was silhouetted on the ridge in the other direction.

Up on the level, at last, the crawler came to a stop. "This is where we get out," Pip said.

And Arne said almost apologetically, "Dave and I will take the tractor and go to the winch shed to bring up your luggage. It's only a little distance for you to walk from here."

We scrambled out of the trailer and the tractor rattled off. Within a few paces, we'd turned the corner. "Here we are," Pip said. And there was our home, perched above the road, in a shallow gully where the hillsides weren't too awfully steep. There was a sprawl of low trees on the bank behind it and a wire fence separated it from the grazed pasture of the hills. Higher up, the island was capped with low bush, but, below, the gully grew steeper and steeper.

Like The Palace, the house had white weatherboard walls and a red corrugated iron roof. It was quite alone and I liked the way it sat there all by itself. The other keepers' houses, and the lighthouse and all the rest of the buildings, were out of sight nearly half a mile further to the north.

On the road below the gate we stopped. "Thanks for coming down to the block with us," Pip said.

"Of course we wouldn't dream of not coming," Cis said. "You'll be wanting to be on your own tonight but we'll have you around for a meal as soon as you're properly settled."

"Thanks," I said. "That sounds great. Say 'goodbye' to everyone, Freddy."

"Bye," Fred said, obligingly, in his clear little voice. "Bye, bye." It was the one word he could enunciate perfectly. He stood waving and they all looked back and waved as people do to little children.

"Bye, Fred," called Alison, suddenly not so shy now that she was safely distant. Then they slipped out of sight around the near corner.

At last our family was alone. We were watched only by the cluster of lichen-covered boulders which lay about on the ridge above the road like big domestic animals. Pip, who wasn't insensitive but not publicly demonstrative, now stretched his arms around us. "It's been a long time," he said.

I could have stood, thus enveloped, forever, but Helen had other ideas. The motion of the uphill journey had distracted her from her hunger for a while, but this moment of stillness was all too much.

"Ah ah. . . " Pip said. "It sounds like she's at the end of her tether. We'd better get you all home." Up the steep gravelly track we walked, past the corrugated iron coal bunker at the wooden gate and around the house to the back entrance. Here, Pip bent and untied his bootlaces.

"Around here, everyone takes off their shoes before going inside. I think it's the same on all stations. . . I've had the fire going hot and there's a roast in the oven. It's a real house, lovey, much better than any of the others we've been in." He dashed ahead of me through the large, concrete-floored porch. I kicked off my white leather jandals, approached the door, and, on peering through the internal window into the kitchen, was just in time to see him swiftly gathering up newspapers which he had spread across the floor to keep it absolutely gleaming and spotless until the moment of our arrival.

I felt overwhelmed. Not only did we, at last, have a 'real' house, but I had a man who really cared about me as well.

It was as though the house, itself, had been waiting for us. Pip's proud smile, the polished surfaces, the smell of roasting mutton, all drew us into its central warmth. Our voices echoed in the moderately furnished and, as yet, uncurtained rooms, and, suddenly overpowering all else and quite beyond ignoring, rose the full-throated screams of our starving daughter.

The new life had begun.

Above: Pip and I. "Four new tyres for the Landrover" sparkle on my finger.

Left: At the wedding, with my parents Jim and Clova Kerr.

Pip

Mac

Tramping trip 1963.
Left: Pip, myself, Dave Massam, Mac. Right: Pip, Dave Massam, Mac.

Pip and his mother, Frances Aplin, with Fred and Helen.

My sisters Paul (left) and Barb.

Pip and I, Fred and Helen.

CHAPTER 3

Into the Night

In the living room we knelt on the red vinyl seat of the rather ugly settee, peering through the fly-screen of the single sash window. Below us the shadow of the island, which had briefly floated, dreamlike, in the air, had joined the deeper shades of dusk which had spread across the sea. I knew that the sun had sunk, at last, on the far side of the island; and in Tasman Bay, beyond, it would have disappeared as usual behind Nelson's familiar mountains.

I looked down at the darkening gully which fell away steeply below us. It ended in mid-air, with the cliffs and shore out of sight beneath. Just east of this, a huge rock outcrop jutted up from below, perhaps two hundred and fifty feet. It was a solid, jagged formation, eerie in the twilight.

"That's the Big Razorback," Pip said.

"It reminds me of something pre-historic," I said.

"Yeah, like a giant tuatara."

"Waiting to gobble us up. . . Do they bite?" I asked.

"Not unless you grab them. Then they try. The others say that once a tuatara latches on to you its jaws lock up and it won't let go. . . "

As I digested this information Pip went back to contemplating the Big Razorback. "You can get down there," he said. "That's the emergency landing."

"Down there!" I shivered, looking at the sheer walls. I'd always been hopelessly chicken-hearted on heights. I'd despised myself for this and tried to overcome my fear by putting myself, over and over again, into situations that people like Pip took for granted, but which turned me into a quaking idiot. I had improved, but not much.

"How do you get down there?" I asked, keeping my voice even.

"There's a track down this side. It's not too bad."

A track? I knew what some of Pip's 'tracks' were like. I should have known that landing by crane, here, was the easy way and there was bound to be some nightmare alternative for emergencies when the crane wasn't an option.

At this moment Helen gave a cry and we both stole over to admire her. I was glad to have my thoughts temporarily diverted from the emergency landing.

"Do you like her name?" I asked anxiously. I'd been so sure that our second baby would be another boy that we hadn't even discussed girls' names before Pip had departed for the lighthouse and when the time had come for me to register her birth before leaving the mainland, I had had no name to give her and no idea of Pip's preferences. I could have sent a telegram with a list of likely names to him via the coastal radio and awaited his reply, but I hadn't thought of that.

However I had remembered his telling me, once, about a special girl whom he'd got to know in some tramping club or other before he had met me. I was sure she must have been ravishingly beautiful and brave and. . . At any rate, though that was just a flight of my jealous imagination, I remembered, very clearly, her name, Helen.

Helen! I'd known, without a doubt, that this would be a good choice for our daughter because Pip would be bound to approve.

Now he repeated her name. "Helen. Yeah, it's pretty good."

"I knew you'd like it," I said. "I named her after that Helen you told me about once."

"What Helen?" asked Pip.

"You know. The one you used to like in that other tramping club."

"Oh, her," he said vaguely, looking away.

I looked at him suspiciously. Had there been such a girl or had he invented the story to show he'd 'been around a bit' before he met me?

"You made her up!" I accused. "You told me a fib!"

"Did I?" he answered sheepishly.

In my mind, my guess became a certainty. "Yes, I can tell, now. It was a lie. . . "

"But I do like the name, though," he said.

It wasn't a cuddly settee. It looked as though it could have withstood a horde of children for half a century with no ill effects, but, now, with our arms around each other, it seemed a pretty comfortable place to sit waiting for the night.

At first it crept in with tranquillity and stealth, but soon birds came flocking in from the sea. Through the open window, their cries echoed from the hillsides; strange cries, the like of which I'd never heard before, cooing "gook-a-look-gook, coo-coo-coo-cook," and rattling laughter.

I was impatient to go outside but Pip said, "Wait until things really get going." He wanted to be able to take me to the door and say, "Voila!" And there would be the miracle.

We sat there, in the dark, by choice because we were reluctant to spoil the evening's magic by flooding the room with light. The houses and the lighthouse were powered by three diesel generators which were used in weekly rotation; the old days of candles and kerosene lamps were well past.

A little earlier, I'd been startled when the loud bleat of alarm bells had resounded through the house.

"Is that normal?" I'd called to Pip.

"It's just the alarms," he'd called back. "Arne's down at the lighthouse turning on the light."

"Oh." Busily unpacking my bags, I'd had other things to think about. But as darkness enveloped the room, I listened to the curious sounds about me: the belching of the hot water cylinder behind the stove, the maniacal orchestra outside.

"Those alarms," I said. "What were they all about?"

"They're tested every evening and we keep our ears tuned to make sure they ring in the houses." Pip's curly hair brushed my chin. "I can hear your heart," he murmured.

"You mean I've got to listen for them?"

"Mmm—you soon get used to it."

"But what if I don't hear them? What if they don't ring?"

"If they don't ring, we try to fix them. If we can't get them going, one of us has to keep watch all night."

"Keep watch? You watch for ships—in case they bang into the rocks? What good would watching them do?"

Pip gave up on my heart. In the darkness his voice held a smile. "No, we don't watch the ships. We watch the lighthouse and the radio beacon to make sure they're still doing their job. Normally the alarms are on watch for us so we can sleep all night. If there's any sort of malfunction they ring and wake us up."

"Clever things, aren't they!" I said.

"They make life easier," Pip replied. "In the old days the keepers kept watch every night."

Our conversation and the strange cacophony of birds' voices were interrupted by a resounding, loud 'bong-g', as if someone had plucked at the string of a giant guitar just outside the house. I jumped. "What was that?"

"Just a dovie hitting the wire," Pip said. "Come on. It must be time to go and see my big tuatara. I hope he's out tonight."

The concrete path and rocky banks at the back door were flooded with light coming from a bulb on the corner of the house. Pip regularly left this light on at night to bring the moths around for his 'friend'. Now, there he was! My first tuatara, only a couple of yards away from the door. He stood sturdily upright on his four lizard legs, his head high, obviously ready for action.

"He's a big male," Pip said proudly as though it was his own creation.

Big? His body and head together were about the size of my forearm from wrist to elbow but for a "big male" I thought he was disappointingly small. In my imagination tuatara had had the proportions of fearsome little dragons at least big enough to make me nervous but, if I'd felt inclined, I could have grabbed this one with one hand.

· "Is that the biggest you've seen?" I asked.

"Yeah, they don't grow much bigger than that. The males are bigger than the females and they have a bigger crest."

I crouched down in front of the big tuatara and looked into one of his scale-framed, old-gold eyes. It was a jewel in an aged and time-worn face. "He looks old!" I whispered. "How long do they live?"

"Maybe a hundred. Some say more. Nobody knows."

The tuatara and I remained motionless. There wasn't anything threatening or sinister about him. Instead, he had an indefinable quality, something I sensed as an aura—almost, I could call it, charisma. I was mesmerised by those jewel eyes. With frilly necklaces of gold layered within them, they were bright as gems between creases of dusty brown leather. And, somehow, they seemed as expressionless as gems as he stood with hardly a flicker of movement and let me peruse him. Along his spine was an erect, tooth-like crest; on his flank, treebark skin; and on his belly, snake scales in a mosaic of white and gray. A jointed stick of a tail tapered out behind and he looked ancient and passionless, neither good nor evil, but as though he came from an era when joy and sorrow didn't exist. I had been told that, two hundred million years ago, reptiles virtually identical to this had walked the earth, but I had difficulty with such unimaginable aeons of time. I'd also been told that tuatara were living relics of a dinosaur species, and this I had no trouble in understanding at all.

Finally an awareness of my intense scrutiny must have penetrated the big tuatara's ancient reptilian brain and he scuttled, in speedy but clockwork jerks, to his drain behind the house.

"I dunno what he does when it rains," Pip said, and, for months to come, his diary faithfully recorded the coming and going of this big male tuatara because it turned out that the drain was not his only dwelling.

"Gook-a-gook, coo-coo-cook"—the combined calls of birds, far and near, reminded me of distant cheering from a children's sports day. From the bush further up the hill came cackles, shrieks and wails. Pip turned off the light at the house and we entered the darkness flashing our torches, first to the ground to avoid walking on other tuatara (which we found up the steps, on the banks and in the grass,) and then into the sky. It was alive with the dove-like shapes of fairy prions. They swooped erratically, jaggedly, as though they had no idea of direction, seeming to land just anywhere and yet, presumably, they knew where they were going or they would never have been able to find their home burrows. They were uncountable; hyperactive in the air, yet awkward and shuffling on the ground, which didn't seem surprising to me considering the freedom they enjoyed out in the great wide world of air and ocean, perhaps without touching land for weeks at a time. I remembered back to when I was a child and how hard and strange the ground had felt under my feet when I had got down off my rope swing beneath the wattle tree— after a mere half hour, or so, of being suspended in the air.

I could see why the fairy prions were nicknamed 'dovies'. They were gentle-looking, nicely proportioned little birds, their plumage soft blue-grey above and white beneath. I held one in my cupped hands and felt its rubbery little blue feet kneading my palms. It seemed a trifle confused but not afraid. Pip said these birds never really tried to dart away from people, and, I could see, they didn't seem to panic when they were handled. It was as if we, with our flashing torches, were just another small part of that confusing earth-world onto which they had descended; toward which they had probably navigated not by sight alone, but by using other senses that we sight-dependent mortals couldn't comprehend. It struck me that to crawl into the damp darkness of an earthen tunnel, (which was more than likely to be inhabited by a carnivorous pre-historic reptile), was a very strange thing for these pretty little ocean-going birds to do.

With our torches switched off we stood beside the tangled ngaio trees on the bank above the house. Looking up at the sky, I thought I'd never seen so many stars. I listened to the nattering of the birds, their crash landings through the trees and the scuffling sounds about our feet. I had never experienced anything like this. It was as though I could see the thread of time stretching back through the ages, with this island and its reptiles and birds enduring forever.

Pip said softly, "It's a real night-time place."

My eyes and ears were wide open straining to catch the many different sensations. Somewhere in the branches overhead, I heard a familiar sound a little like the scratching of two pieces of dry bark against each other. "Hear the weta?" I whispered.

"That funny little scritch-scratch noise," Pip said. "You like your wetas, don't you!"

I shone my torch in the direction of the sound, hoping to catch a glimpse of the big, brown, cricket-like insect, but saw only the cracked grey bark and shining leaves of the ngaio and taupata trees. "I used to keep them in a glass case by my bed when I was a kid."

"You told me!" Pip said. "There's enough wetas out here to fill our whole coal bunker. Arne and Cis say the giant variety is as big as an egg."

"As big as an egg! Gosh!"

"Yes, but it's quite rare, and it lives in the grass, not in trees."

"Do the tuataras eat them?" I asked.

"Yeah, wetas and beetles—anything like that, but my big fella likes little bits of raw meat as well."

We made our way down past Pip's garden—a very small plot

sheltered by a low wall of corrugated iron. In it were the plants he'd brought with him to the island: tomatoes, lettuce, and cabbages—all standing up bravely, beaded with dew and showing good growth, but with a few gaps where the wind had already claimed its first victims. "But they were too close together," Pip said. "I should have planted some of them up in the top garden."

This was only the house garden. In the bush, about five minutes' climb up the hill, there were several plots, well hidden and sheltered from the wind. I thought it would be strange to have gardens so far from the kitchen, but wonderful, too, because it was such a Robinson Crusoe-y sort of idea.

Down the steps, our torchlights illuminated the white walls of the house, and a small tuatara, with much softer and more mottled-looking skin, had taken the place of the big fellow at the door. It wiggled away quickly at our approach and Pip said, "That one'll be a female. It's got hardly any crest."

The distant cheering of the birds' voices seemed to have eased a little, or perhaps we'd grown used to them. As we left the canopy of stars and entered the porch, I saw that it was dimly lit by shafts of light escaping from beneath the kerosene refrigerator. Earlier I'd packed the belly of this great creature full of vegetables and I'd found that, inside, it looked much the same as any other older type of fridge, but Pip had given it such an ominous character reference that I wondered what lay ahead.

"She's a cranky old girl and she's got a few tricks up her sleeve!" he'd said.

Beside 'her' was a bench where the cream separator, wooden butter churn and shiny milk bucket were arranged in old-time country-dairy style. I shone my torch onto them and they reflected back a beam of pure nostalgia, sweet as a stream of milk fresh from the cow.

Then we opened the door into the house itself and warmth billowed out. Pip flicked a switch and it was as though I'd emerged from a dark theatre after being immersed in a movie. I had to remind myself that the fantasy was still being enacted—but it was reality, and we were the intruders—the aliens.

CHAPTER 4

The Real House

S itting up in bed at five o'clock in the morning, I watched the new light of my first day come pricking through the fly-screen of our bedroom window. I'd woken to hear the last, demented cries of the birds as they departed the island before daybreak and soon the first rays of sun brushed the silver sea with pink. It tinted the white curve of my full breast and lit up the downy head of the helpless little human being who so rhythmically and hungrily suckled there.

As I nursed her the tired paint on the walls of the stark, underlit bedroom took on a rosy hue. In the room next door I could hear the dampers of the stove rattling and the kettle whistling because Pip was already up and dressed. Soon the aroma of coffee mingled with that of smoke and Pip joined me on the bed, his face lit by the sunlight flaming up across the sea.

Arne had given him the day off which meant he had to do no official work or routine duties. After he had milked the cow he'd have the whole day in which to tell me more about the things he'd done and learnt in the six weeks we'd been apart. He said that anything he didn't yet know was bound to be in the *Lighthouse Keepers' Manual*, a fat volume which lay beside the hairbrushes on top of the painted chest of drawers. It held all the regulations governing life on a light-station. It covered everything that anyone could possibly have an argument or an enquiry about, right down to minor details of general life such as housekeeping—yes, the housekeeping standards of the wives, not just lighthouse keeping itself.

Pip leaned back against the bed-head, sipping his coffee. "In the old days," he said, "the principal keeper used to come into your house and run his finger over the ledges looking for dust."

"What!" I gave such a squawk of outrage that the baby momentarily stopped sucking. "How do you know they did that?"

"Arne told me. It wasn't very long ago. He remembers it."

After contemplating this for a while I said I thought the Marine Department sounded far too strict—not just strict, but nosy.

"Well," said Pip, "those blokes in the office are miles away. Mostly it's just commonsense and so long as we get our job done properly there's no problem."

"But there's Arne," I said. "What about him?"

"He's good value. Quite a strait-laced bloke in some ways, but sometimes he surprises you."

"He looks quite stern."

"Yeah, but he's all right. He can get really wild at times and he gets fed up with the guys in Head Office. A lot of those old-fashioned rules are a hangover from the navy. Besides, the whole manual's being rewritten."

"Is that why they couldn't give us a copy of our own before we got here?" Manuals were automatically handed out to intending lighthouse keepers but there hadn't been one available for us. I had found it very disappointing.

"It's out of print, now," Pip said. "At any rate, Arne just goes his own way. That's how we come to run a generator here, all day and every day. He doesn't see why we can't have power in our houses all the time."

"So we do have power all through the day?" I asked, surprised because we'd definitely been told, at our interview, that this wouldn't be the case.

"Yeah, the rules say the generators are mainly for running the lighthouse and can be run for only a few hours each morning so you can get your washing done and things like that. But Arne reckons that sort of thinking should've gone out with the ark."

"So I'll be able to sew and do the ironing at any time of day?"

"Daytime, yeah, but not at night. The lighthouse draws so much power that we can't use anything that puts a load on the generator—no electric jugs or frypans at night."

"What about other stations?" I felt suddenly concerned for our seemingly wayward principal keeper.

"They're all different, I guess, but it's island stations that have generators. Most of the mainland ones are on the national grid. What happens on each station depends on the P.K. really."

"What's the P.K.?"

"Principal keeper. He's always called the P.K. The other thing is, while the radio beacon's on we've got to have a generator running to power it."

"When's it on?" My mind's wispy grasp of technology allowed me only a vague understanding of what function a radio beacon would perform.

"Well, apart from all night just like the lighthouse, it goes on whenever there's a bit of fog or rain. We have to be always looking out to sea, watching the visibility, and we keep a bit of an eye on boats that go past, too. It's sort of becoming second nature to me." He had always had an interest in the weather and an eye for boats and I was glad he'd found a job where these interests were of value.

I slung Helen up onto my shoulder and rubbed her tiny back. "And when you're not on duty, you fix fences and do stock work and paint buildings?"

Pip nodded eagerly. "And we shift the gear up the hill from the block—that can be quite a picnic, especially if the weather's lousy—and we keep everything working properly. It all takes ages. We only get maintenance blokes out here if we can't fix something ourselves. And, you should see us, we're like a bunch of old women down in the lighthouse and the engine room—polishing the lenses and the brass and cleaning everything."

I continued rubbing the baby's back and thought back to the long days I had spent alone on the orchard while Pip was at work. "What time do you finish work each day?" I asked.

"Three-thirty or fourish."

"Heck!" I exclaimed. "You'll be a man of leisure!"

"Don't forget when we're on duty we do weather reports from six in the morning and I have to learn about all the different sorts of clouds and be able to tell what speed the wind is and how high the waves are, and on wet days Dave and I practise our semaphore and Morse code and learn dozens of different signal flags. You wouldn't believe how much there is to do out here!"

"I would. I would," I protested, laughing. "You're going to be the best lighthouse keeper in the whole world." I balanced the baby on top of the mountain made by my knees under the blankets. Her head wobbled a bit, her eyes looked vaguely away into the corner of the room and a hint of a windy smile lit up her face and made her look fleetingly human.

Pip took her from me. "It's just the sort of life we've always wanted," he said happily. Then his voice changed into a squeak as he addressed his daughter. "And your mummy is the very best mummy in the whole world," whereupon as if on cue Helen gave a burp worthy of someone ten times her size and milkily overflowed all over his leg.

For many people the cogs of their metabolism don't really mesh into gear much before lunch time, but Pip and I were always alike in starting each new day with our throttles out and our engines racing, waking up with an immediate eagerness to find out what each new day might bring. We found that the routine of early waking to feed the baby and milk the cow, and the three-day cycle of morning lighthouse duties were perfectly suited to our 'early bird' personalities.

That first morning I tucked Helen back into the bassinet and wheeled it out into the kitchen, (or should I call it the diningroom?) and, in seconds, I was dressed and viewing my new indoor surroundings with hopeful curiosity.

So this was the house in which I would reign as queen. It gleamed and shone beneath the bright electric bulbs. Every surface clean and glossy, hard, shiny paint on all the walls, the new wonder material, Formica, on the benches. Even the top of the traditional wooden table had been 'modernised' with it. The doors had been 'modernised', too, with sheets of plywood tacked on either side so that we could only guess at the panels and mouldings that lay beneath. It was a modest sort of castle for a queen but it didn't look a bad sort of prison, either, and, as Pip had said, it was a 'real' house, respectable and permanent and obviously built by tradesmen. It had withstood the test of time and bore little testimony to seventy years of island storms and a continuous succession of lighthouse families.

Of course Pip had put everything in its place; not for me the traumatic first arrival on station with a tired family and our gear still packed in boxes. I had only to open the cupboard doors to find all our belongings.

Our books were on shelves in the glass-fronted cupboard near the stove and our old clock ticked away on the mantelpiece. I'd already noticed that its chimes were switched off. Pip was inclined to think of the sweet melody of Big Ben ringing though the house every quarter of an hour as being a 'heck of a din' that we could well do without, but I loved the sound. It had been my grandfather's clock and I treasured it for the sense of security I felt when its chiming brought back early memories. Though it had spent its early life in more genteel surroundings I knew it was happy with us, and now I looked up at its round, faithful face and promised silently that I would set its music playing as soon as diplomacy allowed.

My gaze shifted from the clock down to the stove, a Shacklock '501' with a temperature gauge on the oven door. It was obviously much superior to the little black stoves I'd learnt to cook on, and Pip had already sung its praises to me the night before. "She's a beaut. The oven gets hot in no time and the hot water doesn't turn the bath orange like that useless blimmen thing we had on the orchard."

I knew I would never forget that last 'useless blimmen thing' which had turned all my washing the colour of rust. I had been glad to leave it behind, together with the dry rot and the unfinished rooms in the house and the chemicals from orchard sprays which had fogged the windows. The boss had been a very clever man but he and his wife hadn't believed there was anything wrong with the stove in that last house. They had lived in that house, themselves, twenty years before while they had been renovating their own—and the stove had been wonderful back then. They had kept saying to me, "It must be the way you're driving it. . . "

As a girl at home, I hadn't been taught to cook. Mum had said, "Hah, girls don't need to waste time cooking. They'll get plenty of it when they're married," so my earliest, rather blackened, efforts had been on campfires when we'd been away on tramping trips. Then, when we were first married, I had set to work to teach myself to bake 'properly' with my *Edmonds Cookery Book* beside me and a good hot manuka fire burning in my little black stove in the place where we'd lived for a start—a quaint hut beneath tall gum trees at the back of an orchard. Then, before Fred was born, we had moved from there to a one-bedroom cottage which had been equally quaint and rustic. In both I had cooked on simple, free-standing cast-iron stoves and had soon nursed the secret belief that I had a talent for doing things in the old way. But when Fred had started walking, the boss had shifted us into the larger dwelling (a horrible barn of a place) with the 'useless blimmen stove'. It had kept the ugly building moderately warm but the 'hot' water cylinder and wet-back must have been half-full of rust and debris. And as for the oven—nothing good could be said about it! After a while, however, I had got better at driving the 'useless blimmen thing'. Though it had had its limitations, some of the problem had been mine after all—but, at any rate, the rusty water could never have been cured.

So now that I had reached Stephens Island I had behind me three years of experience on three different wood stoves, and when I saw the gleaming cream and green enamel fire-god which presided over the living room in 'number three' house I knew I had the ability to tame it and that Pip would be proud of me, and that nobody would find this new lighthouse keeper's wife crying over her coal range (as Cis had told Pip that new wives were wont to do). For a minute I stood basking in its heat, feeling the energy throbbing out of it—a radiating benevolence that seemed to warm the whole house.

From a crouching position, I flicked open the cream enamel door of the fire-box and peered into the fire-god's red-hot throat. With a rattle and a bang I scooped a couple of lumps of coal from the tin scuttle on the hearth and fed him. Then I closed the door and screwed the lower air vent shut. Like feeding an animal, it was a very satisfying thing to do.

A bunker at our gate was filled with good West Coast coal which burnt cleanly and was provided by the Marine Department. With the passage of time I was to realise that, no matter how much coal we burned, the department would send out more, and although I was also to learn that the department could be petty over trifles, I would never hear it query the amount of coal used on station.

I rocked backwards from the stove and sat cross-legged on the gleaming gray congoleum. "Just look at these floors!" I crowed. "So shiny!"

"Everyone's floors are like this," said Pip, beaming modestly. "There's polish, gallons of it, government issue and industrial strength. You just wipe it on with a cloth and she shines up real beaut."

Standing up, I skated in my socks from the stove through the door into the adjoining room, singing in my off-key voice, "It's a real house! We're living in a real house!" Only much later would I come to realise that the layout of the livingrooms was strange and inconvenient.

At this moment I saw the bright shiny stove and the wonderfully functional stainless steel sink bench without a thought about the fact that they were situated at opposite ends of the house, and that I would be traipsing back and forth between the two on endless marathons with my hands full of pots and food and dishes, skirting around toys and babies and avoiding the outstretched legs of anyone who might be sitting in one of the peculiar armchairs—which were all in unsuitable positions because there was nowhere else for them.

Although the tiny room with the stove was the heart of the house, it had a door in all four walls and not much room for furniture. The dining table and chairs were jammed against one wall and the red vinyl settee fitted nicely below the window —but it was fortunate that it had no armrests or we would have had to be athletes to get into our bedroom. There was space for one armchair only and that was beside the stove so that I would always be saying "Excuse me" to its occupant.

I saw none of these things as defects. To me everything was perfect. The adjoining room in which I now stood was a livingroom of sorts but was strangely long and narrow, being just three paces wide and two-thirds the length of the house. It was almost like a passageway in shape, and against its walls were two more of the peculiar armchairs and an assortment of benches and cupboards. At the far end, facing a bright yellow wall, was the sink bench, and, behind that, the window. Outside was a cluster of water tanks which obscured all of the view and most of the daylight but with strong electric bulbs blazing down from the ceiling the rooms were well lit.

All my life I'd been taught to switch off lights when they weren't needed but now Pip said, "The generators run better with a load on the motors so we keep the lights on all day."

"That'll be hard to get used to," I said. "I'm so used to trying to save power."

"Well, you can save water, now, instead. There's no natural water on the island at all. It's all tank water from the roofs."

What about the animals?" I asked, thinking a few hundred sheep and a handful of cattle might drink quite a lot during summer.

"Still tanks," Pip said. "There are tanks by every building. Did you see those big ones down by The Palace?"

I had seen them and they were huge—nearly as big in volume as a house.

"They're quite new," Pip continued. "Water must've been a real problem before they were built. But we've still got to be a bit careful, and from now on, with summer coming, we can't leave taps running when we clean our teeth or anything like that. And don't flush the dunny every time. Flush dunnies run away with more water than everything else, much more than washing machines."

I went to the back door and studied the wash house which was really part of the entrance with just a wash tub and a copper. Pip put an arm around me and mine slid over his shoulder. It was our natural position because, at five foot three, he was nearly two inches shorter than I was. He looked dolefully at the empty space beside the tub. "I was going to have the new washing machine here as a surprise," he said. "But it won't be coming until the next boat."

"Never mind, I can use the copper," I said, not without pleasure because Mum had always used a copper. Even after she'd acquired a washing machine when I was a teenager, she'd insisted that boiling was necessary to "kill germs" and it was only in my last year on the orchard that I myself had had no copper and had, therefore, felt terribly guilty about not being able to purify the linen, particularly the baby's nappies, as she had taught me.

I had begun to think, however, that some of Mum's ideas were old-fashioned and belonged back in less enlightened times. Sometimes I was torn between respect for her wisdom and a residual resentment about the dozens of little eccentricities that had set me apart from the children in our neighbourhood. I'd envied the more relaxed standards of other families towards health. My friends hadn't always been made to wear woollen singlets throughout summer, or horrible starched sunhats. What is more, they'd often shared combs and cups and licked each other's icecreams, all without coming to any apparent harm. Nor had they been subjected to a litany of the vitamin and mineral contents of their food every time they sat down to dinner and they'd been allowed to eat lollies and cake and drink cordial instead of milk. It was true that most of them had tooth decay, but by and large other families had seemed as healthy as our own. Mum had boasted that her children never broke bones or had boils, or school sores, or ringworm—and she had been right about that—but my close friends had all seemed to be healthy and their mothers, being younger and more modern than mine, had kept clean houses with shiny floors (much cleaner and shinier than Mum's), and, although they had used washing machines and not bothered with coppers, they hadn't been attacked by armies of germs.

Nevertheless, during the previous year on the orchard when I had had no copper, guilt had gnawed at me for not boiling sheets, towels and nappies, particularly as my mother had just died of cancer (I was told it wasn't infectious but how could anyone be sure?) Now, with Pip apologising for not being able to get a new washing machine to the island before my arrival, instead of feeling disappointment I thought this would be my chance to do the right thing by my mother. I'd be able to boil up the linen; maybe I'd keep on doing it even after my new machine arrived. It wouldn't hurt to give those germs a nasty surprise. Within seconds my mind was planning a laundry routine for the weeks ahead.

But Pip said, "It doesn't work."

"How do you mean it doesn't work?" It was just a matter of lighting the fire underneath the copper and the water would be boiling in not much more than an hour. All you had to do was dump in some bar-soap and the dirty linen and poke it around with a stick every so often as it bubbled and seethed. The result, clean hygienic linen, no school sores, no boils, no ringworm. There was nothing to it! I had done it heaps of times before and it was a simple process. "How can it not work?" I asked disbelievingly.

"It smokes."

"It'll just need its chimney cleaned."

"I've done that and it still smokes."

"I could leave the door open. . . "

"No, it smokes too much and the fire sulks. Arne says we'd better pull it out. It's shot. The other houses don't have coppers in them. Nobody bothers with them nowadays."

"Oh!" It was loyalty to Mum's values versus my delight at the thought of having an up-to-the-minute washing machine of my own.

Pip said, "We could cut the top out of a kerosene tin and you could boil the nappies on the stove in that."

"Yes," I said in confusion. "I could do that."

"And we'd still have a washing machine for when you didn't want to go to the bother."

"Oh, yes," I said looking down beside me at the reality of a pile of dirty clothes and a bucketful of nappies and remembering, with a sinking feeling, that I had hardly ever washed a garment by hand in my life (even though Mum had done it for years). Just at that moment Fred came waddling out of his bedroom with his night-time nappies and pyjama pants in a wet heap around his ankles, and, suddenly, I didn't care about the copper. Though I thought the kerosene tin might be a help, I even began to wonder how I could survive without a washing machine until boat day.

As with everything, there are techniques to washing clothes efficiently by hand but I had never been taught them. When my washing machine arrived the following week I almost hugged it with gratitude. Fortunately I had no idea what a cantankerous thing it would turn out to be, or that I would end up giving it away within the year. I gazed at it with awe and pride but also with a little suspicion. I saw two flimsy plastic lids with flexible plastic where proper hinges should be. And I saw a spinner! I had never before seen such a thing. Doubtfully I packed the washed garments into it, careful to balance them evenly as the instruction book said. The machine vibrated and I packed them again. It vibrated less. I listened and watched in amazement as it roared and whirred, then I pulled out the clothes.

"They're almost dry!" It was astonishing. This was, indeed, a clever machine, and with a good windy day out on the clothes line most of the crumples and wrinkles would be blown away. From now on it wouldn't be so difficult to dry clothes during wet weather. That spinner was so much more efficient than an old wringer. And the hinges? They wouldn't last but were a small thing—as long as they weren't an indication of the machine's overall quality.

Although machines hadn't hitherto played a big part in my life I was already besotted with one, my sewing machine, a modern Bernina with all the fancy attachments. Therefore I knew I had the capacity to love a machine and I knew there was room in my heart for another. I was ready to embrace my new Norge washer with its wild spinner if only it would let me, and although it didn't quite fit in with my vision of the perfect pioneering lifestyle, I was willing to make a few concessions. Meanwhile Pip watched its vibrations with incredulity and wondered about the power supply and said that perhaps the current was a bit down by the time it got to our place. He predicted gloomily that, at this rate, the washing machine would shake itself to death within a year. . . but I preferred to believe he might be wrong.

It wasn't long before I saw the truth of Pip's statement that the kerosene fridge was a "cranky old girl with a few tricks up her sleeve" but, being still in the first stages of a love affair with everything on Stephens Island, I flirted happily with the fridge as well and was quick to inspect the mysteries of its hidden parts. I thought the strangest thing about its running on kerosene was the fact that it used heat to cool things off. At the bottom of the fridge was a small door. When I opened this and got down on hands and knees and peered inside, I saw a fuel tank with, at the back, a little flame burning like a lamp inside a glass cylinder. Above this was a hidden chimney which led up through the bowels of the fridge and emerged right on the top through a little china chimney pot. What happened to the heat from this flame as it travelled upward on its intestinal journey was a mystery to me. I knew only that it somehow cooled off the interior of the fridge and the food inside it. Even more mysteriously, the bigger the flame, the cooler the food became and the smaller the flame, the warmer the food. This funny little miracle didn't make much sense to me—the more heat the colder the food and the less heat the warmer the food—and, to make matters worse, if the flame was too high, the chimney smoked.

In the beginning Pip and I were unknowingly battling each other as well as the fridge. For instance, it happened one day something like this. When putting away the cheese, Pip saw that the lettuce was partly frozen so, going down on his knees, he opened the door across the bottom and peered in at the flame way back in the far left-hand corner. He twiddled the knob that lowered the wick (remembering that the less flame the warmer the food) then, feeling well pleased with his little adjustment, he went off, promising himself to check it again in a couple of hours.

Soon after this, along came I, the pioneering wife, to fetch a jug of milk (rich with cream) and what did I spy? That same lettuce that Pip had seen, going dark with ice crystals in its outer leaves. "Hmmm," I said and, being quite unaware of his correction, I, too, went down on my knees, peered in at the flame and turned the knob that lowered the wick—and went away well pleased with myself, intending to check again in a little while.

The flame, (being now very small indeed because of its double adjustment), began, in its own mysterious way, to actually heat the food-chamber, and, when Pip came along later to check on his carefully calculated correction, he found warm lettuce and thawed meat in the icebox. Down on his knees again he turned the knob just so—just a little higher—and went away.

Pretty soon after this I returned and found, (as Pip had before me), that the food was warm. Down I went onto my knees again and turned up the flame, high (but not so high that it smoked) and told myself that Pip had certainly been right about this "cranky old girl".

Next time when Pip passed by and checked on the food inside, he found that everything was frozen. I heard his swearing from the kitchen and, going out to the porch, I said half angrily myself, (beginning to suspect that we had been working against each other), "What's wrong? What are you swearing at?"

"I can't understand this bloody fridge. . . " he said grimly peering in and trying to adjust the little flame. "You haven't touched it, have you?"

"Of course I have. It's being playing up all day—"

For a few moments we stared at each other in angry silence and then we realised that we had to unite against this cranky old girl. From that day on it became Pip's responsibility, once a week, to fuel her tank, trim her wick and clean her sooty little chimney—and mine, every day, to deal with her temperature control by adjusting the flame. But a kerosene fridge has no thermostat and is affected by both the daily temperature and the number of times its door is opened. I, myself, had to be her thermostat, and every time I looked inside I had to mentally note the state of the icebox. It soon became a habit for me—but the fridge always did have tricks up her sleeve (just as Pip had warned) and, after several days of smooth running had lulled me into complacency, something would be bound to upset the cranky old girl and she would freeze all the fruit and vegetables right through.

There would be six weeks before Dad and my sister arrived for their Christmas holiday. In that time I hoped to have mastered all the skills I needed in our new lifestyle. I confidently believed I could achieve anything I set my mind to (being one of my mother's capable daughters), but there was one every-day, very important task that became my greatest challenge. This was the baking of bread. From now on, if we wanted to eat it, I had to make it—most of it. We could order a few loaves to come out from Picton with the fortnightly supplies, but they ran the risk of arriving sodden and squashed, and in any case they were already going stale and would keep only a few days. Besides, lighthouse keepers' wives always made their own bread. That's what they did. It was part of the pioneering life.

I had grown up with bread from the bakery. It had seemed as natural to me as were eggs from fowls and milk from a cow. It had been unsliced, often had a burnt crust, and was never wrapped. Kids carried it home from school under their arms, picking out the soft, tasty centre with dirty fingers, and, at tea time, we had eaten it stale or fresh, and the crusts burnt or not, regardless of its unwrapped travels.

Nobody I'd ever known had made bread. As far as I knew, bread-making was a lost art of 'the olden times', dead and forgotten except by those few people who still existed in remote outposts and hidden valleys—those mysterious places unheard of by New Zealanders at large, except in the picture pages of the _Auckland Weekly News_ (which all lighthouse keepers received free every week). Now I was one of those same far-flung people, so, almost straight away, I plunged into bread-making. Up to my elbows in yeast and flour, I tried to follow the instructions Pip had got from Cis.

I kneaded the dough. I set it to rise. I kneaded it again and set it to rise again, baked it and brought it from the oven—joyfully, expectantly, for it certainly smelled good. But it was as hard as boulders. A few days later my second effort was spongy like toasted crumpets, and my third was rubbery like toasted boots.

Time went on and though, with my stove, I was in my element twiddling knobs and levers and got the temperature just right whatever the weather, I couldn't get the dough right for my bread. When the wind howled outside, making the fire roar exuberantly inside its firebox and its top-plate glow a dull red and the needle of the thermometer go to the far edge of its dial (past six hundred degrees Fahrenheit), I got the temperature down by simply closing dampers and shovelling on ashes to bury the flames—but I still couldn't get my bread mixture right. Even when the day was damp and quiet and the fire inclined to sulk I raised its temperature by rattling the poker about among the hot coals to get air flowing through them—and I chose good solid lumps of coal and my oven went up to four hundred degrees which was just right for putting in the bread—but still my bread was a flop.

With every batch, Pip commented favourably, always beginning with, "It's not like 'real' bread, but—" Sometimes he ended his statement with, "But it's yummy," sometimes with, "But it still tastes all right." One day he said, "It's not like real bread, but it's—palatable."

Palatable! I wanted it to be like 'real' bread from the shop. I didn't want it to be merely palatable.

"Palatable's a horrible word," I wailed.

"Well, my efforts weren't any better and we won't starve. It's just different."

"What's Cis's bread like?"

"It's not like shop bread, either."

I looked at him with disappointed eyes. "But it's better than mine, isn't it!"

"Yes," he mumbled, "It's better than ours—sort of softer."

When the men were working near the lighthouse they were often invited to Cis and Arne's house for smoko. Pip, therefore, knew much more about the way they lived than I did. Finally admitting defeat, I went to Cis for advice and she helpfully told me that, in her early days, she'd been advised to 'knead the dough until it squeaks'.

With renewed enthusiasm I went home and kneaded the dough. Then, in desperation, I thrashed it, but never a squeak did I hear. Through trial and error I would learn, eventually, (squeaks or no squeaks) to make a presentable loaf just as Cis said I would. I would also find that other people adored fresh bread and that the way to get a reputation for making good bread was to let them scoff it all up, while it was still hot, and before it could turn into a rock.

I was to find, too, that we needed bread most when there were extra people in the house—when I was at my busiest—so I would make it more from necessity than for enjoyment. It was destined to become a routine chore which I would sometimes tackle with pleasure, turning out interestingly-shaped savoury loaves and spicy buns. But, on the whole, I would make it doggedly (and with reasonable efficiency), determined, as always, to be a good true lighthouse keeper's wife.

CHAPTER 5

Secure and Well Cared For

A s for the lighthouse itself, the reason for our coming to Stephens Island, much as I was determined to love everything about our new life, I couldn't help feeling a sneaking disappointment that it was so far from where we lived. True, it was only five minutes' walk away, but, because our house was situated in such a totally different area, I still felt timid about wandering around the more official parts of the station without Pip.

Occasionally I accompanied him when he did his routine duties, carrying Helen and leading Fred by the hand. The mere sight of the tower and everything about it thrilled me. I looked on its symmetry with the kind of awe and fascination I felt for cathedrals with their stained glass windows, ornate architecture and spiritual aura. It seemed to be symbolic of permanence and hope, and even mystery and drama. I'd had a mental image of what the classic lighthouse should look like, and it fitted perfectly: the close-cropped green-grass hillside, the overpowering sweep of seascape beyond, and the tower, pure, virginal white as a gull's breast with not a blemish to be seen. There was something in the upward angle of the wall, from ground to ornate balcony, something graceful in her proportions, that suggested gender—definitely female.

One fine night, soon after my arrival, I said to Pip, "I want to go and look at the lighthouse. . . I want to see it when it's really, properly dark outside. . . "

"I think you should," he said. "I get a real kick out of seeing that blimmen great, beautiful light going round. . . shining out over the sea for miles and miles. . . and the birds diving about everywhere—and me being part of it all."

In the back porch I took the torch from him and slid my feet into my gumboots. At the gate I kissed him on the nose and bravely set off, flashing my light in front of me, my heart beating quickly because I suddenly felt enormously afraid at being outside and alone in the blackness. There was no moon and every one of the million stars that pierced the all-enveloping night winked the same message to me—that I was helplessly frail and small and in danger of being swallowed up by some dark and mighty force.

Almost running as I followed the beam of my light along the dry earth of the road, I avoided stepping on tuatara of all sizes and half bent my head down, fearing that a flying dovie might collide with me. The rabble of birds' voices grew louder as I neared the place where the bush grew lower down the hill, and I slowed and listened, my fright subsiding as my torch picked up the glistening grey and white of their plumage. They huddled here and there on the hillside, benign and innocuous, their eyes bright and black and decidedly alive. Together with the tuatara they made me feel not quite so at the mercy of the unknowable. Around the corner I saw the lights of number two house above me, and then the road ahead was lit by the moving beam from the lighthouse. And there it was—the tower, just a shape in the dark with the light slowly turning in its upper storey.

I felt calmer now. I could hear the thumping of the generator, and, passing the white picket fence of number one house, I saw lights from windows and imagined Cis and Arne, safe in their livingroom, watching their television. Only a few yards further on I came to a wire gate and opened it. There were a couple of sheds in front of me and the lighthouse beyond them. This was the paddock where the cows spent each night after being milked. It was called 'the night paddock'. It was also the heart of the light-station. The office and relieving keepers' quarters were here, on the hill, just above the lighthouse while, below it, was the powerhouse with its three generators.

I leaned against the wall of the tractor shed and stared. It was a real lighthouse, beautiful by day and magnificent at night. At fifty feet the tower was tall enough to have presence, yet its lantern was close enough to show off the entire intricate arrangement of lenses and prisms. Half frightened, half in awe, I gazed up at the slowly revolving spectacle. The light from the bulb at its centre gleamed and reflected through a multitude of crystal facets. Originally I'd had no idea it would be like this. I had expected to see some sort of globe that flashed on and off intermittently, but the light didn't flash at all. The bulb at its heart burned steadily throughout the night, and the flashing effect, so familiar to mariners at sea, was created by the lenses and prisms which focused and magnified the light into beams. These, I now saw, were sheer shafts of brilliance wheeling through the dark night, almost invisible in the clear air except for haphazard flashes of white light which were dovies, briefly illuminated as they swifted erratically earthward. I now saw that the beams of light were like the arms of a giant windmill revolving above me, quite narrow at the base and widening as they disappeared into infinity. Try as I might, I couldn't get my eyes to follow the path of those beams to the far-away sea but I knew that, if there were a sailor out there in a boat, as each beam passed him he would see it as a tiny, bright flash.

I thought it strange that light could pass through air and space undetected until it hit something, anything, like the flying dovies, vapour in the air, or the sailor at sea. And when it hit them it seemed to disappear. Would there be a hole in the stream of light after it had hit the dovie— that would be a shadow, wouldn't it? But after light had passed over a dovie the bird became dark again. Where did light go? What happened to it?

My eyes strained again towards the sea and then swept across the scatter of stars overhead, which seemed not so bright now. Their light had travelled millions upon millions of miles—light years, in fact— only to die when it hit something. Where did it go after it hit the earth? How could it just stop? I shivered, feeling dizzy at the wild depth of the universe. I turned away from the lighthouse, and clutching my torch as if it were the only thing between myself and oblivion, I set out for home, my fickle shadow looming ahead as the revolving beams passed over me. Once past the lights of Arne and Cis's house, I began to run and didn't slow down until I saw the lighted windows of our own number three house.

Pip was at the table writing a letter. "You were quick," he said. "It's a nice night. I thought you would've stayed out longer. . . What did you see?"

"The lighthouse," I said. "Stars."

"Was it a good night for tuatara?"

"They were everywhere." I automatically crouched in front of the stove and put on more coal. Then I swept the hearth and stood with my back to the warmth, an acrid whiff of coal-smoke in my nostrils. My thoughts flew about as if I had been to the outside of the universe and back. Those lumps of coal beside me in the scuttle were plants and trees that had once lived way back in pre-historic times; and the tuatara on this island, they had lived here for millions of years, and were still here when all other dinosaurs had disappeared. . . inside my head was a swirl of darkness splashed with stars and an image of the lighthouse, itself. I thought about its light system, with its giant set of revolving prisms and lenses; people still sometimes called it a lantern but it was like an enormous crystalline seed sparkling at the heart of the station and it was as if its well-being was now the entire reason for our existence, as if our lives would, from now on, be forever devoted solely to its service—to the service of the light.

I could see it wasn't called the lighthouse *service* for nothing and I understood now why it was often said that lighthouse keepers 'tended' their lights. Keepers really were proud of their lights and they did tend them with loving care. They often spent wet days in the tower. With soft cloths they whisked the dust from the lustrous facets of the prisms, and with less delicacy they cleaned the glass window panes both outside and in. As Pip had said, they were generally like a lot of old women polishing brass and mopping floors, making sure that their lighthouse was a showplace—even though it was rarely on show.

Another regular and curious task which they did in the tower was the testing of the 'standby equipment'. This was the old system which had kept the light burning before the days of electrification. Now, the only likelihood of its being used again in earnest was if all three generators should fail at once and leave the station without electric power. The standby equipment was kept in perfect order in readiness for such an unlikely emergency. Instead of electricity, this old system was fueled by kerosene and clockwork, and every few weeks the keepers tested it to ensure that everything would be ready if it were ever needed.

The old lamp, itself, was a kerosene burner with incandescent mantle, and the power for turning the lens system was provided by a giant clockwork mechanism. This had weights which, after being wound up by hand, slowly descended—down through the centre of the tower.

Had they been in serious use, these weights could have descended right down through a hole in the middle of the first floor and on down through the ground floor and into an underground room with a pit which we called 'the dungeon'. During their practice sessions, however, the keepers never allowed the weights to fall this far because of the time it took for them to slowly unwind—and also the human energy required to wind them back up.

When the old-time keepers had kept watch each night, one of their major tasks had been winding up the weights. I often thought about how they'd had to remain awake and alert through the hours of darkness. Although it excited me to picture the lone keeper in the tower sitting through long winter nights—through thunder, lightning and gales—trimming the wick and waiting to wind the weights back up every hour or two, I also thought that those keepers of old must have had to be much more staunch in their devotion to their duties than the keepers of our own time. I was glad that the station had been electrified and we could fall asleep at night happy in the knowledge that alarms would waken us if the system failed. I liked the way it was for us.

I always found it cool in the lighthouse and felt as if it were welded to rock. This building didn't shake and rattle in a gale and I felt its strength and durability as soon as I entered and saw its walls—a patch-work of nuts and bolts, row upon row, line beside line, both vertical and horizontal, joining the cast-iron plates of which it was built. There were not just a couple of bolts joining each plate to its neighbour, but regiments of bolts side by side, marking lines of latitude and longitude on the interior of the walls. It looked gloriously indestructible and was coated thickly with layer upon layer of paint, white on the wall and red on the concrete floor. Red, too, on the metal hand-rail of the curved stairway that led up to the first floor and the same on the second which led up to the light-room itself.

The lower wall of the light-room was matchlined with wood but, again, thick with paint, and the stair-rails and other fittings were of polished brass which I always tried to avoid touching, knowing how much effort those 'old women' put into keeping them that way. Occupying the centre of the room was 'the mechanism'—gleaming brass cogs and mechanical bits all showcased behind glass, (glass on all four sides of the cabinet, more glass for the keepers to clean). Above that, above head height, was the lantern, that is the light system itself, with its giant prisms and lenses all reflecting and refracting light in a multitude of ways.

The light mechanism was activated from the ground floor. On first entering the tower the duty keeper would flip on the alarms, thereby causing a brief commotion in all the dwellings and proving that they were in working order. Then he would flip on the switch for the light mechanism and the alarms would fall silent as they were designed to do while the light was functioning correctly. Up in the lightroom, a mercury switch governed by centrifugal force kept the alarms quiet as long as the lantern revolved, but, if its movement stopped, the mercury ran down to the wrong end of its cylinder and set the alarms ringing. There was another mercury switch on the automatic bulb-changing mechanism. The bulbs that provided the light were 1,000 watts. Two of them sat side by side, one in use and one spare. If the filament fused in the one which was in use, the break in current would somehow affect the mercury switch which would automatically activate the other bulb into taking over. This was all a far cry from the old keeper of the past trimming the wick of his kerosene lamp and replacing its mantle when it disintegrated.

After testing the alarms on the ground floor, the keeper climbed the iron stairways to the light-room where the 'showcased' brass cogs and mechanical bits were now performing their nightly function of rotating the giant lantern. Above his head the huge glinting assembly of prisms and lenses turned silently with the bulb shining at its core. The keeper's last task was to climb the stairway to the iron catwalk and clamber up between the lens structure and the curtains which were drawn at sunrise to stop the sun from shining through the lenses and starting a fire.

Sometimes, if I went to the tower with Pip at sunset, I didn't go up into the lighthouse but waited on the hillside with Fred and the baby and looked at the view. Often there would be ships passing out at sea and in very clear weather the mountains of the North Island, Egmont and Ruapehu, stuck up from the horizon in a dreamlike surreal way. Looking up at the triangular panes between the balcony and dark, domed roof of the tower, I would see a shadow-play reflected on the curtains. I saw the geometric shapes of the prisms and lenses split and fractured as they moved around the gathers and folds of the fabric. Then I saw

Pip's distorted, witchety shadow as he climbed up onto the catwalk. It disappeared when he ducked inside the lantern to test the bulb-changing mechanism, and reappeared when he emerged to walk to the far side of the catwalk. Then I saw him appear in the flesh, tugging back the curtains and releasing the lantern's radiance to chase away the last rays of the setting sun. He would look down and wave and, for a few moments, he'd survey the panorama of sea and sky, observing from habit the pattern of clouds, height of swell, atmospheric visibility and any vessels that might be out at sea.

More than anything else, at such times, I was overcome with amazement that we had found an island with a lighthouse—such a beautiful, hauntingly romantic place on which to live and which we could almost call our own. Cis had told me that two-thirds of lighthouse keepers never became principal keepers because they left the service within a few years of arriving— "disillusioned and unable to put up with the isolation. . . It's not everyone's kettle of fish, you know!" Well, of course I knew that—but it wouldn't happen to us. We had our heads screwed on pretty well. I couldn't imagine why people weren't all clamouring to become lighthouse families. I couldn't understand it at all.

Loneliness was the spectre that had seemed to haunt most people's imagination when I had mentioned that I was going to live on a lighthouse. They had almost all said, "But, won't you get lonely out there?" And I had always answered that I never got lonely anywhere. Some had accepted this because they'd known me to be the sort of person who went walking in lonely places but many had obviously thought of me as friendly and outgoing and didn't like to think of my being so isolated.

As a child I certainly had become used to being relatively alone because I was so very much the youngest in the family—and with Mum in poor health we hadn't exactly been a rollicking, good time, gregarious bunch. I hadn't really recognised loneliness in myself—well, not as a bad thing. It was a challenge that had always been with me and I hadn't called it by name. Mum had taken pride from the fact that I had roamed by myself from an early age and that I was happy to be 'independent'. And that's what I saw myself as, still. Independent. I didn't need people around me all the time. This was rather fortunate because although Pip's working days were shorter than on the orchard and I saw more of him, I saw little of the other families. Weekends were a time for relaxation and a certain amount of fairly informal visiting, but, on weekdays, like young mothers all over the country, my life was centred around my home. During Pip's working hours I couldn't leave the children and I couldn't travel far with them.

When mothers, elsewhere, went walking they took their toddlers out in pushchairs, but, with their small wheels, these machines were almost impossible to use in the countryside. When Fred was a baby Pip and I had met an American couple with a child in a backpack so we'd manufactured one for ourselves. Pip had welded up a frame and I had sewn the canvas seat. It worked well but I couldn't carry a toddler as well as a baby in the frame, and if Fred walked we took all day to get anywhere.

We did go out often and look at the world outside our gate, but as both Cis and Peggy were shut inside their houses supervising their children's correspondence school lessons, visiting them was out of the question. Besides, I found there was an unspoken code about casual visiting. It wasn't done lightly. Not here, on Stephens Island.

Sometimes, however, Cis would ring up mid-morning and invite me to join them for smoko and I would drop whatever task I had in hand. I would put Fred in the backpack and, carrying Helen in my arms, I would struggle down to number one house as fast as I could in case the others had dispersed before I arrived. The first time I was invited down in this way Cis sat down with me, after the men's departure, and talked. She showed me her marvellous shell collection and gave me magazines to read while she worked with Anthony on his school work. She invited me to stay for lunch, and Pip came in with Arne and the lunch hour extended well into the afternoon, but I sensed that this departure from normality was because I was new on the island.

At first I was surprised at how often the telephone rang. On the orchard we hadn't had a phone and now we could speak to our neighbours at the mere twist of a handle—but we weren't connected to the outside world. It was an internal system and through it we could speak only to each other. All the houses, the office, The Palace, the two winch sheds and even the landing were linked on one line. With every call the bells rang in every house. Each phone had its own Morse code number of dahs and dits, which we rang manually by cranking the handle on the side of the phone. Some people gave long-drawn-out rings with dits as long as dahs and their dahs going on forever, and some gave several brief, peremptory rings in quick succession. I soon found myself guessing who was calling by the way the rings came through.

But, for some weeks after my arrival, the calls were nearly always for others and rarely for me. I'd prick up my ears at the first tingle, only to have my hopes dashed, and then—imagining that the other two women were gaily chatting to each other—I'd listen to the silence in my own house and feel isolated. But I soon learnt that the men often used the phones, too.

They'd ring their wives from the office or even the landing. Perhaps they were asking "What's for dinner?" I didn't know, and, as we settled into the system, it became less disturbing to me and I began to receive calls myself.

"Dah dit dit. Dah dit dit." That was our call and it rang for me. Yes, for me! It was one of the first calls I'd received. I had finished bathing the baby. Had trussed and safety-pinned her tiny pink bottom into a bulky nappie. Had pulled a woollen singlet over her fuzzy head. Had wiggled her doll arms into the sleeves of an embroidered Viyella matinee jacket.

Dressed for the day and ready for her breakfast, she smelled as sweet and warm as a sun-touched rose as I scooped her up from the bench and ran to the phone. "Hullo?"

"Hullo, lovey. How's your morning?"

"Good. How's yours?" Waiting, hoping for some little diversion.

"Yeah, okay. You're getting a visitor. The district nurse. She'll be there soon. About quarter of an hour. . . "

I forgot to ask how he knew she was coming or where he was calling from, and I flew about my bare and spotless kitchen. I let the baby's bath-water out of the sink, (the Plunket mothercraft manual admonished, "Never bath baby in the kitchen sink.") I tidied away towels, put the kettle over the hottest plate of the stove, told Fred, "Lady's coming to see us." Checked his face for smears and dribbles, checked my own and combed my hair. Only then did I settle down on the red vinyl couch to feed Helen with Fred beside me, his face pressed to the window, both of us watching the road below.

Helen drank quickly. I was like a good cow with plenty of milk and it was all over bar the burping when a lone figure rounded the corner.

I was surprised that a district nurse would make routine visits to such a remote place. After I'd ushered her inside and we'd introduced ourselves, my first questions were, "How did you get here? Where did you come from?"

She was new to the district and she had come out from French Pass "with Pat on the *Spray*". He'd dropped her off on the rocks with her bag and she'd walked up alone. She was fairly young looking and boyish and seemed quite capable of looking after herself.

On hearing that Fred would shortly be two years old, she gave him his 'two-year check-up'.

He was healthy and happy and sturdy for his age and she made out a card for him saying all this plus his vital measurements, and she added a final comment which I read with curiosity. "Very intelligent." I wondered how she could work that out.

Helen was weighed and measured. She was a 'bonny baby' and I answered questions about her feeding and her motions—and that was where we had a problem. Her motions were yellow, curdy splats, the same as the yellow splats that Fred had produced at the same age, but they were infrequent. The nurse wrote in the book. "Constipation."

"But, she's breast-fed," I protested. "And they're really soft and runny. . . "

"Far too infrequent," said the nurse blithely. "She needs milk of magnesia. I'll find a way of getting some out to you."

Confused, I let the matter rest. The kettle was whistling and I offered the nurse tea, but she refused. No, she'd better be getting on to the other houses, and, yes, she'd be waterlogged if she accepted all the drinks she was offered.

After we'd seen her to the gate I went back indoors feeling somewhat let down at the shortness of her visit. I laid Helen in the bassinet and thought about the infrequency of her motions, which the nurse had translated as 'constipation'. My instinct and experience told me that everything was as it should be but I wished I had someone else's opinion. The kitchen suddenly seemed empty and frightening.

"The Western Side".

The box descends to the *Enterprise*.

Routine mailday at the landing.

Dad fishing from the box.

Above: Pip checks the
bulb-changing mechanism
inside the lens assembly.

Left: I make butter.

Opposite page:
Busy day at the landing.

Pip crosses the gap at the Little Razorback.

The sacred tower becomes a butcher's shop.

Bill Kemp, the lighthouse inspector.

Stephens Island lighthouse.

Later in the day I consulted both Peggy and Cis about the matter but neither of them was inclined to express an opinion. I suspected this was because they felt the nurse would know best. I didn't think she knew best at all—but she was the nurse—and, true to her word, she 'found a way'. Two days later Pip brought in a package containing, in a beautiful blue glass bottle, the milk of magnesia. Like the nurse, it had been 'dropped off on the rocks' by a fisherman. Hesitantly I tasted the cool white suspension. It was mildly peppermint in flavour and it seemed to be a very foreign thing to feed to our still tiny baby. In my heart I felt sure there was nothing wrong with her and that it was normal for very young, breast-fed infants to have motions like a mix of egg yolk and mustard—and if this mix was runny, how could it be called 'constipation'?

Pip watched me doubtfully. "I don't think she's sick. She looks okay and she never cries."

He held her and peered thoughtfully at her little face as, in a quandary, I measured one small, white dose of the milk of magnesia into the plastic spooon provided. I dribbled it into the tiny, perfect mouth of our tiny, perfect daughter and it seemed to be a completely silly thing to be doing. In fact, I was sure it was an absolutely unnecessary thing to be doing. I would follow my own judgement and put the pretty blue bottle away in the first aid cupboard with all the other pills and medicines that I hoped we'd never need.

Our baby was completely normal. Her 'constipation' was normal, too. The nurse was wrong. It was a pity I couldn't believe in her, I thought wistfully as I dwelt briefly on the other, more complimentary things she'd said about my babies.

Over the folllowing weeks Helen continued to thrive and the one tentative dose of milk of magnesia had no visible effect on her. On the whole I was taking everything in my stride.

When I had time to spare, I was busy at my sewing machine. I made two cheap summer frocks for myself with zip-up fronts so I could feed the baby unobtrusively; I made summer shirts for Pip and I made curtains from material I had bought in town with the 'curtain allowance' we had received from the Marine Department. I was very frugal, making each curtain from only half a width of material. I lined them with 'tobacco cloth' which my country-bred aunt had suggested was the cheapest available. It was like unbleached muslin and had no body to it. There was no need for blinds or anything to shield us from prying eyes. There were no prying eyes on Stephens Island.

I threaded the curtains on wire and they hung down the sides of the windows in rather mean little drifts but I felt proud to have 'got my curtains up' so soon. They made the place look even more like a 'real house', and, by now, I had grown used to looking through the flyscreens on the windows and resigned myself to the fact that no amount of energy on my part could remove the mist of aluminium oxide from the glass. Arne said it was caused by the sea spray's reaction with the aluminium of the screens. I rubbed away at it with steel wool and succeeded in making scratches on the glass that reflected rainbows when the sun shone through them.

Throughout most of the house there was one window in each room and they were the old-fashioned, push-up-and-down type whose sashes are suspended on cords running on pulleys hidden in the sides of the frames. I had been warned as a child that these windows lay in wait for little children such as myself. If I were foolish enough to lean out over the sill, at that precise moment the frayed cord would be bound to break and, 'Whoosh', the window would fall, and my severed head would fly out into the garden and come to rest under the hydrangea bushes. In my childish imagination they had always been hydrangea bushes.

Arne obviously had a similar understanding of the predatory potential of these venerable-looking old windows, and, on his first visit to our house after my arrival, he instructed Pip in the mysteries of what lay behind their wide, fluted sashes and how to replace their cords— thereby ensuring that the heads of countless unwary lighthouse children would, henceforth, remain joined to their bodies instead of rolling about under hydrangea bushes.

"But, oh!" Cis told us. "It's not just heads!" Other appendages, she said, were at risk, too! And she launched into a story about a drunken maintenance man (on some other station than ours, of course). In the dead of night he had shoved open his bedroom window—a window with frayed and broken cords hidden behind its sashes—a window which had been lying in wait for a drunken man who was too lazy to find his way to the toilet—a window that could well have felt insulted at being mistaken for a urinal. Beneath that window there was a garden which belonged to the principal keeper's wife. She took great pride in it and it had flourished under her care in spite of the harsh climate. It was a garden simply full of flowers. . .

"Oh," I gasped, immediately picturing hydrangea bushes with something unspeakably ghastly—something which was much smaller and more pathetic than a child's severed head—resting beneath the leaves; but I bit back my words and almost held my breath as Cis continued with her story.

It was a story that hardly bore contemplation. In my mind I saw the window with the screaming man in its agonising grip and I wasn't sure whether to be shocked or amused as Cis brought her story to a close. "And that Mrs. So-and-so, the principal keeper's wife. . . was such a hard thing. . . and had no sympathy. All she could say was, 'Serve the dirty bugga right!'"

Arne said that Pip would be able to use his new skill at repairing the sash-cords of windows on whatever station he was transferred to in the lighthouse service because nearly all the houses were the same and their windows were all in the same dangerous state. The only garden outside our windows grew nothing but a couple of succulents (too small to conceal anything which might fall from above) but, in it, I carefully sowed the seeds of a 'cottage garden mix' that my thoughtful aunt had given me. I had never grown flowers before but every day I went out and studied the plot, searching for flower seedlings among the emerging weeds. Every day, too, I saved the rinse water from the washing machine and carried it to the gardens in buckets.

With Pip's working day finishing between three and four o'clock we often spent the late afternoon in the gardens. Arne was adamant that gardening was one of a lighthouse keeper's duties. He said that, in the past, on some remote stations, some families had suffered from scurvy, the old sailors' disease caused by a lack of fresh fruit and vegetables.

It was a quaint reminder of our vulnerability and this, plus the Robinson Crusoe atmosphere in the gardens up in the bush, was volatile fuel for my imagination. I wasn't born too late to be a pioneer after all!

When we arrived in the clearing we'd make a nest for Helen in the shade at the edge of the plot and we'd show Fred where he could dig and play while we worked at weeding and planting. The bush around us had been dwarfed by wind, and its canopy was only a few feet above head height, but it provided extremely effective shelter and it almost camouflaged the fact that we weren't many yards away from the seven-hundred-foot plunge of tangled scrub and rock and scree that we called 'the western side'. Among the twisted trunks and beneath the tortured branches of the ngaio trees, the dovies and tuatara had beaten the earth smooth by night. By day, the tuatara basked in dappled shade at their burrow entrances and sometimes a little brown skink would slip, as smoothly as silence, over the rug on which our baby slept. Because there were no rats, mice or cats on the island these little lizards were everywhere—sliding quickly out of sight as we passed.

With all this one would expect a special atmosphere up in the bush gardens: a whiff of the primeval past, or maybe ambient spirituality. Whatever its definition, it was present in the sheltered air. Whether the day was hot and still, or wild and screaming, there was something almost tangible that made me feel complete, yet still hungry for something that eluded me.

The thing that amazed us most was that Arne would often send the men home early from work with instructions to spend the afternoon in their gardens because gardening was a duty spelled out by the Marine Department. And it had been so ever since the regulations had been laid down for 'the conduct of the Light Service' in the 1860s.

Most of the rules that governed our lives as a lighthouse family were equally as old, and, although Pip had assured me that the department was too far away to be a worry, we were always aware of its presence in the background—a mixture of stern employer, pernickety landlord and benevolent parent controlling us, or perhaps watching over us, almost like God. I saw evidence of this in the scrupulous manner that station duties were executed; in the careful routines of cleaning and polishing; in the meticulousness in the engine room; the tidiness of the sheds, and the general high standard of maintenance for everything on the island.

All equipment had to be accounted for and the P.K. was always filling out forms: requisition forms for what was needed, and other forms to allow items which were worn out or damaged to be 'written off'. Pip said that the wooden chairs around our kitchen table had been written off. "They still look new," I protested.

"I know, but we're going to get new ones."

"But they're good chairs."

"Apparently they were too heavy for the wives to lift."

"What wives?"

"They had a couple here who were pregnant—I dunno. It was probably just an excuse to get new chairs."

"I get sick of useless females," I said crossly. I had already told Pip I could fill my own coal bucket and that, just because other men ran around after their wives as if they were invalids, it didn't mean that he had to do the same for me.

Nevertheless, because I had been brought up in an orderly home and yet had also been allowed plenty of personal freedom within the boundaries my parents had marked out, I was on the whole happy to accept the strange blend of restriction and independence imposed on us by the lighthouse service.

I didn't see the reproving letters that arrived in the mailbag for the P.K. if anything was lost or broken. I wasn't really aware of the days he spent in the office. As well as the day-journals, he had to write up a monthly report. This was quite an epistle which covered everything that had happened on station during the preceding four weeks. Standing orders governed the whole procedure. There were engine-running sheets detailing oil changes, and the number of hours all engines were run daily. This included the tractor, the winches, the crane and, even, the lawn mower. There were 'met' sheets which covered all meteorological observations and there was also a standard procedure for stating that the ordinary tasks had been done. Examples of this were: that the characteristics of the light (flashing twice in succession every half minute) had been checked daily, that the alarms were operational, and that the chronometers were accurate—(they rarely were).

All work undertaken, and all miscellaneous incidents, such as iron being blown off a roof, or medical advice being sought by radio, were reported, and such things as 'accident reports' could generate a chain of correspondence. Letters would arrive from the Secretary for Marine with a stream of trifling questions, such as: how many keepers were employed on this task; was this a station job involving departmental material; did the accident occur during working hours—and the answers that made their slow way back from the lighthouse were likely to be based on strategy rather than truth.

Presumably somebody in Head Office read all these reports. It would have been a time-consuming task, for there was no limit to the trivia they contained. Everybody's arrival and departure was recorded, and no sack of coal or drum of fuel, no empty sack or drum, was unaccounted for. If there were personality problems, the P.K. could also mention these.

The long lash of the Marine Department whipped out around all of New Zealand's twenty-three manned light-stations, and licked us neatly into shape. I should say 'shipshape', because, although we were a far-flung community of landlubbers, our lives were ruled by the sea and by 'The Department'.

But all these matters became only slowly apparent to me. On the whole, instead of feeling burdened by the patriarchal regime which regulated our lives, I began to feel secure and well cared for.

CHAPTER 6

Christmas

Time passed so quickly that I hadn't even had a chance to learn to milk the cow before Dad and my sister, Barb, arrived for Christmas. I was looking forward to their visit. The previous Christmas had been awful, with Mum just gone and presents to open that she'd left behind and Dad telling us how she'd insisted that he take her into town so she could choose them for us, knowing they would be the last, and I appalled, knowing what effort that had cost her. It had been awful, just awful, and with the coming of Christmas again I couldn't help but remember.

But that hadn't been all. I remembered, too, that apart from Christmas Day I had spent most of that following two weeks at home on the orchard with only one-year-old Fred for company. To make matters worse, he had got bronchitis and had clung to me all day, wailing and wheezing, and I had felt worried, bereaved and alone.

Why was I alone that Christmas, and where was Pip? He had gone away into the mountains on a Christmas-trip—which is what earnest young mountaineers traditionally did each year during their two weeks' annual holiday. For them, Christmas-trips were an institution, their only chance to get a long break in the mountains. It was also a sort of status-enhancing activity, and, by marrying me, Pip had missed two whole seasons, the first because he was 'getting hitched', and the second because we were 'having a sprog'.

Earlier that year he had done an Easter-trip into the mountains and I, determined not to miss out, had sewn up a canvas pack to fit beneath the 'sprog's' carry-frame, had stuffed it with clothes, sleeping bags, food and nappies, had swung a billy and a teddy bear from the top corners, and, with Fred perched on top of the whole amazing assembly, I'd staggered off intending to have my own Easter-trip in the valleys below. But I'd quickly realised that babies and 'adventures' could be a recipe for disaster. By day I'd been afraid I would drown Fred during river crossings, and by night I had shared the hut with disgusted young men who'd viewed me and my baby with sulky eyes.

On the third day I had tramped back to the empty camping ground, pitched my little yellow tent in the most remote corner and spent a fearful night while a gang of hoodlums roared around outside on motorbikes, boozing and shouting and guffawing hideously.

It was enough to scare any young woman on her own, and, for the first time, I realised how little protection a tent provided against anything but the weather. After that I knew when I was beaten. I had wanted marriage and babies—well, I was a girl so of course I had—so I had better become a 'proper' wife and mother. And I'd better not hold back my man, either. This was why, when Christmas had come, in spite of Mum's death, Pip had gone with my blessing on his Christmas-trip; down south to Mount Earnslaw with his friend, Mac. Malcolm Riding was his full name.

Mac was more than just an ordinary friend. Ever since they'd been skinny boys he and Pip had hefted their packs among hills and mountains, dreaming of peaks they'd climb, boats they'd sail and countries they'd explore together; but this had come to a sudden halt. When Mac was seventeen he'd had to return 'home' to England with his parents. Having been brought up as an all-New Zealand boy he had pretty soon been casting around desperately for the means of getting himself back to the country that *he* called 'home'. He'd made it, eventually, with the help of a loan from Pip.

During his absence, Pip had finished his building apprenticeship and left home to 'see the world'. He had climbed a fair few mountains, including Mount Cook, and he had met me. Then I, too, had left home— tucked under Pip's protective arm. We had got as far as Christchurch, found a boarding house, found jobs and spent every weekend 'in the hills'. When Mac had returned from England, there I was, the traditional ball and chain threatening to spoil everything. Not that anyone had said such a thing. At the boarding house I had been the only female boarder among seven young men. We had all got on well and several of the others also had girlfriends. The difference had been that these others would all one day be engineers and accountants, and wives would fit into their lives and be assets. But Pip and Mac had long had their hearts set on adventure, just the two of them, together.

Had I really trapped Pip into marriage? Why had he let himself be caught? Right from the start there had been times when I'd felt crab-pinched with guilt.

"Four new tyres for the Landrover," he'd joked after we'd become engaged. "That's what it cost me!" Was it a joke?

"You were the one that proposed," he'd said. Another joke—or had it been an accusation?

In a way it was true. We'd idly stopped outside a jeweller's window, inside which were dozens of dazzling diamond rings. I had always preferred emeralds so I'll never know what possessed me to say, "We should get one of those."

He'd immediately said, "Okay," (no discussion, no planning), and in less than ten minutes we'd walked out of the shop with a diamond ring sparkling traditionally on the third finger of my left hand. It was worth 'four new tyres for the Landrover'.

Pip had traded in his green truck for this Landrover, and sometimes, while lurching over back-country tracks, Mac or I would ride on its roof rack—with not a care in the world. "Four new tyres. . . " That's how he'd broken the news to Mac. It was a joke—definitely like a little crab pinching inside me, but I'd had to laugh.

Mac hadn't even smiled. He'd just sat dragging on his pipe, his gaze fixed on an imaginary point somewhere in the distance beyond where his long, outstretched legs ended, and I had known that he was thinking of the adventures he and Pip weren't going to share. But he was too good a friend to be churlish. Too good a person, all round. Men and women of all ages were drawn to Mac. With his beard and fine features, he resembled the typical picture of Jesus Christ, handsome, charismatic and with the look of the seer in his eyes. He was my age, just over a year younger than Pip, and much 'better looking'. They were odd companions—Jesus Christ and a wise little gnome—in my opinion, a blend of the very best of male virtues.

Pip's next adventures being marriage and babies hadn't included Mac (except for the Christmas and Easter trips) but when we'd had the idea of joining the lighthouse service, Mac had decided to do the same.

In fact, because he was unmarried, he'd been accepted and taken on straight away as a relief keeper.

The Marine Department employed seven or eight single men to stand in for married keepers when they were absent from station and there was a good chance that, before long, Mac would arrive on Stephens Island to relieve. Knowing his likable personality and his unconscious ability to influence everyone he met, we were sure he'd be able to talk Head Office into sending him to relieve either Dave or Arne as soon as one of them took leave.

The home base of all the relief keepers was The Brothers Island Lighthouse. Three at a time manned the station, all of them part of a continual rotation that gave them each six weeks on The Brothers and six weeks elsewhere. Typically, an R.K. would have a stint of four weeks at another station—perhaps Cape Reinga at the north-western tip of the North Island—then two weeks at somewhere like Farewell Spit at the northern tip of the South Island, then an overnight stay at the Federal Hotel in Picton before his next six weeks on The Brothers.

Each time the *Enterprise* made its fortnightly mail trip to The Brothers it carried out one incoming keeper and took to shore the keeper who had just finished his six weeks on the Rock; for a rock was all it was, the largest of a group of rocks of varying sizes, known collectively as The Brothers.

The only one of these rocks of importance to us was the one which bore the lighthouse. It was the one we thought of when we mentioned The Brothers. We could see it from Stephens Island. Our houses didn't face south-east but, if we were out and about on a clear night, our eyes always lingered in that direction, searching for a spark of light in the ocean blackness. "There it is," we'd say, "there's The Brothers," and, with the whole sparkling universe of stars arching over our heads we'd focus on that flashing pinpoint, seeing only that one friendly little light in the vast expanse of night. Knowing that it was a manned lighthouse made it special, and knowing that one of its residents was likely to be Mac made its message warm and personal.

On a clear day I needed to go only a few paces up the hill from our house to see The Brothers. They made up a little pebble of blue out in the sea, well beyond Cape Jackson with Cook Strait and the hazy Wellington Headlands fading on the distant horizon.

It was from this south-easterly direction that the *Enterprise* came to us but, after rounding Cape Jackson, it was halfway to Stephens Island before it could be seen with naked eye. At first a dot, ("I can see it. . . no, yes. . . there it is"), it grew bigger and bigger, climbing up and over the swell like a beetle over rippled sand.

Our mailday was always different from the rest of the fortnight, but, because of the babies, even by Christmas week I hadn't yet made it down to the block to watch the unloading of the supplies. Instead I knelt beside Fred in the grass on the ridge and directed his gaze towards the south-east. "Grandad and Aunty Barb are coming on the boat."

He gazed out obediently. Perhaps he saw Sentinel Rock. I doubted that he saw the *Enterprise*, at first no more than a flea slowly, slowly ploughing over ripples, then a beetle. The gusty wind took his breath away. I was glad my sister, Barb, was a good sailor. She hated heights even more than I, but she was happy on the water. Dad, too, was never seasick. He'd spent a fair bit of time fishing from a dinghy and he'd been to the other side of the earth and back during the First World War.

A couple of hours later Pip delivered them safely to the gate and surrounded them with suitcases, boxes of Christmas goodies and cartons of stores. And what was this? Something huge and secret packaged up with plenty of tape and string around it.

"For Fred!" Dad whispered. I looked in astonishment at him and received an unpractised wink in reply. Fred, himself, was more interested in his grandfather than in anything else and was already clinging to one leg of his rough saddle-tweed trousers.

I was suddenly aware of the sky and the great expanse of sea and the quiet hillside, and a gap that needed filling with words. "Come inside, come inside," I said. "What sort of a trip did you have?" And my smile felt wider than my face as we carried the boxes and cases into the house.

The big package was left alone beside the coal bunker. Already I had guessed what it contained. Just for once, Dad had wanted to do something really extravagant. Something to show the gratitude and love he felt for a little boy who'd brought new warmth into his life. He'd talked about it before I'd left Nelson—not in a soppy way, of course—he'd simply told me he'd seen this shiny, new pedal car in town that would be "just right for Fred".

As a father, Dad had always been poor. First the depression and then his war pension had made sure of that. Mum would never let him fritter money away on 'rubbish'. She'd made sure that everything we bought was, first, necessary, and, next, good quality. Money didn't grow on trees, and a pedal car or anything else as frivolous didn't come into the equation. Prince Charles had had a pedal car. I was older than Prince Charles but had been still young enough to envy him his car. I'd seen the picture in a magazine, the chubby little prince looking like a toy himself, sitting in a limousine that looked like the real thing. Mum had said it 'wouldn't do him any good'!

Now that Dad had so obviously and rashly followed his own inclination and splurged his money on a pedal car, recklessly ignoring the code of frugality that had been integral to our family life, I myself felt twin pangs of excitement and guilt—but, in Dad, I saw only the former. He was a little boy waiting for Christmas morning. Later, as we carried the big package up the concrete steps to the dog-box, our dark little shed in the corner of the section, he whispered, "It's got a hooter and real lights."

Arne had promised that between Christmas and New Year there would be only minimal station work for the keepers. Now it was the day before Christmas. Pip would be finishing work earlier than usual, and, though we were miles away from the rest of the world, we were all affected by the Christmas spirit. I had that summer holiday feeling of freedom, a hangover from childhood, not yet crushed by adult responsibilities

Barb and I sat at the kitchen table, bowls of black currants between us. Their deep, aromatic tang tickled the backs of our noses. The crimson juice stained our fingers as we searched for stalks and leaves that might spoil the jam. Black currants had featured in our lives since childhood. Our parents had had the knack of supplying dung, grass clippings and water in just the right amounts and at the precise moments to ensure they got bumper harvests on their half dozen bushes. Our tea table had always been graced by a large pot of jam. There'd been no fancy dishes or ceremony at our meal times but Mum had had an instinct about what was vitamin-rich and nourishing. Already, since her death, Dad had learnt to make jam, himself, but from now on I was going to be the recipient of the bulk of his black currant harvest.

As we sorted the fruit I chose the biggest, juiciest and blackest and put them on a saucer for Fred. He stood beside the table picking them up delicately one by one. Chewing, screwing up his eyes and swallowing. "More. More."

I wiped his fingers with the dishcloth. "Just a few more. There, that's enough for now."

The screen door banged in the porch, followed by the voices of Dad and Pip as they unlaced their boots. Dad's face crinkled with pleasure as he came in. "Aw, you're getting on to that jam. That'll be good."

Pip went straight to the stove which was roaring in expectation of the jam making. "Cup of tea, Jim?" Then he turned to me. "What have we got in the way of presents we could give the others? I've found out we do all give presents—all the families."

We'd wondered about this but decided that, in a place without shops like Stephens Island, it wouldn't be practical. Maybe we'd swap a pot or two of fresh jam and share a few treats but there'd surely not be a great, inter-family gift-giving occasion.

Pip said, "The others are calling in later tomorrow afternoon, after Christmas dinner. I know they've got things for us."

"Oh, no! What sort of things? We haven't got anything special for them." At the back of my mind it had been troubling me. How could we know, until the moment arrived, whether or not we should have presents to exchange with the others? I should have prepared for this eventuality before I arrived on the island, but at that stage I hadn't understood the nature of the lighthouse community. Also I was realising more and more that I was hopeless at choosing presents and that, though Pip was just as bad, being a man absolved him from the responsibility. Between the two of us we didn't bother much for ourselves, but bought things when we wanted them, saying, "This'll be our Christmas present," or "I'll give you this for your birthday," never on the right day, sometimes two presents for the one occasion and sometimes none. I tried to be thoughtful about other people and I spent hours agonising over choices for my family, my immediate desire to be flagrantly generous always tempered by the prudent parsimony of my childhood. How I envied those happy souls who swept through shops confidently gathering up gifts. Why couldn't I do the same?

Above the bowls of black currants my startled eyes met my sister's, deep and calm as vats of treacle. Slowly she arched her dark brows, "Well, we'll just have to set to and make a few things, won't we."

Of course we would. We weren't our mother's daughters for nothing, and as my mind accepted the challenge, my panic began to subside.

Almost gaily, Barb said, "Necessity's the mother of invention." It was one of Mum's favourite and oft-repeated maxims. She'd had a saying for every exigency; comforting little rules, like safety nets designed to support us when we faltered. I remembered another, "It's easier to give than receive."

"Oh, really," I said savagely to myself, "for other people, maybe!" As I weighed the black currants and added a pint of water for each pound of fruit, my mind raced through a maze of possibilities, considering the means at our disposal for creating something out of nothing in time for tomorrow. I recalled presents received and given over the years—past Christmases and birthdays revisited, inspected, picked over, rejected. None of these memories were particularly memorable except for one Christmas I'd spent with an aunt. We'd received crackers and clickers and things that made a racket when you blew through them. And, best of all, my aunt had given me a book with only a paper cover, which Mum had, later, called a "bloomin' old penny dreadful", but I'd savoured every paltry word of it, over and over. That had been my best Christmas—the only one with a tree and decorations. We'd heard the queen on radio for the first time and my cousin had driven me mad for hours afterwards by mimicking the posh English accent. It was December 1953 and we should have been feeling sad because of the terrible Tangiwai rail disaster, but it had seemed a long, long way away from the infinite safety of my grandmother's seaside bach.

All that was now a very long way from Stephens Island where my two tin trunks full of material and knick-knacks seemed to offer the best hope for creating something out of nothing by midnight. I heaved the trunks out from the wardrobe in our bedroom, parked them in the middle of the floor and threw open their lids, exposing to view my hoards of materials and scraps. I riffled through them. There was fake fur and velvet, gingham and corduroy; florals of all kinds, and felt; braids, threads, yarns, patterns, buttons, buckles and beads.

My usual self-confidence returned with a rush of ideas. "Cushions, we can make cushions—and look at this pattern for a fluffy dog. It's really simple and we could make it for the little ones. . . or a mouse, with this teddy bear fur we could make a mouse. What do you think about the men?" Here my imagination failed me. Coming from a family both inspired and dominated by women, I hadn't much understanding of males

I looked hopefully at Barb. Her answer was glib. "The way to a man's heart is through his stomach." This wasn't one of Mum's sayings. It was too flippant, too silly—and yet, wasn't it so true? I thought back to the bags of peppermints and brandy balls which I'd inflicted on Dad, Christmas after Christmas, and which he'd always accepted with a credible show of honest delight. Now that I was an adult I'd progressed to more interesting presents. This year we were giving him a sleeping bag. From the Marine Department I'd received a maternity allowance for the six weeks I had waited in Nelson and, as Dad had accepted nothing in payment for accommodating me, I had spent the money on a sleeping bag of excellent quality —the kind of bag mountaineers would die for. It was the sort of bag I'd coveted on many a cold night spent in trampers' huts while Pip and Mac had snored away quietly beside me. At this stage I was only just becoming aware that Dad had a super-efficient circulatory system and that he slept hot. Even as I contemplated what a sensible and useful gift this was, I had the uneasy feeling that it might be excessive, because Dad did seem quite comfortable using his simple bedroll and would probably be just as happy to receive peppermints and socks. But at least Dave and Arne would be easy. They would need no more than a little something to put into their stomachs.

After dinner, with cushions in mind, I cut out and sewed patchwork squares while Barb cut a cat from some white fake fur. It was a willowy creature (somehow, everything I drew, myself, seemed to look overweight). Such an elegant cat needed a sumptuous background and we'd found just the right stuff. Side by side on the red settee lay two exotic garments, the blue satin 'Suzie Wong' dress I'd made for my sixth form dance, and the black velvet dress Mum had worn during her flapper days, its scalloped hem bound with bright orange braid.

Barb fingered the cloth. "Gee whizz!" she said. "They don't make nice velvet like this these days."

"No, and fancy her keeping it all these years! I s'pose it was too good to throw away."

"She didn't throw much away."

"Well, it's a wonder she didn't make it up into something for you during the slump."

My sisters had always made sure I was aware of my good fortune in not being a child of the depression, which was a time when they had had to eat dandelion greens and wear bloomers made from flour bags. And they'd put their naked dolls to sleep between newspapers. "We had only one doll each, Jeanie. One doll! And old Mrs. Sparrow took pity on us and gave us some stuff for dolls' dresses but Mum swooped on it and made clothes for us out of it instead. She didn't want to take it off us but we were that poor. . . "

Family history! Stories repeated so often around the tea table they had become legends to me. So much had happened in our family before I was born that I'd grown up believing I'd missed out on a lifetime of character-building experiences but now I was making my own history and creating my own family legends. I was 'living on a lighthouse' and the tuatara were stalking about outside in the darkness and dovies were making their usual fuss as they swooped in from the sea.

Through the open window the night air rolled gently down onto my hands as I cut a large square from the skirt of Mum's flapper dress. The black velvet was soft as night, a superb background for a white fake fur cat. Next, feeling no compunction, I sliced a same-sized square from the dark satin of my slimline 'Suzy Wong'. I had been seventeen the first time I'd worn it and I'd felt like a beautiful and desirable woman, but its magic had later evaporated when the hands of the drunks at Saturday night dances had slid over the satin in a way that had made me feel like a tart. After that I had joined a tramping club and spent my weekends wearing boots, shorts and jerseys, and a year later I'd met Pip whose hands stayed where they belonged until they were invited and whose funny sayings made me laugh.

"Dancing!" he'd said. "It's just a vertical impression of a horizontal intention," and, from then on, the closest I had come to a waltz or a quick-step was linking arms to make a safe river crossing.

The skirt of the 'Suzie Wong' looked great as the back of a cushion.

The satin, the velvet and the elegant white cat made an opulent combination. We completed the picture with glittering rhinestone eyes— (relics from an old friendship with someone who had tried to woo me with gems rather than jokes). We would give this cushion to Cis. She was an expert dressmaker and, like me, she hoarded materials. As well as this she possessed a quality I defined as 'flair'.

At last the frenzy of creating and gift-making was over. Pip had laboriously poked foam chip stuffing into the toys and cushions and Barb had stitched the gaps closed. I'd found a book about explorers that seemed suitable for ten-year-old Anthony. It was one that I'd received myself at the same age and, now, I tore off the old, Christmas-paper slip-wrap that I'd put on it so long ago and found that the cover underneath was still as bright as new. I relaxed, relieved that we wouldn't lose face over presents and felt pretty sure we'd be holding our own in our microscopic community. It would be a good Christmas. I had nearly all my family captive at home and nobody was dying or giving birth or going away on a Christmas-trip.

As I prepared for bed I planned the day to come. In the morning while Pip was reporting on the weather and milking the cow, I'd get the chook stuffed and ready to roast. Later we'd eat it with the green peas and new potatoes which Dad had brought from his garden, and we'd finish the meal with the Christmas pudding my aunt had made and sent out with him. In it, as usual, there would be threepences and sixpences 'for luck' and we'd swamp it with cow's cream thicker than custard. Then, when we were totally bloated, we'd start on the top tier of our wedding cake which we had been saving for 'the christening'— an event that neither of us now believed to be likely or necessary. We'd laze about and, later on, the others would visit and we'd swap presents. The men might have a few drinks and Dad's eyes would grow bright and his nose would grow red and, as usual, this effect would be caused by his drinking only one or two glasses of beer. Maybe Arne and Cis would tell us more of their stories.

As I brushed up the threads and scraps of material I looked with satisfaction about the room. It was every bit as spotless as the kitchens of the other houses. Cis and Peggy both had electric floor-polishers. Maybe I'd get one, myself, one day. It could be my late Christmas present. I had the washing machine, of course. I supposed that was my present.

I had serious reservations about that new-fangled thing. No matter how I packed the clothes into the spinner the machine bucked and pranced like a Christmas reindeer. Already it had vibrated off its outlet hoses and flooded the floor. Pip had cursed it and repaired it and had tried to demonstrate how to balance the clothes in the spinner. It had continued to jig about derisively and, again, he'd blamed the power source and speculated gloomily about its future performances, but I had faith in his ability to fix anything—well, almost anything.

A ghost-pale gecko clung to the outside of the window-screen, watching for moths. It was just one of the millions of lizards that scuttled about on this island. These little mottled geckos prowled about at night and hid during the day but there was a different species, a vibrant green one, that lived its life in the open, relying on its colour to camouflage it among leaves. I'd seen only one of them. Cis had found it "on top of the island" and now kept it as a pet. One day I, too, would own a green gecko that would lick honey off the end of my finger. One day!

For the first time in hours I noticed the ticking of the clock. We had compromised over its chimes and it currently struck only the hours. Already it had gone midnight and I was the only person not in bed. The fire, now barely warm, was banked up with fine coal and dust, its dampers and vents closed until morning. Next to it, on the sideboard, stood two dozen shining jars of black-red jam and, beside them, an unexpected pile of wrapped presents which had arrived both in the mailbag and with Dad. Friends and relations didn't want us to feel neglected "stuck out there in the middle of nowhere". I looked at the packages with hopeful and childish excitement. No doubt there'd be some really sensible gifts but I was sure there'd be others that were less serious and more trifling, even just a wee bit trashy—such as crackers and chocolate Santa Clauses and Christmas trinkets.

The pedal car, which had been brought in and unpacked with appropriate respect, gleamed scarlet and white in the centre of the room. We'd squeezed its hooter and tried out its lights. To me it looked particularly flimsy and flashy and I imagined that, in our salty atmosphere, it would rust away in no time. I knew exactly what Mum would have thought of it. I could hear her voice at the back of my head and, yes, I agreed, it did look as if it would "fall to bits in five minutes". In all those years she'd had Dad doing things her way she hadn't managed to change him much. It seemed rather sad, and yet, on the positive side, surely there was a lesson in it for me. Maybe there was even cause for celebration that, in his quiet way, Dad was still his own man.

I felt as pleased about the pedal car as if it were intended for me. At first Fred would be too young to pedal it but Dad would be down on the floor pushing it and 'demonstrating' the hooter and lights. I could picture them both. I could picture us all; but it was high time I was in bed because I could also picture Helen, in just a few hours, snuffling in her bassinet, wanting her early morning feed, and then there would be no more rest for me until Christmas Day was over.

And, by the end of the day, almost exactly as I had imagined it, that was the way everything had turned out. The gifts, the Christmas chook, the pudding with threepences and sixpences, my father's flushed cheeks and red nose, Barb and I the only adults drinking lemonade, and the children squabbling over the pedal car. Fred was in a two-year-old's heaven, a place where anything of importance was painted bright red and ran on wheels. As well as books and a pink drum he had received a red and white pedal car, a red and white Tonka jeep, a red and black wheelbarrow, and a tractor and trailer of die-cast metal which had been one of Anthony's own toys. Anthony had restored them with a coat of bright red paint and given them to Fred with no visible signs of regret. Among other things Helen had received a wobbly clown but was too young to care.

That night, after everyone else had fallen into bed, I said to Pip, "I'm making my New Year's resolution here and now. In future I'm gonna make sure we've got a whole lot of things on hand to give to people for presents. . . things like smelly soaps and face flannels and tea towels. . . colouring books for kids and. . . maybe we should keep that box of chocolates we got today. Not eat them yet—just in case— somebody might have a birthday soon."

"It's all right by me," Pip said. "I've eaten enough today to last the rest of the year. How long can you keep chocolates?"

"Maybe a year," I said. "But we wouldn't keep them that long." A thought struck me. "Maybe we won't keep them after all. You shouldn't give away your presents—and what if Aunty C. already kept them a year before she gave them to us? What if they were already old when someone gave them to her. . ." I broke off, intrigued by the idea of an everlasting gift being passed on year after year until, one day, someone decided to open it up and eat the chocolates. "You never know," I said. "That box might already contain just a heap of dust and weevils."

Pip had begun to yawn. He yawned so long and hard I thought he was going to be sick. "Oh, ah a," he groaned. "I'll have to go and hit the sack before m' eyes drop out—what'd you say about weevils?"

"Nothing really," my mouth and lungs were already aching to stretch into a yawn. "It was a good day, that's what. . . " I yawned. "Oooh, aah. . . and everyone really liked all the presents we made." I yawned again. "And Cis, she really loved that cat cushion. It turned out so good, I wished I could have kept it myself."

CHAPTER 7

Land of Plenty

"It's such a waste," I said to Barb as I sloshed an almost full bucket of milk over the patchy grass on the bank outside our yard. "But I don't know what else to do with it."

"It's pig-food," Barb said. "You'll have to get a pig." In a way she was right. I'd already set aside a couple of jugs for the table and separated the cream off the rest so that what remained was the 'skim', traditionally pig-food, but it still seemed such a waste.

"We don't need a pig. I could feed an orphanage with the food we've got here. So much mutton and fish and eggs, milk and butter and cream. . . " Every morning as I heaved the skim milk out over the paddock I felt the eyes of the starving children of the world boring into my back. Eyes like empty wells and pleading hands outstretched.

I had been brain-washed at an early age by Barb, by my other sister, Paul, and my mother. "You eat up your dinner. There are poor little girls and boys in Korea"—(in India, in Africa)—"with nothing to eat." They had had to educate me. I, the little one, the baby of the family and, therefore, in grave danger of being 'spoilt'.

"Eat up your dinner. Starving children. Poverty worldwide." Now, as an adult, I didn't question my feelings. The concept welled up from deep inside me. If you waste food you're somehow responsible for causing pitiful distended bellies in Africa and the plight of whole families who live in drainpipes in India.

"So much food we could start an orphanage," I said again.

"You and Pip will have to have lots of kids."

"No. Too many people in the world already. We should really have only one kid each—sort of replacements for ourselves." (Worldwide over-population! Not enough food to go around! My early tutors had done their job well.) "But I could borrow some. Have you got any little orphans in the 'home'?" Barb was 'mother' to dozens of needy children at the Methodist Children's Home in Christchurch.

"No, they've all got parents of some sort."

I sighed inwardly. Hardly any orphans in this country; just kids with inadequate parents. Still, I could borrow some of those. More and more as I enjoyed this land of plenty I dreamed of fattening a horde of happy children with the fruits of the earth—with this new profusion that was ours. Every day this faceless tribe of barefoot boys and girls, patched but clean, free but well cared for, arose in a vision before my eyes to keep at bay the spectre of the hungry children who watched at my back as the wasted cascade of milk sluiced across the grass. And I, too, felt in danger of being wasted. I could see myself spending the years of my youth in mothering just two little children when a few more couldn't possibly make much difference—when we had this abundance of food which should be for sharing with people who had less, when we had so much to spare but nobody in need.

This was Boxing Day, and Christmas Day had been everything I had hoped it would be, but what is it about Christmas? Pip and Dad had been glad to make their escape this morning. After milking the cow, a job they both enjoyed, they'd taken their lines down to the block to fish. More fish! More food! More good eating—and tonight we would be feasting at Cis and Arne's house. We were all too rich, too well-off, too well-fed, while elsewhere in the world so many people were starving.

Down at the block Pip and Dad were unworried by thoughts of over-supply. They had handlines with heavy sinkers and were trying out some new swivel-hooks. Pip put the landing-box onto the hook of the crane and Dad climbed into it with his knife, bait, cutting board and line. Then Pip swung him out and lowered him until he hung, spinning just above the water. To stop its rotation they anchored the box with a line to the shore and thus they fished, Pip from the rocks and Dad dangling from the crane—"just thinking he was Christmas," as Pip commented when they arrived in for lunch. The swivel hooks had been "a waste of time" but the morning's tally, caught on traditional hooks, was "a good-sized trevally and three blue cod".

The block wasn't the best place to fish but it was easily accessible and usually yielded enough for a feed within a couple of hours. The keepers had more favoured fishing spots which were all at the bottom of cliffs accessed by routes that required rock climbing skills and a brave heart.

Of these, the most popular and closest to home was the Little Razorback, a quarter-sized brother to the massive Big Razorback. It jutted out in the same direction directly below the cliffs between our house and number two house. One afternoon, while Pip baby-sat, I had taken a walk around the cliff-tops wishing I could somehow reach the sea which was still about two hundred feet below. I went further down the ever narrowing ridge toward the Little Razorback until I found myself edging around the brink of vertical walls sheer as skyscrapers. Then, seeing the route ahead disappearing steeply out of sight, I knew I could never go down there. But Pip sometimes raced down there after work, taking less than thirty minutes from home, and within a couple of hours he'd be back with fish for dinner.

Dad wasn't particularly a climbing man and perhaps he'd never make it down to the Little Razorback, but I could see by the look in his eye after the morning's fishing expedition at the block that he was, himself, firmly hooked on the lighthouse experience. In less than a week he'd seen more of the station than I had in six. He'd followed the keepers about as they'd shifted gear by winch and tractor. He'd accompanied Pip to and from the lighthouse. He'd had his turn in the milking shed and he'd rambled alone up and down gullies and in and out of patches of bush. He'd also casually trespassed through other keepers' garden plots in a way that Pip and I wouldn't have dreamed of doing. Seeing him passing, the others had invited him in for cups of tea.

He had come home delighted, especially with Cis and Arne. "Such fine people! They made a real fuss of me."

I was beginning to realise that people did treat Dad with respect. When I was a child I had thought that other adults had regarded him as just 'poor old Jim'. Later I hadn't been so sure that they'd been making fun of him behind his back. Perhaps it had been just a childish worry of my own. It was true that until he had got a car at the age of sixty, (after the death of my maternal grandparents), he had ridden around town on an old bicycle with a canvas bag on his back—this at a time when my friends' fathers were driving off each morning to work at 'proper' jobs. It was also true that Mum had frequently reminded me in a tone of teasing sympathy that I was "a poor old war vet's daughter". This was probably her way of challenging me and my sisters to get our education and become a success in life, but I had resented her implying that there was something wrong with Dad, not perhaps in her own eyes but in the eyes of the rest of society.

Of course she had probably been simply hoping that, one day, we'd make our father proud, or at least justify that pride he already had for us, because there was no doubt that, where his family was concerned, he was bursting with it. Pip and I were all too aware that he'd already used the time he'd spent with Cis and Arne to sing our praises shamelessly and fish for compliments that would confirm his belief that we would one day (if not already) be the most brilliantly capable couple in the history of the service. To our surprise, in spite of his artlessness, Cis and Arne had treated him like a respected elder. Then, when Pip had privately tried to apologise for all Dad's boasting about us, they'd gently made it plain that his behaviour was perfectly acceptable and that he wasn't at all "a silly old coot"—and that as a man of seventy, with knowledge to share, he deserved respect—and I was grateful for that.

One aspect of Dad's life that I'd always envied was that he'd been the middle child of thirteen. As a youngster I had often thought wistfully of the fun he must have had growing up among six brothers and six sisters—on a diet, so it seemed, of hearty country fare such as porridge, jam roly-poly and steak and kidney pudding.

My idealised perception of their family life was partly responsible for those visions I now had of raising more than just two children. It seemed to me that our two would never learn to give and take and rough and tumble if their positions as prince and princess in our family remained unchallenged. Compared with thirteen, our one boy and one girl seemed to be hardly a family at all. They were just 'a pigeon pair' and the term sounded as derogatory and as alarming to me as that other—'an only child'.

Anthony was an only child and I'd seen how, day after day, Cis laboured with him over his school work and deluged him with all the love and care and annoyance and frustration that my own grandmother would have had to divide into thirteen and allot in small dilute portions to each child. In the isolation integral to our lifestyle, Anthony's 'only-ness' scared me and I wondered if our pigeon pair would be any better off. We wouldn't always be on a station where there were other children of a similar age to our own, and, although it was always said that two's company and three's a crowd, to me two sounded dangerously cosy.

So far I hadn't laid out these thoughts and treasured dreams for Pip's inspection. He'd been suspiciously quick to agree that with too many people in the world already we definitely shouldn't produce more than two children of our own. I wasn't sure that he'd be as quick to see that we, nevertheless, needed a larger family. He would, of course, eventually see it my way (such a reasonable man with plenty of commonsense) but to me it was all so obvious—as if I had received a message from the angel Gabriel himself.

That evening spent at Cis and Arne's wasn't in any way particularly memorable but it was important in introducing us to the social ritual of the years that lay ahead. It seemed that in the absence of theatres, shows, shopping trips, church services and most of the other entertainments that 'normal people' enjoyed in the company of one another, lighthouse folk would dine together in a slightly formal way. There was a sense of dignity that had to be preserved. We would dress tidily—the men usually wearing white shirts but stopping short of ties—and we'd set off through whatever weather the heavens were in the mood to hurl at us. Traipsing through mud, dust, rain, fog, through the last long rays of sunshine or leaning half-horizontally into a gale, we'd home in on the aroma of roasting meat that almost invariably wafted out through open windows. In the porch we'd kick our feet free of gumboots and, on the doorstep, our host would appear still fresh-faced from the shower, smelling of shampoo and, though quite dressed up, he'd often be barefoot.

About this time Arne had repainted their kitchen-living area. I hadn't seen the job since its inception but Pip's progress reports and comments on the colour scheme had filled me with curiosity. He had said, "It's very modern I s'pose, but I'm not sure about it really. You'll probably like it. You know more about these things than I do."

Now I entered the house prepared to see something outrageous that I'd either love or hate on sight—something deliciously extreme.

Beneath the bare electric bulbs, harsh reflections echoed off all the usual dazzling surfaces: the highly polished floor, the stainless steel and

Formica bench tops, the Shacklock '501', but now the stove's hearth and recessed surround were newly painted bright scarlet and, all around us, the walls were glossier than glass—white, white, white and, standing out against them in stark contrast, a sheer coal-face of cupboards (there were more than a dozen of them in the kitchen) and they were black, shiny as wet tar—black, black, black.

As I gazed in awe at this black and white phenomenon I became aware of a moment of expectation in which Cis and Arne were watching for my reaction and waiting for me to express (oh lord!) my intelligent opinion. I couldn't simply say, "It's lovely." That would sound too corny and, besides, they deserved better than that. But I was unpractised in the art of flattery, and 'gushing' was a bad word from my childhood. Gushing was for hypocritical old ladies and flighty females—not for the likes of my sisters and me. In my mind I heard other warnings from my past. "Fools rush in where angels fear to tread. You're a bit blunt sometimes, Jean. A bit too honest like your old Grandad Atkins." It was a wall of warnings which dammed up my brain. Pip had an easy knack of turning a phrase to make light of any situation—but not I. I was much too intent on my quest for sincerity and I had long schooled myself up with admonitions such as, 'If you can't say something good, you should say nothing at all.'

Nothing at all! But a long silence would be an answer in itself, so I opened my mouth and words leapt out.

"It's so—so striking! The black and the white together. It's just like you two!"

Then I saw their two faces side by side—the Norwegian white and the Maori dark—both wearing curious expressions. Expressions which reminded me of the warning, "where angels fear to tread". With the despairing feeling that tact was never going to be my strong point I plunged into the strange little silence. "I mean it reflects your strong personalities so well."

Cis chuckled. "I suppose you could say that."

Phew! I thought, still gazing around me and digesting the black, the white, and the red together. It was indeed striking. And, although I might not want the same in my own house, in spite of my haste to say the right thing, I had nevertheless managed to tell the truth.

I was beginning to realise that, on a light-station, there was no excuse for anyone to complain that there was nothing to do, because there was always something to paint. Walls, roofs, water tanks, motors, gates, and (on some stations) boats: all could be chipped and stripped and rejuvenated with paint. Keepers quickly learnt to wield a brush effectively. Some did it under sufferance while others almost took it up as a hobby and routinely redecorated each house they occupied after being transferred. And it could be infectious. On seeing Arne hard at work, Dave had decided to tackle his own bathroom. He was a man whose enthusiasm came in short-lived bursts and he was in far too much of a hurry to do any preparation—or even to change his clothes. In the course of a day he managed to transform himself as well as his bathroom and emerged splattered with paint from the top of his tousled head to the soles of his brown leather shoes.

"His good town-shoes!" Peggy had lamented. We were mystified. Why had he worn shoes of any sort when painting his bathroom?

"Kept ma socks outta the paint," he explained. "Nobody'll notice a bit on ma shoes."

As for the room itself, we'd noted that its mainly white walls had several streaky blushes of pink that had deteriorated here and there into dribbles. This effect was the result of Dave's impatience to get on with the job, using the brush he'd just collected from Arne after it had been used to paint his fire-surround scarlet.

Later I chortled gleefully (nastily) to Pip, "Nobody'll notice! He must think everyone goes round with their eyes shut."

"Not much worries old Dave," Pip said, "but Arne's pretty disgusted."

There were no streaks or runs in Arne's paintwork, though he made much of pointing out to us a couple of faint imperfections on two of his highest cupboard doors. Straining to see them, I mentally noted that my own painting technique had better improve if I were ever to have a paintbrush in my hands on this station. Paint had a mind of its own. It knew exactly how to wait until your back was turned and then it would dribble and accumulate in waves across the walls. If you tried to brush them out it would be too late and you'd end up with an even bigger mess. Since the interior painting of light station dwellings was considered to be a privilege usually carried out in a keeper's own time, it wasn't surprising that Dave showed no further desire to enhance his home.

In fact, he and Peggy were starting to wonder when their first transfer to another station would take place. Assistant keepers could expect a move any time after their first year. It was Department Policy. New keepers needed experience on different stations. They began on islands and were transferred three or four times before becoming P.K.—by which time they should have learnt to cope with a selection of light systems and different kinds of equipment. I found it hard to imagine that we'd be gone from Stephens Island within eighteen months or two years. Such a change seemed so far in the future that I seldom thought about it.

Principal keepers were transferred less often than assistants, and Arne and Cis were confident that they would be on Stephens Island for a while yet. In ten years they'd lived on several stations and had grown used to a passing stream of assistants who had brought their own stories of their previous experience, shared their lives for a while and then moved on.

Now the table was laid for a dinner party with white plates with a pale blue border and gleaming silver. I had helped Cis prepare the vegetables and she had caught me popping a stray piece of raw carrot into my mouth and munching it. "Spoiling your appetite!" she had chided gently. "Didn't you think about that?" And I had felt myself flushing. Fred rushed up to me, laughing and bright-eyed after playing games with Anthony. He had already been fed and it was time to tuck him into his sleeping bag. Before long, feeling equally bright-eyed, I found myself sitting at the table between Pip and my sister, spooning down a bowl of fish soup that could have come straight from our mother's kitchen— and I had been sure that she was the only mother in the world who would boil up fish heads, complete with eyes, to make a tasty soup!

Dad slurped it appreciatively and began discussing the merits of various types of fish heads with Cis. We were all under her spell, and, as we began the main course, Barb told her about the sow thistle and dandelion greens Mum had served up to our family during the slump.

"Oh, those are proper Maori vegetables!" Cis laughed and when Barb said how strong they'd tasted she said, "It's easy to get the bitter flavour out of the puha. You rub it in a bucket of fresh water—between your knuckles, just like washing your clothes. The water goes completely green. . . " She glanced at me, "You come down, one day, and I'll show you how it's done."

I glowed and thought my 'real pioneering' thoughts. This was the right way to live. But then, (I couldn't believe it), Barb and Cis began to share their memories of flour-bag bloomers. It occurred to me that people who had lived through the slump and the 'war-years' were like old soldiers when they got together.

Cis said, "There was a girl at our school who lived with her aunt, and that aunt—she should have known better—didn't boil the label out of the flour bags. When that girl bent over there was the name of the flour-mill, branded in red and blue right across her backside. She was a laughing stock—the boys gave her such a hard time. That aunt should have thought about what it would be like for that poor child."

Now, here I was feeling like the little sister again, knowing that the salt-bag handkerchiefs I'd often had to blow my snotty little nose on just couldn't compete with the flour-bag bloomers that my poor little bottom had, so unfortunately, missed out on. So I let them talk and, before long, the subject changed back to lighthouses.

East Cape, Cuvier, Moko Hinau, Cape Campbell, Dog Island; place names I'd never heard before were becoming familiar. Just discussing their geographical positions, their lighthouses, the methods of getting to and from them and whether they were one-man, two-man, or three-man stations, kept us going for hours. Anecdotes thrown in were a bonus but Cis and Arne had little to say in the way of malicious gossip. At first I attributed this to their own particular high-mindedness but it hadn't taken me long to understand that, with staff constantly rotating around the twenty-three lighthouses, careless words could ricochet from one end of the country to the other.

We were hungry for information about lighthouses. We stored and savoured every little snippet. I had soon learnt that my own arrival on station with a new baby had been a tame affair. Just a few years earlier one new baby had arrived home to Stephens Island in bad weather and with the crane out of order. And that baby had flown ashore. Yes, the guy on the boat who was holding it had thrown it. Just like that. . . "Here, catch!" and it had flown through the air into its father's arms. Arne was shaking his head about it. Oh, yes, it was true all right, but just imagine if. . . It didn't bear thinking about.

Some stories had been handed down over generations. One of these told how a madman, a complete lunatic, had burnt the Puysegur Point Lighthouse to the ground. This had happened in 1942, the year before I was born, so it was ancient history. I was more interested to hear about Puysegur Point, itself, and what Cis and Arne had thought of it. My mind became a jumble of the things they told me. It was a rugged place on the edge of Fiordland.

Everything about it was legendary: the weather, the isolation and, particularly, the sandflies. The latter descended in ravening swarms, relentless in their lust for blood. They were much bigger than those little bloodsuckers you got everywhere else. Oh, much bigger and you couldn't escape them. There were so many of them. They drove animals crazy. Especially one bull, a white one, (black ones fared better, somehow, but this one was always black with sandflies), and finally it was driven mad and just charged to its death over a cliff. The animals down there suffered. And the people—the children had to be clothed from top to toe before they could venture outside and at Puysegur Point insect repellent arrived by the carton—by the boat-load—but it still wasn't enough. Maildays were three weeks apart. It was the most isolated of all the stations and it had been suggested many times that it was no place for women, children or animals. . .

It was all nonsense, of course. It wasn't nearly that bad. Not bad at all. As well as the sea, there were hundreds of square miles of bush between you and civilisation and it attracted a particular sort of hardy individual: fishermen, deer hunters, prospectors, all in search of their quarry. On the whole they were a good lot, but there were some blokes who were real wild ones. It was a wild place and on the station itself there had been a family who were half wild themselves. This family had older children who were always away out in the bush hunting game. They were frightening—those boys—and there was one of them, he was barely fourteen and taller than Arne and had already sprouted a huge ginger beard. He had such a crazy look in his eyes and was constantly watching you, saying nothing—and tinkering with his gun.

The mother! She was a big strong woman—and capable— made bread and scones and mince pies enough to feed an army (you should have seen that family eat!) She said to the new assistant's wife, "Come on over in the morning and I'll show you how it's done." The younger woman had turned up for her lesson next morning. She'd waited while the woman finished scrubbing her floor. She'd watched her swish dirty, black water out of the enamel bowl. She'd seen her wipe the bowl roughly with a filthy floor cloth and then she saw her measure the mincemeat into it—into the same bowl!

In spite of the intervening years, Cis was still comically outraged. Her mouth was a scallop of disgust as she seasoned her words with just the right amount of humour to make us laugh.

I snorted through my mouthful of potato and gravy, at the same time thinking that lighthouse families were obviously all different and at least the woman would have had a clean floor! Any dirt that had got into her pies would have been well cooked. Another of Mum's old sayings came to mind. "You have to eat a peck of dirt before you die." What was a peck?

Anthony helped his mother take the dinner plates to the kitchen. Once again I was struck by his nice manners and his quiet solitariness. He brought the pudding to the table. It was sweet and fruity, served with home-made icecream.

"Our own recipe," Arne said. "Half sweetened condensed milk and half cream." He licked his lips and his wide face split in a naughty-boy smile. "Is very rich!"

It undoubtedly was rich but on top of it we managed to blob dollops of custard and more cream. It slid down as easily as oysters.

"Another helping?"

"I shouldn't but it's so delicious." I passed my plate. "Just a little, thank you."

Later I was to look back and see myself stuffing down that second rich helping. Really it was too much. Next time I must not be so greedy. Also winking at the corner of my eye, I would see a monstrous paua shell on a stand. It was on display in the living room. I had never seen a paua so huge. Arne had polished away its chalky exterior until it reflected back a thousand broken rainbows. It was just one of the many curios they had gathered up during their life in the light-service. I had wondered where, in New Zealand, paua would grow to such a size, but now I knew—Dog Island, south of Bluff, down in the 'roaring forties'. It meant little to me then, but by the end of winter we would be begging Cis and Arne to tell us everything they could remember about Dog Island.

By the time I had finished my meal the voice of my conscience was already roaring at me, "What about the children starving in Africa, India, Korea? What about the families living in drainpipes!" It's Christmas, I told myself, and I'm doing justice to my hostess's hospitality. And I'm eating for two, aren't I? (One of us is very small but she's growing fast.) Tomorrow I'll go on a diet. Tomorrow I'll worry about the hungry children again, and soon I'll find some orphans—or at least some children nobody wants and I'll bring them up as my own.

Later in the evening I retired to another room to breast feed Helen. I still felt full and the same thoughts chased each other around in my head. Too much food. Too much over-eating. But was that a crime? Or was I again being my mother's 'over-conscientious' daughter. She had always said that of me and I had hardly understood what she'd meant. But, more lately, I had begun to be aware that my conscience followed me around like a sneaky pack of hungry dogs, and that I worried too much and sometimes I tried too hard. It seemed a trifle pathetic and that must have been what Mum had meant with the word 'over'. It was all right to be conscientious but not 'over' conscientious. Well, perhaps I wouldn't be any more. I was a young woman of sturdy build and hearty appetite and I could enjoy a surfeit of food if I liked. I didn't have to be always worrying about the starving children in India. But somebody should care. If everybody cared nobody would starve. But nobody cared, (not enough to really do anything at any rate), so why should I? It was hopeless really. People were hopeless. I found myself drifting into sleep, sitting on the floor with my back leaning against the wall and Helen a warm little ball in my arms.

Through the wall I heard the distorted artificial voice of television. Cis must have given in and let Arne turn it on for the news. In the five or six years since television had come to New Zealand, people all over the country had rearranged their living rooms and changed their focus from the open fire's rosy flickering to the impersonal black and white flickering of the screen. Standing out on its own in the sea, Stephens Island picked up the full force of the signals from Mount Kaukau behind Wellington, and reception was good here. Although television was another modern intrusion that my earlier visions of lighthouse life hadn't included I knew it was important to keep up with the news—so perhaps we, too, would one day succumb to its charms.

I forced my eyelids open. I must be very tired. It wasn't normal for me to sleep anywhere but in my bed. Wiggling my finger up the leg of Helen's bulky nappies I found they were still dry, so without waking her I laid her in her makeshift bed in the corner of the room. Then I went out to enjoy what was left of the party.

It was the end of the evening but there was one more thing before we could leave for home. I looked towards the far end of the kitchen where, on the bench between the amazing walls of freshly painted black cupboard doors, sat a delicacy concealed beneath a cloth. It was about to be unveiled and served for supper with coffee topped with cream—lashings of it, whipped and sweetened with a dusting of cinnamon across the top.

Half despairingly I thought of my figure and how well I had been doing losing the weight I'd put on during pregnancy. Fleetingly a procession of starving children staggered through my mind, but they were receding and unreachable. Cis must have spent all day preparing this banquet especially for us. I suspected she would do the same for Peggy and Dave in another day or two. I didn't know how often they saw each other. It was a different world down here at this end of the station.

With the supper unveiled in all its chocolatey glory I turned two deaf ears to my conscience. Just once in a while all this indulgence didn't hurt. Tomorrow we'd get back to normality. We wouldn't be greedy with the chocolates and cake and for a while, at least, we'd live on cold meat and salads.

CHAPTER 8

Helen is Provided For

Life had loosened up over Christmas and New Year with visits between families, a couple of combined picnics at the beach and the child minding shared. After that, for a while, my days seemed quiet but I soon fell back into a routine. Through most of January my washing flapped out horizontally. The clothesline creaked and grizzled as the wind barged from one quarter to another, unable to make up its mind but determined to bring us a selection of weathers—cloud, rain, fog and a little sun.

Back at work, the men painted inside the tower, the office, the workshop and, on the few blue sky days, they painted fuel tanks and several smaller items such as a chimney, a gate, the crane motor.

In his diary Pip noted the movements of tuatara and the finding of lost dovie chicks. By this time they had grown up to be fat grey handfuls of fluff which sometimes waddled away from their burrows, never to make their way home again. Occasionally we found them headless after they had run foul of marauding tuatara and often we tried to rescue adult birds caught by a wing or a webbed foot on the barbed wire of the fences. It was inevitable that, of the thousands which came ashore, some would come to grief, and for a while we tried to nurture the ailing ones, keeping them in boxes, anxiously poking mashed fish down their throats, all to no avail.

Meanwhile, down our own throats we continued to poke fish, eggs, mutton. Mutton! It came on the hoof and, before it was ready to go into the oven, it had to be rounded up from the paddock, killed, skinned, dressed, hung and jointed. Pip didn't have much of a killer instinct but he had the usual young male's hearty appetite for red meat. That, and the sense of providing for his family, made the task easier for him. His dread was that he would 'botch the job'. He was a small man and Stephens Island grew large, healthy sheep.

Arne gave Pip the task of building a small pen to hold the animals prior to killing. It was behind The Palace not far from our house, and when it was finished I took a walk to admire his handiwork and show Fred the three sheep standing within it. They were fine creatures, a wether and two fat lambs—romneys in full wool. Turi was due to come and shear the flock later in the month.

They watched us quietly. Fred clambered up onto the wooden rails and leaned over, his white cloth sunhat flopping about his head. I turned the brim back above his face. "Baa-a," he bleated.

"Nice woolly sheep, aren't they," I said. And my gaze was drawn into the depths of three pairs of alert, yellow eyes—hypnotically drawn inside by the soon-to-be-extinguished life force within. I recoiled. I hadn't been really close to sheep since I'd raised a couple of pet lambs as a child, orphans from my grandfather's farm. Each had had its own personality and I'd loved them as maternally as I now loved my babies. Suddenly I could hardly bear to look at these sheep in the yard.

There was a proper way of killing a sheep—a sharp knife at the throat, the head twisted back, the blood flowing. It was so personal, so intimate. My man, the man I slept with each night, had to do this to feed us. It had definitely been a mistake to look into the eyes of the sheep on death's row.

After a carcase had been hung over night, I helped Pip to cut it up. It was the least I could do. With the recipe book open to show us the various cuts, we sawed through bone and sliced through meat, trying to recall how the various joints had looked in the butcher's shop. Our kitchen, itself, became a butcher's shop. I wouldn't let myself dwell on the fact that this had once been a living animal—this raw-blood smell, these piles of flesh and fat, this pink stickiness on knives, saw-blade, bench and hands. I would simply get on with the job (but a human body would be just like this).

I had been raised to love animals and, of course, we would teach our children to do the same, but how could we do that when we voluntarily carried out this grisly operation? How could I love animals and yet eat meat? How could I *not* eat meat?

Dairy foods didn't produce the same ambivalence in my mind and it didn't seem strange to me that we spent so much of our time in their production.

For a while, that summer, one way or another, lactation dominated my life. The cows, myself and the baby were all involved in this precious, mysterious, life-giving process which has succoured all mammals since their beginning. And, this time, I was determined to breast feed as long as possible. Before Fred had turned three months old I'd had to put him on the bottle. The Plunket Nurse had suggested I had lost my milk because I'd 'overdone it'—worked too hard, done too much walking. This time would be different, or so I thought until late in January when, without warning, Helen's fingers slipped into her mouth and remained there. It seemed that they were a whole lot more appetising than anything I had to offer her. And I blamed the butter.

Yes, definitely, it was all the fault of the butter—four and a half pounds of it. I had decided to make it on my own while Pip was at work.

It was boat day with a blue sky, only a little cloud and an easterly wind that brought up the sea at the landing. It was a rough sea with four-metre waves and Peggy left, that day, with the children. It was their first trip to town for months and they would be away for a fortnight. Fred and I waved to them over the front fence as they trundled along the road in the trailer behind the little crawler, Dave in the driver's seat, fat and relaxed.

I went back into the kitchen and finished washing the separator. I had to do this every morning and though I had memories of myself as a little girl happily helping my mother to wash and wipe the many separate parts, (threading the thirty-six shiny discs onto a thing like a giant safety pin and putting the pieces into the bowl out in the sun so they could air off during the day before being put together again at night), although I could clearly remember the pleasure of pottering away at my mother's elbow under the umbrella of her eternal patience, I now had to remind myself of this simple pleasure, and reason with myself that one task was the same as another and that it was my mind, itself, that influenced my feelings about it. The separator was nothing more than another heap of dishes that needed washing each day. It was merely a part of the morning's clean-up and I had to squeeze the breath out of the gust of nostalgia it brought to me in order to put a tiny wisp of pleasure into a task which threatened to become a terrible chore. And it *was* a terrible chore, but I mustn't let myself think so.

And I really did love the separator. Again, I could see myself as a child, turning the handle for my father; winding it up to just the right speed so that its little bell stopped ringing and the cream ran out of the spout not too thick and not too thin. It had been tempting to wind the handle faster and faster but this made the cream dribble out slowly and, later, it would be so thick that it would have to be dug out of the jug with a spoon. Even now I always wound a little faster than necessary because I liked the cream thick and globby.

Having washed the separator parts I put them all into the bowl and took it out to the porch where the separator base was screwed to the bench beside the fridge. From the fridge I took five quart-jars of cream and carried them into the kitchen.

On previous occasions Pip and I had made butter together but, today, I was going to be a real farm wife—a real lighthouse keeper's wife. I brought in the wooden churn. It was fat-bellied, jocular-looking. Arne and Cis owned a glass one with metal beaters—a clinical, unfriendly thing. I liked the way mine steamed with a wet-wood, sweet-sour smell when I scalded it. I turned the handle and the beaters inside sloshed boiling water into the pores and cracks of the wood. I pulled out the bung and drained it into the sink, then I poured in cold water to cool it. Empty again, it was ready for the cream. This I coaxed from the jars with a rubber spatula, drinking in the aroma of the countryside transformed into the sweet scent of fresh cream.

If I wasted no time I would have the butter made when Helen was ready to be bathed and fed. After that I would finish the morning's chores before Pip came home at midday with the mail. I had everything planned but, unbeknown to me, the butter, itself, was about to take a hand in my calculations. Everything was the butter's fault. I saw that later. There was no other explanation as to why Helen's fingers should pop into her mouth and stay there clenched between her gummy little jaws as if those two wet little digits were the most valuable form of sustenance she'd ever get in her life.

But that happened the next day. As I began turning the handle of the churn the mysterious drama of the vanishing breast-milk hadn't yet begun.

"Chucker, chucker, chucker," the cream slapped over itself and over itself. In about fifteen minutes it would become thick and, after a few more grunts and heaves on the handle, the cream would 'turn', that is, it would change into a mass of fat granules all about to glue themselves to each other and become butter. Then I'd drain the butter-milk out through the bung hole and save it as an ingredient in a loaf, and I'd wash the butter with fresh water before upending the churn onto the clean, steel bench.

We were proud of the way we'd 'got the hang of' making butter. With Dad's first-hand advice and my own memories we had become experts straight away.

"Chucker, chucker," time passed. Fifteen minutes, twenty, thirty, forty-five. "Chucker, chucker," no change, the handle still turning easily and I bored and tiring of it.

Taking a break, I bathed Helen, dressed her in a lace-edged petticoat and fed her. I set up the bassinet outside the door. "Healthy babies, like adults, benefit enormously by being kept in pure, cool air," said the mothercraft manuals of the day. Helen was going to be the healthiest baby in the land, with Stephens Island's pure air swirling past the bassinet, the health-giving sunshine beating down on her little arms and legs, her tummy full of mother's milk. I laughed into her dark eyes and she kicked her legs and clenched both fists at me.

The day before this, the district nurse had appeared for her second visit as unexpectedly as she had done before. She had written "12lbs 4ozs" (twelve pounds, four ounces) in the record book and extended the blue line on the graph. It climbed steadily just inside the upper limit of the band of red—the band of 'normality'—which swept diagonally upward. She was still a 'bonny baby', but, this morning, because of the butter making, I cut short our mutual mother-daughter admiration session.

I carried the churn into the porch and, sitting on the cool, concrete step, I continued with my task.

"Chucker, chucker—blurp, blurp." The cream had thickened. Full of air, now, it fluffed up around the lid and the handle was harder to turn. I wound one way then the other. I wound with my right hand, I wound with my left, but still the cream wouldn't turn.

At eleven o'clock Pip dashed in with our boxes of stores. "Boat was late—quite a swell but nothing's wet—see you at lunch time."

Every mail day we sent out a letter to Black's Foodmarket in Picton with a list of what we would require two weeks later. If we found, by the time the fortnight was up, that we'd forgotten some essential items the men would radio a last-minute order through to the Marine Department office and, from there, it would be relayed to Black's. But that was like a game of whisper with a big potential for error, so the main order was always sent by mail.

Glad to take another break from the churn, I opened the crates. They were slatted boxes in which oranges had been imported. In the first I found a cabbage settled comfortably on the bag of bananas. I muttered aloud, "Those silly old fagots at the store!" They never seemed to learn to put the squashable things on top of everything else. But what could we say? They were quite good at the store, on the whole, not sending out too much over-ripe stuff, and, this week, the tomatoes were sitting safely between two loaves of bread. It would all depend on who packed the boxes.

Boat day divided our lives into stretches of fourteen days instead of the usual seven. It was a special day which brought the arrival of mail and stores and there was often somebody coming or going. It was the day we treated ourselves to fresh food and tidbits. Dave had been known to tear into his stores while still at the block. I could imagine him munching away, cheeks bulging. "Gotta beat the kids to the chocolate." The rest of us tutted disapprovingly.

Fred and I ate a squashed banana each and I returned to the churn. I wound the handle fast. I wound it slow. Perhaps the cream would never turn?

But, finally, it did. When Pip came in for lunch (with a mere handful of mail, this week), dirty clothes still lay beside the washing machine, but, at last, I was shaping butter into cubes; batting them this way and that with ribbed, wooden butter-pats, trying to square them up nicely before wrapping them in 'greaseproof' paper. I said, "I'm starving. I've taken all morning to make this blimmen butter. The cream just wouldn't turn."

For lunch Pip sawed into the last of the weekend's hard little loaves. (I still hadn't got the breadmaking right.) "It's hard to tell whether I'm cutting through the bread or the chopping board," he commented. We eyed the pathetic pile of builders' offcuts and, by mutual consent, consigned them to the scrap bucket—for the chooks to break their beaks on. Then we hacked into a town-bought loaf, sliced up some cold mutton and tomatoes, and, in the course of our simple meal, we completely ravaged one of my precious blocks of butter.

Over coffee we opened our newspapers and the *Weekly News* which came to us free as a lighthouse family by courtesy of we knew not whom. We made a paper dart for Fred from the 'Two-minutes'-silence', which was the newsletter of the Women's Christian Temperance Union. When it arrived in the mail bag it was awarded to the family who had the most miserable-looking pile of mail. That morning we had sent off a dozen letters, had both sat writing far into the previous night—and now felt content that we could wait for replies to come rolling back to us.

It was the day after this that Helen discovered that her fingers were infinitely tastier than anything else and it was as puzzling to me as the turning of cream. Folklore was based on such things: babes at the breast, the turning of cream, the souring of milk, the making of bacon—never at the full moon, never when you have your monthly. It was all influenced by goblins and strange forces—but that was nonsense. It was all the fault of that damn butter and the effort I'd put into it. I had 'overdone it' again and lost my milk.

Or had I? At first I wasn't sure. Helen still smiled up past her fingers and she didn't cry. When Fred had been hungry he had roared—so, was Helen hungry or wasn't she? For myself I whisked up huge milkshakes and drank them down. By the end of the week it was obvious that someone was putting on weight—and it wasn't Helen. I emptied the cane fruit basket, stuffed her into it and balanced it on my kitchen scales. And there it was—12lb 3ozs (twelve pounds, three ounces)— evidence that she was starving just as Fred had been at the same age. I had overdone it again. It was the butter-making. What I didn't suspect, for some time to come, was that little pill I was taking each morning. That new invention that the doctor had assured me was the safest and surest method of birth control ever invented.

Of course I had come to the island well prepared. I had bottles and 'Karilac' for sweetening the cow's milk. There was no problem—except that I'd wanted to give my babies a good start and three months of breast-milk was hardly more than a beginning.

And now Helen drank exactly a third of the amount recommended by the mothercraft manual. Instead of quickly slurping and gulping, she mouthed the rubber teat and smiled her message up into my eyes, "What's the fuss, Mum? I don't need this stuff." Then her fingers would slip back into her mouth. Nevertheless, her plotted line again began to climb up the graph, but, now, it was below the centre of the red band.

It was Saturday afternoon and Cis and Arne stopped by on their way to The Palace. We had just finished churning another four pounds of butter. This time the cream had turned like magic, so what had I done wrong the time before?

"You didn't use fresh cream? You know you can't use it the same day?"

"Yes, I know that—but, well, it might have been a teeny bit fresh—some of it from the night before but it had been in the fridge. . . "

"You never can tell," Cis said. "Sometimes it's the cow. . . the feed she's on. . . the time of year."

She knelt down to where Helen was lying on the floor and held out her forefingers for her to grasp. "Look at her! She's as cheeky as one thing."

"She's still not drinking anywhere near as much as the book says," I protested.

"Oh, you worry too much. She's as strong as a little ox, and, before you know it, she'll be rolling over!"

And Cis was right. In what seemed like no time, she was.

CHAPTER 9

A Quiet Old Chap

As a youngster I had sometimes claimed to my friends that I could milk a cow; but it was a lie born of a sense of loss and outrage that, when I had reached my teens, Mum and Dad had moved house, leaving country for town, and sold their cow—our cow. And the most I'd ever done was squeeze a few cupfuls from the teats into my father's bucket.

I'd had a friend who milked a whole herd before and after school and, though I had suspected that with my faint heart I'd never have her sort of courage in the presence of large quadrupeds, I had held on to a secret image of myself—that, one day, I'd be a strong country woman, as at home in the cowshed as in the kitchen.

At first, on Stephens Island, it seemed that the men were the milkers. Although Pip had been as much a greenhorn as myself when he had arrived, he had, straight away, fallen in love with "our nice placid animal". He said he "wouldn't call the king his uncle," sitting down there in the milking shed on the brink of a cliff with the early sun streaming in. Not that it was always like that. On some days he arrived home like a drowned kitten with milk diluted by rainwater. On other days the wind would swirl dust up off the road and deposit it into the milk—or sweep the milk, itself, up out of the bucket and spray it over Pip's legs and into his gumboots.

I had soon begun to feel that the men had all the fun. Their lives were constantly enlivened by struggles with the elements while mine spread about me like a still sea.

Right at the start I'd asked Pip, "Do the other wives milk?"

And he'd answered, not that he knew of. I'd said I didn't want to offend anyone but did he think it would be all right if I milked the cow sometimes? He'd said he didn't know—but he thought it should be.

Without much justification, I'd felt a twinge of resentment and I had quietly brooded about the matter until Christmas. Then, with Barb happy to baby-sit, I knew that my time had come. I went with Dad and Pip to the cowshed—and, of course, nobody gave me so much as a sideways glance; (with my father and husband both so possessively proud of my performance, nobody would have dared!)

Our cow had stepped straight out of a nursery rhyme book. She was brown and white with a crumpled horn and, although mature and matronly, her name was Heifer, which was about as original as having a dog named Pup. By this time we had also acquired from Dave a flighty young cow called Tammy, so there were two cows to milk. It was no wonder we had enough dairy produce to feed an orphanage.

On Saturday and Sunday mornings the cowshed was our equivalent of the town square. Half the population lounged about there: leaning over the rails, rubbing the cows behind their ears, and watching the milk "zeet, zeet, seeting" into buckets. But into my bucket, that day, the milk had squirted painfully slowly—erratically. The others came and milked, watched and yarned, then left me to my task.

"Had enough yet?" Dad and Pip asked kindly—hopefully—but I was determined to milk both cows myself.

My arms ached and my hands cramped but, after about an hour and a half of dogged perseverance, I had two buckets nearly full—one for ourselves and one for the calves. I felt a flush of pride, (I was already flushed and hot from the strain and concentration I had put into the milking), and, as well, I felt the beginnings of affection for our motley little herd of milkers.

There were five in all because Arne also owned two cows—ordinary old Milly with brown spots and fiddly teats, and the venerable Granny, originally named Tinker. She was a greying brindle and quite a curiosity. Her hoofs had grown forward and upward like the shoes of elves and, as she walked, they creaked in unison with her joints. Her nose had rounded out and become fleshy as do the noses of some old people, and her bones were bent and knobbly like the bones of old people. Somebody had once told Arne that somebody had told them that they had known somebody who had known Tinker as a calf—and that had been about a quarter of a century back. Year after year she had produced a calf of her own and given her daily quota of milk. We wondered how long she could continue.

To have survived to such an age Granny had to have been either particularly cautious or just plain lucky. Few cows grew old on Stephens Island. The cliffs were largely unfenced and, sooner or later, they all met the same fate. Some fell as calves—others later. Some onto rocks—others directly into the sea. This awful process of natural selection ensured that cattle numbers never became too high.

Once, from the window of number three house, I spied something floating in the sea far below, and, on looking through binoculars, I saw that it was a dead cow. I had seen plenty of animals' corpses in paddocks but, for a while, I was haunted by the sight of this one being carried away by the tide—head just visible flopping down toward the green depths, tummy buoying it along. I pictured those cliffs with tufts of succulent herbs growing to their very edges—horrible, threatening, seductive—and I shuddered knowing that, for my own self-respect, I, too, must brave some of their narrow pathways.

Two things had always fueled my nightmares, and Stephens Island had them both. It had heights and it also had a bull. More often than not, in order to have the pleasure of milking the cows, I found I had to brave that bull.

If asked to imagine a bull—any bull—a craven coward such as myself would conjure up a picture of something black, thick-necked, enormous. If you add to this vision an encrustation of mud where the beast had pitted his strength against the might of the earth, itself, you will have a fair enough picture of Toro. For good measure, put a malevolent leer into his eye and you will see him as I saw him.

Most of the time Toro did as he liked and what he liked best was to be with the cows—his wives—which was an understandable aspiration. But, repeatedly, his puny but powerful two-legged masters banished him to the place they considered to be his rightful home—the Ruston paddock where the drystock lived.

There, the winch-shed stood on a vantage point that would give any bull delusions of grandeur; and, there, Toro paraded around exerting his authority over the trolley which was always pulled up at the top of the rails in front of the shed. Fortunately it was built like everything else on a light-station. It had enough strength and reinforcing to withstand anything, even Toro. The brake on the winch stopped the trolley from hurtling away down the line and from flying sideways into the gully so, apart from the ignominy of being upended, it survived Toro's moonlit attempts to teach it a lesson.

From the moment I learnt of his existence I became an excellent observer of the whereabouts of this bull. Even if he was a mere dot on a distant hillside my super-honed eyesight would seek him out. At close quarters I became skilled at watching his every move while pretending to be looking in the opposite direction.

I soon observed that he had a grotesque habit of stretching his neck and sniffing the air: nose pointing upward, eyes rolling, top lip curling up like a distressed paua above fleshy pink gums. And, though I knew nothing about the sex-life of a bull, I quickly came to the conclusion that this fascinating display had something to do with the detection of the sweet perfume of a cow coming into season.

Whenever the wind carried a whiff of this perfume to Toro in the Ruston paddock, he paid no heed to the mere spider-web inconvenience of a fence in his path. Without a backward glance at his companions the steers and calves, or at his old rival the trolley, he'd charge off to meet the object of his desires. And there he would be when I went out to milk, and there would be another job for the keepers—a fence to fix.

Taking my cue from the men I acted as if I thought it perfectly natural to milk a cow with a huge bull grimacing over my shoulder. I tried not to cast too many sidelong glances in his direction and I avoided the days when I knew one of the cows was 'bulling'. I thought that if the men wanted to milk a cow while a bull was 'trying to hump it' in the bale, then I'd let them do it. (As well as learning new skills, I was learning new words.)

If I happened to be the first one to milk, I had to search the hillside for the little herd which, by late afternoon, was usually grazing in a hollow at the top corner of the main paddock. I'd leave home with my bright metal bucket in hand, preparing to use it as a shield. I'd clutch it tightly as I slapped the least offending rump to turn the cows in the direction of the shed—and I'd imagine the clang it would make as Toro tossed my rag-doll body in the air. I wondered constantly whether a bull could move faster uphill or downhill, and, of course, I always had my eye on the nearest fence.

Only Pip knew what a chicken I really was, and he forgave me because I was a woman. The most pathetic thing was that, even when the cows did not have Toro with them, the same skittery thoughts kept me company. Cows are big and, sometimes when you round them up on a summer evening, they run about with their tails in the air, tossing their horned heads.

I wasn't unfamiliar with this sort of behaviour. As a child, out in the paddock with my father, I had warily followed the cow to the shed. Staying on the farm with my cousin I had flitted nervously in and out among the animals while my aunt had milked.

But, now that I had grown up, why was I still so wary and so nervous? It was terribly wearying to be timid. It could have been so peaceful to be walking around the hillside with my bucket, crying out "Bale up, bale up—come on there, Heifer —get along there, Granny." But of course I had to say it in an extra-strong voice and in my mind I constantly heard the saying, "A coward dies a thousand deaths. . . " The truth of it mocked me every time. If only I could control my fearful heart and have inner courage to match my outer calm, I thought.

Really it was easy to appear calm when milking a quiet old house cow with the grassy smell of her breath wafting back to me, my head pressed into her hairy flank, my hands gripping her sausagey teats, the udder brown and warm with raised veins beneath the skin like the veins in my father's arms. She stood comfortably with her head in a headlock. Her tail was tied back so she wouldn't switch dung in my face and her near hindfoot was roped using a slip knot so she couldn't put her foot into the bucket—and she would have done so if she could because I hadn't, yet, developed much of a rhythm to my milking. She chewed her cud steadily, grinding the day's grass to a pulp before swallowing it back into another of her many stomachs. The chewing of the cud is technically known as ruminating, a word which, not by coincidence, also means meditation. I found it easy to meditate in the cowshed—sometimes.

Sometimes I even found myself believing that Toro might, indeed, be harmless. Then, unfortunately for my peace of mind, one Sunday morning fearless little Alison walked in front of Toro's nose on her way down the chute to the cowshed. As she passed him he lowered his head and knocked her over. He didn't gore her to death or toss her into the air—and her parents quickly whisked her out of harm's way. It was nothing, really.

Pip mentioned the incident casually. "She wasn't hurt. Just a bit dusty and frightened." So that even I was inclined to believe that it had been (almost) an accident. My imagination needed no encouragement to picture the result if Toro had been serious about doing somebody a mischief. Besides, I truly didn't want to believe ill of him.

Nevertheless, shortly after this, the keepers decided that the time had come to get tough on the bull. I didn't know whose idea it was but I could picture them with heads together like the proverbial mice who decided to put a bell around the neck of their enemy, the cat. Ingeniously, the keepers decided to put a yoke around the neck of the bull and, from it, they would hang a heavy hard-wood fence post which would get in Toro's way even if he so much as thought of trying to walk through a fence.

In the workshop they built a wooden yoke and attached a post to it with number 8 wire. It would be light as a feather to Toro but it would impede his progress. I never knew exactly how they managed to bolt this contraption around his neck, but, unlike the aforementioned mice, they were able to use the headlock in the cow bale and they managed to yoke the bull without too much trouble.

Then they chased him back to the Ruston paddock, the heavy post banging into his legs at every step. After his banishment there seemed to be a sort of conspiracy of silence about him. Naturally I never put myself in a position where I could see him at close quarters, wearing his yoke. Therefore I was unaware that the hard wood bruised his knees until they were raw, and that the men, having bolted the thing into place while he was in a good mood, had no idea of how to release him from it, now that he was no longer quite the same quiet old chap. But the mighty Toro could not be vanquished for long.

The first I knew of his return was when Pip came home and said, "He's back. He's wrecked the fence again and he's busted the yoke right off."

"What will you do now?"

"I dunno, but it wasn't much of an idea. It was a cruel blimmen thing to do to an animal."

So, there was Toro again, back with his ladies. We would have to put up with him.

Perhaps, if I had milked more often, I would have become more relaxed around the animals but, that first summer, there were many things to keep me in the home. As well as babies to care for, I had visitors. Dad, himself, returned for a second stay just a month after the first. Being an outdoor man, he found plenty to do. In the garden he weeded, barrowed dung from the cowshed and cut back encroaching branches. He also loved to milk and, even more than doing the milking myself, I preferred to see him having the satisfaction of doing it. In wet weather he was a bit like a caged animal but, between us, we found things for him to do. He and Pip cleaned out The Palace together and spent happy hours there, after work, carving wooden moulds and heating lead in a ladle to make sinkers for fishing lines.

Dad had also begun making very tasty rock cakes. He always arrived with a tinful and when we had eaten them all I'd leave him to himself in the kitchen and he'd produce another batch. On wet days he ached to be outside doing something and I found his forced inactivity as irksome as he did. When he looked bored I felt bored on his behalf. When he paced the floor looking out at the rain I longed for it to clear up so that he could be released outside again. He carved spinning tops out of cotton reels "for Fred". At two, Fred was too young to spin them but he delighted in pouncing on them and stopping them. Dad, on the other hand, wanted to spin them and watch them as long as possible. He wouldn't spin them if Fred wouldn't watch the spinning to its wobbly conclusion. I said, "Oh, Dad! He's too little, yet. All he wants you to do is spin them so he can chase them." But it was an impasse and the tops soon lay idle.

Dad had developed another hobby. It had to do with the Armistice. I had grown up with the language of Dad's war experience; shells, shrapnel, trenches, troopships, armistice. The signing of the Armistice had ended the war for Dad and it was an important word. Now a different kind of armistice had entered his life. Since Mum's death he had begun to collect scrap copper. It was worth money and for an old man on a pension it was worth working for. Scraps of copper were everywhere but he repeatedly told us that the fellows at the garage were good enough to save the 'armistices' for him. These things came from inside a car's engine and they had something to do with electro magnetism. Dad painstakingly unwound yards and yards of copper wire off them and added it to his collection. When he mentioned them, Pip would correct him, "Armatures, Jim, not armistices," but Dad had the latter firmly fixed in his brain. In my mind, too, armistice and Dad and scrap copper were all connected.

Now Dad had discovered that Stephens Island was a veritable copper mine. For years people in the lighthouse service had been replacing phone lines and electrical wires and discarding the old ones where they lay. They'd been tossing scrap metal into hidden hollows, and for Dad it was a treasure hunt. The pursuit of copper got him out of doors on all but the worst of days and I was amazed at how much he brought back. He would roll it up into tidy bundles and pack it carefully into a wooden 'benzene box' which he always brought out with him.

One day Dad found his way down to the beach between the landing and the Big Razorback. It was the most accessible of the beaches on the island. He didn't catch a fish down there and he didn't find much copper. He found treasure of another kind —a dead sheep recently fallen over the bluff. With the help of his knife which he carried in a sheath at his belt, he skinned it and brought the skin up to The Palace where he hung it over the rails outside the killing-shed beside the others which were drying there. I knew that old-style self-sufficiency was second nature to Dad, and I knew that many a thrifty farmer would have done the same thing, but to me this was carrying things too far. It seemed beyond the bounds of good taste. I'd found there was an unpleasant side-effect to living the country life in that something was always dying. My mind was increasingly occupied with the reality of death because we were always making meat of some poor creature and skinning it. In the semi-rural, sheltered life of my early childhood I had seen nothing bigger than a rabbit being skinned, and, to a little girl, that had been a sad enough event. After that, all through my teens, we had killed nothing except the occasional fish. I had grown up to be 'soft', letting other people do the dirty work in hidden places—I could see that now.

Soon after Dad's departure, our insurance man with his wife visited the island for an extended weekend. They came from Nelson to French Pass township and from there paid for their own trip with Turi on the *Belfast*. We thought him a 'very nice man'. He had an unassuming, fatherly manner and he had recently been honoured with some sort of important award for selling a lot of life insurance.

All of his own sons were 'right for life' because of the policies he'd taken out on them during their infancy—so, of course, we'd want him to make sure that Helen was similarly well provided for, just as he'd done for Fred—and, though it wasn't something we liked to dwell on, (but these things did happen), what if I died and left the children motherless? Would Pip be able to cope with them on his own? For a few sombre hours, as I went about my housework, I thought about my orphaned children and the possible circumstances of my death. I pictured my corpse: limp and bloodied after a battle with Toro, white and bloated after drowning at sea, shattered at the foot of a cliff, or, even more sinister, ravaged by cancer like my mother. The blood and gore, the sea lice, the tumours, I saw them all. And, by evening, oh yes, I could see that we all needed our lives insured. Naturally, the insurance man suggested, the other families might also want to make the most of this opportunity. It wasn't every day an insurance representative visited Stephens Island, was it!

The insurance man's wife had brought her knitting. She was happy to sit with Fred and Helen and knit. As the mother of grown up sons, she was fascinated by our baby daughter. "I can't get over how good that baby is. She never cries!"

"No, she never cries," I echoed. "Not even when she's hungry."

Down at the milking shed with us, her husband went through the usual visitor's routine. He scratched the cows' necks and yarned away about the view, the isolation, the mail service and what we might do if we had 'an emergency' (by which people always meant, if we cut an artery or developed appendicitis). "And you've done your first aid of course. And you'd have a medical encyclopaedia?"

"Well, no, we haven't got an encyclopaedia, just a first aid book."

"There's *The Ship Captain's Medical Guide*," Pip said.

"You must bring that home for me to read," I said.

"Arne doesn't like people reading it. They always think they're dying of rabies or anthrax or something."

The insurance man joined in. "But you people have got your feet firmly on the ground. . . "

"Sure have," I said.

The cowshed was forty feet below the road not far from houses one and two. The insurance man sat down on a spare milking stool and leaned back against the corner of the shed. "This is the life! You've got it worked out, haven't you. Y' know, I come across a lot of different ones in my job and I always think. . . " He paused, looking up the clay chute that the cows' hoofs had carved out of the hillside on their way to the shed. "Hullo, what's up?"

My eyes followed his gaze and I saw Arne loping along the road above.

The insurance man's expression sharpened. "There's something wrong," he said.

Pip looked up past Heifer's flank. The rhythm of the milk foaming into his bucket didn't falter. "What da ya mean?"

"He's running. Why is he running?" (This was in the days when would-be runners still sat around their firesides, happily unaware of their own potential for self-punishment.)

Pip said, "He's probably off to The Palace to get something."

The insurance man gaped uncomprehendingly and, as if we hadn't heard him the first time, said, "But he's running!"

"We all run. It's the quickest way. Otherwise ya take all day to get a screwdriver or something."

"Well, you people out here, you'll live to be a hundred if you carry on like this!" The insurance man's plain face had unfolded like a flower to the sun. He glanced about at the picture of cud-chewing contentment in the yard beside us. His eyes rested on the tank-like form of Toro, half asleep among his wives, his dusty coat soaking up the sun. "He's a quiet old chap, isn't he."

"Yes," I agreed. "He's like a lamb!"

Later that morning, filled with enthusiasm for self-improvement, and maybe hoping he, too, might live to be a hundred, the insurance man set off with Pip down to the Little Razorback to fish "for a couple of hours". Pip was on duty that day and, at midday, he had to be up at the station to do his weather report. After that I expected them home for lunch. But at 12.30 he arrived home alone.

"I'd better get some sandwiches. We're going to make a day of it down there." He grinned, "He reckons it might be his last—says, now he's made it down there he might as well make the most of it—says he might never make it back up."

"Freaked out, was he?" I felt a tiny flash of pleasure that I wasn't the only coward in the world.

"Freaked out! You can say that again! He froze on the last bit—couldn't move."

"Poor guy!" I could imagine Pip calmly guiding him down, showing him the footholds, giving him his hand where possible—as he had done with me in many a tricky situation. The insurance man would have been clammy and quaking, floppy as a tapeworm. I knew the feeling well.

"I'll take my climbing-rope down but it'll be only a psychological belay. . . "

I knew a bit about 'psychological belays' and I wasn't fooled by them, but somehow, terrified as I would have been on my own account in the same situation, I felt hardly any doubt that both men would make it safely home for dinner that night. It was the fear that I empathised with, the fear that was always much worse than the reality.

When Pip went back down to the Little Razorback, Dave went with him. To them it was just a playground. A few weeks later they even took pitons down and strung a wire across to an outlying rock, hoping that the fishing would be better further out. Pip made four trips across the wire but, under Dave's weight, it broke. He had already swum the gap to take the wire across for the first time, so another plunge did him no harm.

But as to our poor frightened insurance man that Saturday, having finally made it up from the Little Razorback in time for dinner he came bounding into the kitchen as if he had just scaled Everest in his lunch break. After his reprieve from death he looked ten years younger.

Again I felt envious of the men. Sometimes I wished I had been born a boy; then perhaps I wouldn't be so crippled by fear and convention. In the long hours I spent at home I constantly pondered on the best way to bring up our children. I wanted Helen to grow up to have the physical courage I lacked, and I wanted Fred to have the sort of sensitivity and understanding that most men seemed to lack. I wanted them both to be everything good that could be imagined in both sexes—no frilly silliness for my daughter, no callous arrogance for my son.

I remembered my mother once saying to guests that she believed "society was inclined to put too much emphasis on the difference between sexes." With a ten-year-old's innocence I had wondered why no-one had mentioned this obvious truth in my presence before. "That's right," I had piped up eagerly "It's just that boys have grown a bit more down there. . . and girls grow more up top." I remembered the complete silence that had followed this moment of enlightenment, and how my voice had died away as I'd realized that Mum's meaning hadn't been this simple. But it had been the beginning of my understanding of what Mum had meant. Courage, kindness and intelligence were what I wanted for both of our children. But how could this be achieved in such a biased world?

I coated the cod fillets with seasoned flour, quick-fried them in oil, served them with baked potatoes and salad.

The insurance man whooped in delight. "Fresh fish! This is the way to eat it—nearly jumping out of the pan! This is the life, Pip. You've got it worked out. This is the life for a man!"

On the day that the insurance man left with his wife, Pip's parents were delivered by the new Marine Department supply boat, *Enterprise 2*. She had replaced the old *Enterprise* which I hadn't even laid eyes on. Eventually, I would come to know and love the new vessel, but that was still well in the future.

Two weeks can seem a long time when you have visitors in your home, and now, as well as playing the roles of hostess, mother, and lighthouse keeper's wife, I felt I had to be the perfect daughter-in-law. Fortunately my in-laws were easy going, easy care folk. They loved the island and they even tolerated my insistence that they shouldn't carry Fred about but should let him walk and find his own way around obstacles. (Mum had been so insistent that children must grow up to be 'independent' that I was terrified of producing a child 'with no gumption'.) They were wise in-laws and the fortnight passed without incident, but, by the time they left, the novelty of being the dedicated hostess had worn thin for me. It was already the last day of February and I was looking forward to quieter times ahead.

CHAPTER 10

We Sit A Chook

In the old fowlhouse, the chooks had been laying well all summer. Each day I had negotiated the crumbling dirt steps up to the top corner of the section, had thrown in my billy of wheat and food-scraps and watched with satisfaction. The steady pecking and clucking had transported me back to that not so distant time when, little bigger than Fred, I had peered contentedly at my mother's fowls and marvelled that with no teeth they still had managed to eat.

For the first three days of March, one of the chooks had been sitting tightly on the nest, fluffing out her feathers and giving a squawk of protest when I had stolen the eggs laid there by her companions. The time had come to give her a clutch of her own to sit on and we had swapped thirteen of our eggs (which were infertile) for the same number from Arne and Cis—because they kept a rooster.

This was our second attempt at hatching out a batch of little fluffy chickens. The first had been a total failure. After Christmas we had borrowed both a sitty chook and a coop from Arne and carefully followed all his instructions, but the uncooperative bird had left its eggs to get cold and sulked in the rain at the far end of the coop.

After that I remembered how it had been done in my childhood: a small, wooden box with a stone in the doorway and a water-dish just outside where the chook could reach its head out past the stone to drink. This was the way we would do it this time.

Again it was Saturday, hot and dry with clear skies. The twenty-knot sou'-easterly of the morning had eased to almost nothing. Pip had spent the morning carting sleepers and timber from the Ruston shed to the palace. After lunch, on my instructions, he had built a wooden box, cut an opening in one end big enough to allow a chook to come and go, and had nailed a piece of corrugated iron on top to run off the rain. I had gathered dry grass for the nest from the wild area above the house. Helen lay in her bassinet at the back door, sucking her fingers and absorbing the benefits of the pure, clean air. Fred padded along beside us on his grubby little feet. He was wearing red drill shorts with braces and his job was to carry the nesting material. His arms were full. Pip carried the box and I had a grubber, a spade and the eggs in a bowl. We were ready to sit the chook.

Halfway up the dirt steps, to the left and above the water tanks, and beside a straggly old ngaio tree, we had found an open patch with no tuatara burrows. We flattened out a square in the crumbly dry earth and seated the bottomless box snugly onto it. Crouching, I arranged the dried grass inside so that it looked like the sort of nest a chook might be glad to sit on. We arranged the eggs in it.

I said, "Now we need the stone to block the entrance—just to keep her in until she understands she's here to stay." It had all come back to me from my childhood as clearly as if it had been yesterday. There were stones lying about beneath the nearby trees and while Pip selected one I collected the chook from the nest in the fowlhouse. She gave a croak of alarm but I held her legs and tucked my arm around her. I carried her down the dusty path to the steps and over to the nest site.

On the bank at the edge of our little excavation, Fred stood, obediently out of the way, patiently watching proceedings. I held out the quietly clucking chook for him to stroke. His little brown hand bumped up and down on its back.

"Chooky," he said looking up at me and laughing at the softness. He ploughed his spread fingers through the fluffy feathers around its backside. "Chooky," he chuckled. Then in mid-breath the chuckle became a gasp, a cry. With a puff of dust the bank he stood on crumbled. In a flurry of dry earth he slipped feet first down beside the nest box. It was only a little fall—hardly more than eighteen inches—but the corrugated iron caught above his shin, peeled a thick strip of skin upwards and, below the knee, bit in wide and deep.

For a moment it was as though the day stood still. The summer sun, the dry bank, the sitty-chook, made a picture in two dimensions. Fred, quickly scooped up into Pip's arms, was the only reality. I stuffed the chook into the box and threw the stone across the entrance. Then together we held our child and stared, transfixed, at the chubby leg.

The thick piece of skin, strangely white and made rigid by the outside edges curling under, jutted out at an angle, dark blood running underneath.

This was only a little accident. No bones were broken, no arteries cut, but it was the first time I had ever seen blood flowing out of my child. However, I was not 'one of those helpless types', the ones with no gumption whom Mum had often mentioned so scornfully.

"Some girls faint at the sight of blood," she'd say—implying that our family was made of stronger stuff.

Six months ago, the Plunket Nurse from Motueka had told me, "You will cope. When an emergency comes you will find you have the strength," and she had given me a list of first aid items which we had purchased and packed into a special wooden box, feeling sobered as we'd done so and a little frightened at the thought that such things might, one day, be needed. The reality had seemed a long way off.

Fred, too, was staring at his leg, wailing rather than crying, repeating one unintelligible word. "Diddiup. Diddiup. Diddiup."

Fix it up?

"It's all right, Freddy, we'll soon fix it up. You'll be all right," I crooned.

A few minutes later, in the house, Pip sat with Fred on his knee, holding the bleeding leg over the bath. The first aid box was open beside us, exposing a comforting array of creams, potions, dressings and bandages. I studied the flap of skin with its curled-under edges. If it remained it would rot. That flap would never sit down flat. It would be a terrible trap for infection. I thought no further.

"We'll have to cut it off," I said.

"Do you think we should?" Pip sounded uncertain.

"Yeah, it'll go rotten if we don't."

We were on our own. 'They' had impressed this on us right from the start. There was to be no calling for help for mere trifles. Self-reliance was the first requirement for a lighthouse keeper's family. That's what all the literature had told us and that's what 'they' had made clear to us at our job-interview. That was why they always made a point of interviewing wives as well as the potential keepers. It was important that we women were made of 'the right stuff', too. Only a few weeks back Arne and Cis had given a real-life example of this self-reliance.

Arne had cut the ends off his fingers with the trailer hitch and Cis had efficiently dressed them and bandaged them up like a fistful of little Egyptian mummies. He had taken a day or two off work but there hadn't been the tiniest bit of fuss.

Mum had brought me up that way, too. "Some people," she used to say disapprovingly, "run to the doctor for every little thing." She had got a doctor to me only once. I had dislocated my ankle and spent ten weeks with it in plaster. ("Oh, no," she'd told people, "it's not broken. Our family have got strong bones.") That was the sort of emergency for which we could legitimately get a doctor's help—not for every little cut.

Now, with the sharp scissors sterilised and ready, we positioned the leg favourably for me to give a quick snip. One swift, clean cut; no pulling or tugging, no second attempts.

"Good boy, Freddy. Hold still, Freddy. That's a good boy. Mummy'll try not to hurt you."

He watched fearfully. I held my breath. Tensely I slid the blade up under the protruding flap and gave one swift cut.

The scream that split the air between us set the very walls vibrating. The bathroom, the white bath with its red splashes of blood, reeled about me. He shouldn't have screamed like that. It shouldn't have hurt him that much. Before the blood welled up to cover it I saw the fat and tissue exposed where I had cut.

I looked into Pip's startled eyes. "I've cut too much off," I whispered grimly. He shrugged—a little gesture that said as clearly as words, "Who knows—it's too late now."

We restrained and comforted our sobbing boy as best we could and dressed and bandaged the wound using skills we had practised a lifetime ago on unhurt limbs.

"All better soon," we said as we carried him to the red vinyl settee. "All better soon," the blood already spreading across the white bandage.

It was easy enough to say "All better soon," but I knew it would be a long time in healing. In the weeks that followed, an anxiety that had gnawed deep within me since childhood at last found an opening through which it could escape. It saw its opportunity and began, that very night, to worm its way up through my guts, through my heart and towards a position in my brain where it could not be ignored.

CHAPTER 11

Child Prodigies

One reason I had looked forward to the quiet autumn months of March and April was that we were aware of disruptions ahead. Early in May, Pip and Dave would be leaving the island to spend a fortnight at the lighthouse keepers' training school in Wellington, and Arne had suggested that Peggy and I and the children would be wise to 'have a break away'.

There was wisdom in this. I saw that two weeks on the island without Pip would seem more like two months to me, so I wrote to my sister, Paul, who lived about an hour's train journey from Wellington, asking her if it would be a convenient time to visit. There were still three mail days in which to finalise our arrangements and two months in which to enjoy the quiet time I had contemplated after our visitors had departed. Now, however, no sooner had that quiet time arrived than Fred had hurt his leg and I was worried and anxious.

During that first night after we sat the chook, while Pip slept on quietly causing hardly a ripple in the bedclothes, I wriggled about like a maggot, doing my best to wear the sheets into holes. All the while an endless montage circled within my head: the sitty chook, the injured leg, the scissors in my hand, the bathroom filled with one wild scream. Then infection, blood-poisoning, gangrene and all kinds of fanciful visions made scarier by my ignorance—swollen black flesh, putrescence, death; the little white coffin lined with satin—oh, my god! My god! Trying to be more realistic, I projected myself twenty years into the future and took a look at the leg grown to man-size—hairy, masculine, scarred. But men are proud of scars—thank god he was a boy!

At intervals throughout the night, as I felt myself slipping into sleep, Fred cried out and, wide awake, I found myself kneeling at the side of his white cot in the barren chill of the back bedroom. By morning, like any mother of an ailing child, I felt as lively as a hibernating snail, but when we all went out to feed the fowls, I saw that the day was bright and clear and the sitty chook had taken possession of nest and eggs. When she ignored the wheat that we sprinkled in front of her doorway it was a promise that, in three weeks, she would give us little fluffy chickens.

After breakfast the phone rang a brisk "dah-dit-dit," and Pip answered it. "Yes—no, it's a nice offer. I'd like to take you up on it but I'm not sure whether we can. I'll see what J'nette says." He put his hand over the mouthpiece. "It's Arne. He says Cis'll baby-sit this afternoon if you and I want to go to the beach with him and have a go with his underwater gear."

Underwater gear! We had never tried it but I had always loved swimming and playing about in the sea—oh, why did it have to be today? My glance slid from Pip clutching the phone expectantly to Fred sitting on the red vinyl settee, his legs out in front of him, the bloody bandage dominating the scene. My head ached and my voice became a squawk as I said, "What about Fred? We can't leave him." Then I added more quietly, "But you go. I'm a bit tired today, at any rate."

Pip leaned one forearm against the wall, propping himself upright. He stood on one leg, the opposite foot resting on the inside of his knee. "Yeah, Arne, Fred had a bit of an accident yesterday. Cut his leg on some iron—probably should be kept quiet until it settles down a bit."

I felt irritated. He was always so matter of fact. But the message had got through and within minutes they were at our door—Arne, Cis and Anthony, all looking concerned. It was a relief to see them and to be able to share the story, yet it was gratifying to know that we hadn't gone running to them at the first sign of trouble—and there was no need, now, to make a fuss.

But Cis and Arne were horrified that we had felt that we had to be 'so independent'. Arne, shaking his head slowly, searched for words. "Never—you must never feel that you are on your own."

Cis said, "This sort of thing is so much better shared. We have the telephone and you can ring us any time—day or night. If anything ever happens again you mustn't hesitate." As a final rebuke she added, "You should remember that, as principal keeper, Arne's responsible for the health of everyone on station. It's his duty. . . you know he's got his first aid ticket. . . "

I clamped my wobbly lips into a crooked smile as Pip thanked them for being so kind and concerned.

After they had gone, he humbly tried to earn his afternoon at the beach, by spending some time bringing 'bush dirt' down the hill to enrich my 'flower garden', a powder-pot of dry earth which rain refused to penetrate. After lunch he, Arne, and Anthony set off down the hill with masks, snorkels and spear gun, I assuring them I didn't mind missing out, and Arne, knowing I lied, promising there would be another time soon.

Fred didn't mind being kept quiet. He found that his desperate mother involved him in everything she did. I sat him on the bench beside me. We talked and sang nursery rhymes, and instead of letting him amuse himself, I endlessly shared stories and books with him. In return, he shared his sore leg with me. He spread a small hand over the blood-stained bandage and droned, "Dor leg. Urt. Urt." Then he got into the action, "Fall down." And the climax, "Bump!" It was a major news item, repeated at regular intervals and, probably believing that his leg was ready to fall right off if he didn't sit still, he stayed motionless for long periods of time, directing his young-animal inquisitiveness at his only source of new information—books.

Anchored thus, he became obsessed with an illustrated children's encyclopaedia and was especially drawn to a cutaway picture of a steam-train. It showed the engine parts, interior of the furnace, coal in its bunker, engine driver and (decorously seated in the carriages) the passengers. Having to read the text to answer his questions I saw that my own repertoire of general knowledge was largely a network of great, airy gaps and I saw that if I, myself, didn't take a more serious interest in learning I'd not be able to present the information to my children's questing minds. I was to be their teacher as well as their mother, and who else would educate them if I couldn't? There was only Pip—and he was like my father who had been a mere accessory to my own mother's driving force. She had been the one with all the ideas about education and child-rearing so I had automatically followed her example, charging confidently into motherhood while Pip unquestioningly accepted the same role as my father had.

Without any 'highfaluting' or intellectual theories on the matter, I imagined a child to be a little blob of clay which its mother must somehow shape into a decent, intelligent human being. Everyone seemed to believe that nurture was more important than nature in forming the adult that emerged from the child. This nurturing was a serious responsibility, particularly for mothers, and if we weren't careful we could damage our children's tender little personalities beyond repair. We could create monsters—or psychopaths with terrible complexes about their mothers which they would transfer into a seering hatred of all women.

As a post-war child I had been raised on stories of the holocaust. Also I had seen the movie *Psycho* and I had read *Uhuru* and *A Clockwork Orange*, all of which had disturbed me dreadfully and given deeper meaning to my mother's phrase, "man's inhumanity to man". I hated to see pain in others. It was as if I felt it too. I had never witnessed brutality first-hand and the idea of it sickened me. But now my eyes had been opened and I knew that you had to be strong to survive. I was a woman of the world—and I was aware of what human beings could become.

All this was a burden which sandwiched the delights of motherhood between huge slices of guilt and worry. But there was hope! On public radio at this time, I heard a programme that told the listeners what could be achieved with the right kind of parenting. An Englishman (a professor, too) had raised a child prodigy—his daughter, little Maybelle. Her amazing precocity was entirely the result of the training he had given her. It was not (as one might naturally suppose) due to any ability she might have inherited from the professor, himself. His mission, now, was to enlighten the rest of us so that we could all raise our children to be geniuses, simply by doing as he had done with dear little Maybelle. Ever since her birth he, personally, had schooled her in every possible way. He had fed information into her, had reasoned things through with her, had provided her with every imaginable tool for learning. And now here was the living evidence, little Maybelle herself, speaking on the programme along with her father. She had a nice, educated English accent.

I thought about all this. My own mother had been convinced, like this professor, of the rightness of her methods, and she had believed that her own innovative ideas had produced three superior daughters. We had all grown up believing that Mum knew more about educating children than any other mother, though I felt, myself, that somehow I hadn't measured up to expectations. With some guilt I had reasoned vaguely that my failure might have had something to do with my being the youngest and (as my sisters had frequently told me) that I'd been 'spoilt'. I wouldn't 'spoil' my children. It was one of the worst things you could do, but I would feed their hungry minds at every opportunity. Now that Fred was responding so magnificently to the children's encyclopaedia and its cutaway picture of a train, I saw that he was already on the path to brilliance, just like little Maybelle—if only he could survive the threat of gangrene.

Yes, gangrene! At night a horde of worries descended on me like uninvited guests though by day I was usually able to keep them at bay. We soon became used to the sight of the bandage on Fred's leg, and apart from bath-times and the times that he bumped the wound badly, life continued as usual.

As far as underwater swimming went, Arne was true to his word. Two weeks after his first invitation, we spent a picnic day at the beach with him, Cis and Anthony. When I put on the mask and snorkel for the first time and saw that previously hidden world of open sea anemones, darting fish and graceful seals, I knew that I had found a new passion. Pip and I decided to write away for underwater gear at once.

We also began thinking how nice it would be to own a boat because Arne had a dinghy—the only boat on station. He kept it at the landing and lowered it to the sea with the crane. Sometimes, when the station work was running smoothly and the weather particularly calm, he would decree that the day was for picnicking or fishing. The men sometimes rowed a mile from shore (which was the furthest any of them went from the island without asking official permission) and they almost always arrived back with about half a sack of blue cod, the usual line-fish caught in the Marlborough Sounds.

In preparation for the lighthouse school where they would be expected to 'get their tickets' in signals and basic radio operation, Pip and Dave were now practising semaphore, Morse code and the international code of signals as if lives would depend on their knowledge. I tried to imagine situations in which these skills might be used. I could picture Pip clacking out Morse code to a ship in distress or beaming the Aldous lamp towards an afflicted vessel, but as for running meaningful flags up the pole to signal—to signal what? And the vision of a lighthouse keeper standing on a promontory in oilskin and sou-wester, waving his arms using semaphore to communicate—it didn't fit my idea of reality.

"Don't we have radio for all that?" I asked.

"Could be a fire in the radio room—besides we might be the ones reading the signals from someone in trouble and we won't always be living so far above the water," so I tested Pip on his codes and flags and learnt their meanings with him.

On the knoll above the lighthouse was a wooden hut which contained a lot of mundane and boring bits and pieces. Its rounded front with windows giving a ninety-degree view of the ocean gave it a quaint appearance. To us it was the dry-store but it had been built as a signal hut and was a remnant from that era when keepers had actually used the many flags of the international code which now remained rolled up in cubby-holes in a dresser in the office. I had only a vague idea of what the duties of these old keepers had been. As well as keeping watch all night, it seemed that, by day, they had regularly communicated with ships by flying flags from the signal hut. To our generation all this belonged to a dim and distant past—a time when anything could have happened.

Another old building which was now obsolete stood in the paddock between number one house and the cowshed. It had been built as a school but in later years had been used as relieving keepers' quarters. Now it was to be demolished and Dave was the man with the strength and personality for the task.

At first I thought it surprising that there had ever been enough children on the island to warrant a school but then I remembered that a single family of my father's generation could fill a schoolroom on its own.

Before the advent of the Correspondence School in 1922, young, uncertificated teachers had often taught in remote places. There was a story about one of these girls. While teaching on Stephens Island she had become pregnant—at a time when there were no unmarried men on station! There had been a furore (we could all imagine it) among suspicious wives, each one of them wondering whose husband was the culprit. But at last the young teacher had confessed that the father of her child was a fisherman and shortly after that she went off and married him. It was rumoured that she was living, still, in one of the remote bays of the Sounds. In my mind I could see this poor lonely girl, raging with desire and stuck on this island with only married couples and children and strange reptiles for company. I wondered if she had sneaked down to the landing in the dead of night or if she had spent her days off languishing on the rocks like a mermaid, waiting for her fisherman.

Being a builder by trade, Pip was interested in the demolition of the old schoolhouse for practical reasons but for me its fascination was its age and the fantasies I could weave around it.

I said to Pip, "Dave might find a heap of gold sovereigns under the floorboards."

"He might, but who would have gold sovereigns out here?"

"Well, jewels then. You never know—back in those old days."

"It'd make old Dave's eyes light up, wouldn't it!"

"We could fool him. We could plant some, just to have him on a bit."

"Where would we get jewels from?"

"I've got some!" Pip looked at me in disbelief but, soon, we were prising 'rubies' from cheap Woolworths earrings that I had been proud to wear at the age of fourteen. Then, after tearing a rough square from a piece of newsprint, I singed and scuffed it, screwed it into a ball and smoothed it out again. I held it up proudly. "There! Does that look old?"

"Well, it doesn't look new any more."

I picked up the 'jewels'. "What whopping rubies!"

Pip chortled. "His eyes'll be out on stalks when he finds them."

After wrapping them in the smudgy paper I poked the little package inside an ancient pill bottle which I had found the week before while digging the garden. Pip grinned as he slipped it into his pocket, "There's just the place for it in the wall behind the sink bench."

After that I waited for days to see Dave's eyes 'come out on stalks'. I looked forward to sharing the joke with him. But the weeks went by, the building was demolished and nothing was ever said, so I assumed that the little pill bottle had been lost among the debris.

I said to Pip, "And after all that, he never even found the treasure!"

"Well, we don't know for sure about that, do we?"

"What do you mean?" But his meaning was already dawning on me.

"He wouldn't have let on to us, would he. He'd probably take the rubies off to Wellington and have them valued. He wouldn't say a word. You wouldn't expect him to, really."

"Ooh!" I giggled. "That's just what he would do. Why didn't you tell me that before?"

Pip shrugged. "I never thought of it until now."

While Dave was putting his strength behind pinchbar and mallet in the old schoolhouse, Arne was painting the Ruston shed and Pip was continuing in the power house as well as ferrying coal and fuel up from the Lister shed. It was the old school teacher's ploy of separating chatterboxes and troublemakers—only, in this case, the teacher had separated himself as well. Arne was used to handling young keepers and, with signs of friction beginning to show, he allocated separate jobs so that the three weren't always working together, though there were still plenty of tasks requiring combined effort. Pip found he enjoyed being on his own for a change and the other two probably felt the same.

Apart from understandably getting on each other's nerves from working together all the time, there had been 'incidents'. In the weather enclosure, someone had broken an expensive thermometer, but instead of owning up to the accident had pieced it back together and laid it in its place in the white slatted box so that it fell apart when the next keeper touched it. In the tower, somebody forgot to turn on the alarm and this meant that the lighthouse went all night without its emergency system in place—an equipment failure could have caused a shipping disaster. In the Ruston shed, somebody let the trolley get away so that it tore off down the tracks and then crashed into the gully—its wire-rope a giant bird's nest around the winch drum. And while fencing, somebody threw the station axe over the cliff and Arne demanded that *that* somebody pay for it. That particular somebody came home full of righteous anger.

"It was an accident! Arne asked me to chuck it to him and, when I did, it stuck to my hand because it was so muddy. Then it went clunk, clunk, clunk, down over the edge—I shouldn't have to pay for it." With Arne's old-fashioned values, Dave's casual attitude and Pip falling somewhere in between, there were bound to be a few ructions. But on the surface we were still a happy lighthouse community—which was the way we wanted it to be.

I was sure Cis and Peggy heard the same stories from their husbands as I did from Pip but we never mentioned them to each other. We didn't swap confidences, and, in some ways, I felt young and naive in the face of their greater experience of life. Although Peggy wasn't many years my senior, Dave was her second husband. She'd already coped with the death of her first. I knew she had nursed him through the various stages of cancer, (Dave had told Pip and he had told me), and there it was again—illness and death always lurking around, waiting for a chance to claim a victim. Coils of unease lay in my stomach. It seemed as if we all went on living and pretending these things didn't matter— and they didn't matter really, did they, so long as you kept on as if nothing had happened.

In my relationship with Peggy I avoided talking about her past but I was always glad to see her. She and I had worked out a good arrangement concerning child care so that we could take turnabout for a few hours on a weekend to get out of the house and do some exploring and fishing with our husbands without having to worry about our offspring. Most of the time, however, our children were with us wherever we went; Helen in the carry-frame and Fred uncomplainingly walking in spite of his still-bandaged leg. We were proud of his 'independence'.

On Easter Sunday, very appropriately, there was a cheeping and a peeping from within the puffed-up feathers of our sitting chook. It was immensely exciting—although it turned out to be a practical demonstration of the origin of the proverb, "Don't count your chickens—." From the clutch of thirteen, only five hatched. It takes three weeks for an egg to turn into the miracle of a real flesh-and-blood chicken but, on the injured leg of a child, the tissue-generating process goes more slowly. We weren't sure what lay beneath Fred's dressing. By now it was firmly stuck to the wound and we were afraid of disturbing it and damaging the new tissue. It had no bad smell and it wasn't paining him so surely we should let it be—or should we? It was three weeks now. How long would it take to heal? The hidden worry tainted everything I did.

On Easter Monday we took the opportunity to go to the beach and fossick in the rock pools while the tide was low. Pip said that, according to his father, Easter always fell on the "first full moon after the spud-pickin'" and that this guaranteed that tides would be very low. Fred walked all the way to the beach with us and we carried him around the rocks to search for seals. We swam and found an oar washed up, and, on the home journey, Fred walked all the way back up the hill—all six hundred vertical feet of it! His leg was obviously not about to drop off. Finally Cis said, "We really have to soak that dressing off and see what's underneath it. You bring him down after the mail tomorrow."

The next day the sea thundered in again from the south, and during the landing of our stores everything was saturated. It didn't help that one of our cartons floated about in the sea for about ten minutes before it was rescued. The men got the necessities up to the station by midmorning and then we took the children to number one house for the assessment of Fred's wound. I was relieved to have someone else share the responsibility.

After the sorting of mail, the opening of stores, the drinking of tea, and when Peggy and Dave had taken their children off along the bush track to their own house, Cis filled a bowl with water and we unwound the bandage, layer by layer. Then we bathed the dressing. Terrified of what I might see, I felt all my nights of worry coming together in broad daylight, and as the stained lint was at last lifted away we saw the wound. It was healing slowly from the edges and, although it still had a long way to go, it looked smaller and less disfiguring than it had in my wild imaginings. It was now only five weeks until the lighthouse school. The leg would be healed by then—wouldn't it? If it wasn't, I would be able to get a doctor's opinion at last. Not that a doctor could do much because, as Mum would have said, "Nature simply has to take its course."

At the lighthouse school Pip and Dave would learn first aid and their course would be more comprehensive than the one we had done before our lighthouse life began. They would be taught such things as how to stitch wounds and how to remove a fish hook from a human catch. If wives had been officially taught a little home nursing and follow-up treatment for injuries it would have been reassuring but it was probably assumed that we had learnt such things at our mothers' knees and that a husband's first aid ticket was all that we needed.

Hoping to gain some enlightenment and also pandering to a growing obsession which was simmering at the back of my brain, I begged Pip to bring home *The Ship Captain's Medical Guide* and he, believing in me utterly, was foolish enough to do so. This was the heavy and impressive tome which Arne wisely preferred should remain out of sight in the office drawer. It had pictures in lurid colour of every affliction which could imaginably assail a human being on board a ship, and descriptive detail to match. I read it word by word far into the night, unable to stop, in the grip of an addiction. It was a horror story without the comfort of knowing it was fantasy, and each list of symptoms had me searching for corresponding signs in myself. I saw that so many potentially fatal conditions could strike me down that only pure luck had kept me alive for twenty-three years.

But, in the end, I knew that I had a problem. It had begun way back. Back in my earliest days when disease had ravaged my mother. I had always lived with it and, now, I had a name for it. It was a simple case of paranoia, (or was it hypochondria or neurosis?) Whatever its name I mustn't let anyone else suspect its existence—not even Pip. I would be all right (destined as I was to be the mother of child prodigies all growing up in splendid isolation). Yes, I would be all right, as long as I said nothing about the childish fears and weaknesses that had always been with me, and which now seemed ever more threatening—like an octopus of doom, all clammy arms wrapping me around with lonely chills and shivers. I must be strong and not give in to silly fears. Then I would be all right—as long as I kept myself busy. Yes, that was the answer, keeping busy—it would be my secret recipe for happiness.

CHAPTER 12

A Rare Species

Keeping busy! It wasn't difficult. I knew only a fool would waste time on fear and negativity and I simply would not let myself do that. I would not! There was not enough time in the day. The nights were a different matter. I couldn't keep busy at nights and that's when phantoms came to haunt me, but by day there was so much to do. With cows and sheep and chickens and children—well, raising the latter to be prodigies was going to be even more time-consuming than simply raising them. Every aspect of their surroundings had to be seen, touched, explained and, above all, enjoyed, because learning must naturally be *fun*.

Even Helen's bright eyes now followed and absorbed whatever was going on, and I swore it wasn't simply 'wind' that had made her smile from the age of two weeks onward. I suspected that she too was shaping up to be a genius, a kind of barefoot, New Zealand version of little Maybelle. Meanwhile I, myself, hadn't grown blasé about the island. Oh no! Wherever I went I was constantly moved by a sense of wonder— that feeling that old people often so wistfully lamented as a lost part of their childhood's innocence. Well, couldn't those old fogies just stop and look around them at a sunset or a flower or a woolly lamb or something and see that magic was still everywhere?

I swore to myself that I would always see magic. I would not let myself grow stuffy and old. But I knew I was lucky. Lucky? Was it purely luck, then, that we had chosen to join the lighthouse service? No, but I was lucky to have met Pip and lucky to have been born in New Zealand. Lucky not to have been born in India where I could have been living in a drainpipe. I was indeed lucky to be living on Stephens Island where there was a surfeit of my kind of marvels. Nature's marvels—the marvels of natural history. My mother had spoken of the

Good Lord and Mother Nature in the one breath as if they were sibling rulers of the earth. The Good Lord had given us eyes and ears and two good legs and must have put us on the earth for some good reason, but Mother Nature. . . mankind tampered with Mother Nature at its peril. I could not remember a time when I hadn't thought of Mother Nature as the embodiment of all that life and its surroundings represented. She was the great integrated system of rock, earth, fire and water, air, space and everything else. She was the ocean, the rivers, the mountains. She was all forms of life—all marvels—and if mankind's interference went too far, she was the avenger.

I loved Stephens Island the way it was as I knew it: the skinks that rustled out of sight in bushes as we passed, the colony of giant, egg-bodied weta which I had found living beneath an orange-flowered gazania a couple of metres from the back door, the cluster of leathery tuatara eggs we had unearthed in the garden—after accidentally breaking one, we had ministered to the tiny, slimy embryo for a whole day before it died—and, now, we had a bright green tree gecko just as Cis had had. We had found it and brought it home on the same day we had discovered the dehydrated frog which now reposed on a bed of cotton wool in a cardboard box well hidden in our bottom cupboard. It was hardly recognisable as a frog, let alone the last earthly remains of a possibly extinct species, but we dared not mention it to anyone.

Right from the start the place I had been keenest to visit was the frogbank, a tumble of loose stones in a hollow on the summit. And, right from the start, Arne had warned us that he didn't approve of people poking about up there. He had said that the frogbank was, on no account, to be disturbed. The frogs were rare and endangered and could possibly already be extinct. It was such a small population, such a tiny area, and they hadn't been observed, now, for some years. There was talk of similar frogs being found on an island in the Sounds, Maud Island, and they might be the same species. Last time the wildlife officers had visited here they had not been pleased to see that someone had been up at the frogbank, 'meddling'. They had known this because they had noticed a disturbance in the lichen which normally grew evenly across the surface of the stones; and, actually, it had been Arne and Cis themselves. They had turned over one stone—just one stone—before guilt had got the better of them. Then, to their embarrassment, it had been noticed.

It was such a temptation! Arne couldn't emphasise the matter strongly enough. As P.K. he was employed to protect the wildlife on the island. Such a lot of damage had been done already, damage which it was too late to rectify. One of the first things the lighthouse keepers had had on their conscience was the extinction of a unique flightless wren, a ground-dwelling bird that had lived among the rocks like a little mouse. It had been completely unknown until the first specimen was brought in by the lighthouse keeper's cat. Then, in a very short while, cats had eliminated the whole colony—an entire species gone, just like that! It had happened with appalling ease.

In my imagination I pictured the island as it had been before the arrival of the lighthouse keepers in the 1890s. Until then it had been a pristine wilderness hardly touched by man except for perhaps the annual visits by Maori who came to harvest the fat chicks of prions and shearwaters. I liked to dream, my mind slipping back through those countless, unlogged millennia when an unbroken canopy of forest had sheltered a diversity of animal treasures: the pre-historic tuatara, the primitive Hamilton's frog, the wren which was the only flightless perching bird in the world, several species of skinks and geckos, land birds and invertebrates. The latter included about half a dozen different weta, giant beetles and snails—several of them unique to the island and many of them doomed to become extinct during the lighthouse keeping era.

For so many centuries it had been like this, the island a trim little ship riding at anchor, drinking in rain and sun and weathering frequent, shrieking, salt-laden storms. And then, in a mere seventy years, the assault of the lighthouse people had reduced it to a battered hulk. Seventy years was three times my present lifespan and I could feel no personal guilt. What was done was done, and it had been the way of the times. Even my own father had spent his early years bushfelling, clearing the land for farms and industry—and now he worried that the birds no longer sang as they had done in his youth. It was sad but it was too late to worry about it. The Stephens Island I loved was the one I knew now and there was no point in blaming past generations.

It was a pity, though, that they hadn't erected a few protective fences before they had begun to burn and clear and sow the slopes close to home with grass. In those days, as well as cattle and sheep, they had kept a couple of horses to haul supplies to the station. The patient animals had walked around and around a turntable providing the power to winch the trolley up from the landing. They had been fed on oats which still grew wild on the ridge above the keeper's bush where our hidden gardens flourished. That had been the only area of bush fenced in earlier times. Elsewhere the farm animals had roamed at will, trampling and gobbling up the undergrowth, destroying the tangled and dwarfed plants which had protected the exposed edges of the forest. Then, with bared flanks and gaping wounds in its canopy, the forest had given way before the pestering winds as easily as curling wallpaper succumbs to the picking fingers of a bored child.

Exposed and hungry, their ancient lifestyle shattered, the tuatara, lizards, birds and invertebrates had fallen easy prey to the offspring of the light keepers' cats which had gone wild, and the harrier hawks which now came and bred in their thousands. Even in those early years some authorities had recognized that the flora and fauna of Stephens Island was unique and worthy of protection. Alarmed at its destruction, they had provided rifles and ammunition to keepers and visitors and paid them bounties for the birds of prey that they shot. The slaughter of hawks and even kingfishers had begun as early as 1914 when, in that year alone, 1,500 hawks had been killed. This had continued until the 1930s with tallies of many thousands being recorded. Hawks are large birds of prey and only a glut of food could have enabled their numbers to increase so phenomenally over such a small, isolated area. For them these must have been years of orgiastic feasting as the precious creatures of Stephens Island became obscenely exposed beneath the tortured and wind-scorched remnants of their forest.

But taking up arms against predators couldn't alter the relentless destruction of habitat. Only an early fencing programme could have done that. The last of the wild cats had been eliminated in the 1920s but it wasn't until 1951 that a fence was erected to protect two-thirds of the island from depredation by the farm animals. By then the creatures that had survived the destruction of their shelter and food sources were clinging to niches underground or in pockets of inaccessible vegetation. The hawk population had dwindled to a few pairs which soared and wheeled on the updrafts above the cliffs and were once again having to work for their living. The island, having been stripped almost naked, was clothed, now, in grass—a farmer's delight. The western side, because of its inaccessibility, had retained remnants of its hardy, wind-shorn vegetation and, up at the summit, a tiny patch of bush had been fenced to protect the rare frogs which had been discovered in 1914 by a lighthouse keeper's son.

In actual fact, the frogs lived slightly north of this pretty little pocket of kohe kohe trees and nikau palms. Someone had made a mistake. The frogbank was not inside the fenced area and now lay totally exposed to sun and weather. It was an unremarkable-looking hollow filled with angular stones. Muhlenbeckia vines scrambled around its perimeter and an encrustation of grey lichen coated its surface—the telltale lichen which we must, on no account, disturb!

Arne had been right about the temptation. The allure of the forbidden, plus my obsession with natural history, were an irresistible combination for me. Mere mention of rare frogs so close to home awakened a keen excitement in my breast and it wasn't surprising therefore that, on my first visit to the frogbank, I found myself down on my knees at its edge, removing a few of the top, lichen-covered rocks and putting them aside carefully so that I could fit them all back together at the end of my search. Pip was a few feet from me making his own little excavation, rock by rock. We couldn't possibly do any harm. We were taking such care.

On a clear day from the summit it was possible to see as far south as the peak of Tapaeunuku in the Kaikoura ranges of the South Island, and north to Ruapehu in the central North Island. You could see Kapiti Island and Farewell Spit and the dark hills and inlets of the Marlborough Sounds. You could look back beyond D'Urville Island and see Nelson's familiar hills. This latter skyline had the power to make me feel as if an indigestible clot had congealed somewhere between my stomach and my heart—a feeling of homesickness not specifically for the hometown I had left but for the world of people and activity it represented, and from which I felt more and more estranged. This feeling was usually a minor accompaniment to the soaring elation I felt at seeing seascape spreading to meet distant landscape with myself king of the castle at centre.

I was, however, spared all this on my first visit to the summit of the island because the cloud was low. From the ridge, almost a thousand feet above the sea, we saw only swirling mist close at hand and bright splashes below that told us the sun was trying to shine through. The frogbank was a silent, sombre place, its area not much bigger than the ground-floor of the lighthouse. I supposed that the rocks might go a long way down into the earth and that down there it might be eternally dark and damp, a haven for hundreds of frogs. On the other hand, there might be only one or two survivors clinging to life in an environment that had become too inhospitable to sustain them.

After a short while I sat back on my heels. "We'd better not dig too far."

Pip said, "Somebody's been here before us, at any rate. Not just Arne and Cis with their one rock. Look at the dead lichen on the underside of these ones."

We were on the lower side of the tumble of stones which composed the frogbank. It was the place where anyone wanting to poke around would naturally stop. I wondered if we were simply part of a long line of curious lighthouse people who had come here to investigate and excavate. Pip was peering down at the rocks he had exposed. Then his nose went almost to ground level.

"Look at this." He picked out a small rock and handed it to me. Its sandpaper surface was the same as all the others. There was no lichen on it, alive or dead, just a few strands of dried grass or dead sticks or something stuck to one side.

He said, "It's a frog."

"It's not, is it?"

"Yeah, see its toes there."

We crouched together, heads together. It was a frog—at least, the remains of one. A tiny dehydrated shell of a body with inordinately long legs extended and twisted and skinnier than toothpicks. It was dried up. Dead. But it couldn't have been long since its demise. Months? Perhaps even a year or two? How many scavenging insects wiggled their way among these rocks? Why hadn't they eaten it? Just how deep did these rocks go and what had caused them to be deposited together on the island's summit? If there was one dead frog, surely there must be many live ones hiding below the surface? It was the strangest place for frogs to live, but I'd been told that New Zealand's frogs were different from all the others in the world in that they didn't need a pond—or even a puddle. Their tadpoles stayed in the eggs until they had grown legs, and by the time they hatched they were miniature frogs capable of surviving in cool damp places.

Side by side we contemplated the desiccated specimen, my mind fussy with unanswered questions and regret. "Someone must have walked over the rocks and squashed it," I said. Suddenly I felt very bad about being at the edge of the frogbank with an excavation, small though it was, in front of me and a pile of about ten small stones beside it—looking as though it would be utterly impossible to fit them back together so that the lichen would tell no tales. I half-expected Arne to appear out of the mist. And now that we had found it, what could we do with the mummified remains of a rare frog which might be the last of its kind on earth, and which we had no business to be discovering at all?

We felt duty bound to preserve it. Pip pulled a crumpled handkerchief from his pocket and smoothed it on his knee. I picked the scrawny mummy off the rock and wrapped it in its shroud.

So that was how we came to have the remains of a rare frog hidden in our bottom cupboard. It was an embarrassment even to think about it, but we wouldn't have dreamed of throwing it away.

We did have a more legitimate find on that same day, however. This was our green lizard, a tree gecko which we could happily show off and enjoy because at that time, as far as we knew, there were no laws against keeping them in captivity. We had discovered it on our homeward journey from the summit.

As we slunk from the frogbank up onto the ridge I realized that the last of the mist was, quite literally, vanishing into thin air.

We waded through wild grasses and scrambled over cushiony mounds of muhlenbeckia which had grown over the narrow pathway. We dropped into a hollow, clambered around lichen-covered boulders and made our way down past the overgrown radar station, which was a relic of the wartime presence of the navy. All that remained of it now was a concrete edifice that resembled a tiny hut with something like a rusty iron chimney sticking up from its roof, and a tramway that led downhill. After this, the track sidled below a thicket on the ridge. The ground sloped away below our feet and we found ourselves supported by little else than the interlaced vegetation of the western side. Far below us, blue sea twinkled and skipped about the edges of a rocky shore—a shore I was never to have the fun of exploring. Further out a pattern of cloud shadows glided away across the ocean and, on the northwest skyline, the domed cap of the lighthouse reared up beyond the keepers' bush.

As our right hands clutched at the foliage of ngaio and taupata, our eyes searched among the leaves because Cis had told us that this was where the green tree geckoes were most often seen. I had come this far before and looked for them in a hopeful but haphazard and unpractised way. Now it was Pip who saw the brief movement as a gecko shrank out of sight.

He pointed at the glossy leaves. "It's just there."

"Where?" Holding my breath I peered past his finger, at first seeing only leaves, but then, taking shape among them, a yellow eye, a small green hand, a delicately pale throat.

It was ours! Of all the lizards on the island this kind would make the most appealing pet. As well as being a bright, attractive green, they spent their entire lives in the canopy of trees and shrubs, relying on their colouring for camouflage. They didn't scuttle into dark places to hide when daylight came as the common geckoes did. Instead they basked in bright sunshine and, even when disturbed, tended merely to melt back among the leaves, and remain motionless.

Exultantly I removed the little gecko from its natural home. It was vibrant green in the pink nest made by my hands, and it was neither slithery like the skinks nor wriggly like the common geckoes. There was a gentleness about it, its skin soft as a kiss.

I carried it with care. From there it was less than ten minutes to our house, and before long I had made it a new home in the space between flyscreen and sash window in our kitchen. Then I supplied it with a bunch of shining taupata leaves from our yard, a dish of honeyed water, and a selection of appetizing insects. In the course of the next few weeks, I wasted a lot of time observing it.

On several occasions I thought it must have escaped,—so well camouflaged it was, in its cluster of leaves. And, so anxious was I to catch its every little action, that I watched it until my neck ached from craning. When a fly crawled about just out of its reach I would be holding my breath and willing the unsuspicious insect to go close enough for the lizard to lunge for it. I was always on the side of the lizard (I who would rescue a beetle from drowning and carry spiders from my house and release them out of doors!) And, in the same way that another person might watch a game of rugby or a movie, I watched this mini-drama in my kitchen. It took me back to my childhood when I had happily populated our home with a variety of small creatures: caterpillars, preying mantis, weta, frogs, and anything else I had happened to come across while roaming the countryside.

But it would be a rare person who was not, at least momentarily, captivated by the green gecko, for it was a perfect little creature with wrinkled elbows and a barrel of a tummy which grew fatter by the day. It would cling to your forefinger with miniature green hands, its dazzlingly clear eyes viewing the world with a steady, unblinking gaze. When honey was dabbed onto its nose it would obligingly show off its tongue which was so similar to that of a cat or dog that you watched in fascination as it flicked up over the smooth scaled lips. Up and over the small nostrils it went, reaching further up with each lick—changing colour from pale pink to rich ruby red—and finally sliding up over the eyeballs themselves. In observing this cold-blooded creature, a reptile, no less, I wondered about the differentiation of species; and was amazed that, while yet being so substantially different from a warm-blooded mammal, it could be, in some ways, so astonishingly and endearingly similar to our own species. I was mesmerised by the exquisite miniaturisation of the tongue, the eyes, the arms, not forgetting the little, wrinkled elbows.

The first time it shed its skin I watched the process with voyeuristic delight. Initially I was worried. The normally leaf green skin had become milky pale and the creature looked sick. But then the outer layer split and peeled off from head to tail. It came off like a wispy garment, with every detail still impressed into it. One by one the gecko pulled its little feet and hands free, leaving behind four delicate, inside-out gloves, and then, bright and smart again in its green suit, it walked away from the tissue-pale ghost of itself; left it hanging twisted among the twigs, its tail turned inside-out right to the tip. I could see the shape of the eyeballs and the clear membrane that had covered them, and the tiny holes where the nostrils had been, and, all over it, the imprint of scales.

By the end of summer I had realized that tuatara also sloughed off their outer layer in the same way. The skins blew about the station like fallen leaves—curled up impressions of a pre-historic animal, scales and dorsal spines included. I collected a few pieces and pressed them between the pages of a book.

The lighthouse keepers' training school was to take place during the first two weeks of May. I had always associated this time of year with my birthday and the end of the summer school term, the beginning of holidays and the real onset of winter. Now, the end of April found me sitting at my sewing machine late into the night, creating garments in preparation for our trip out 'to civilisation'. I carried an image in my mind—we must be warm and well dressed and we must not look like country bumpkins—country people, yes, but bumpkins, no.

Before we married, I had spent a year working as a machinist; first in a Christchurch factory, The Paris Manufacturing Co., producing ladies' dress jackets and coats, and later in the hospital sewing-room in Masterton, where we had patched and mended great basketsful of linen and also made shrouds and babies' gowns. This practical experience had added to and consolidated my self-taught dressmaking skills. These I had acquired as a teenager because of my mother's serene expectation that we would all sew, and do it well, if we were equipped with a sewing machine, a Simplicity pattern, and a modicum of the intelligence with which the Good Lord had endowed us.

So now, each night, I sewed with pride and pleasure, the hum of my Bernina blending with the sounds of wind and rain which slashed at the house to no avail. I sat at the fold-down table with Pip often bunched up in one of the peculiar armchairs nearby, reading a library book or writing letters and drinking coffee. Sometimes I would look up and find his eyes on me. . .

On this night I said, "You're looking at me!"

"Yes, I like to watch you."

"Why?" (hoping for a compliment).

"It's always nice to watch someone who's good at what they're doing. . . and I love watching your hands."

I sewed another seam. My hands fed the double layer of corduroy under the foot while the needle flashed up and down, leaving a line of stitching behind. It was as though I saw my hands for the first time; the coppery gold of my skin, my wedding ring a spark of yellow, my nails short and natural. I sat back in my chair and spread them out in front of me in mock admiration. "They are quite nice, actually! They make up for having a fat stomach and big legs."

"You know I like your legs, I'm always telling you that. . . but I like to watch your hands working away. . . like when you made that pocket just now. You put all those pieces together—all inside out and upside down like a Chinese puzzle—and your machine goes 'zit, zit' and then you turn it out and you've got a pocket." Sensing an ineffable sweetness and sincerity in his words, I felt quite overcome and hopelessly unworthy.

I said, "Oh, Pippy, I love you so much. . . " and then, with the shadow of another parting suddenly sending a chill over me, I said, "And even though I'm looking forward to staying with my sister, I'm going to miss you terribly while you're at the lighthouse school." I felt my bottom lip beginning to pout. Leaving the corduroy trousers on the sewing machine, I went over, knelt down in front of him and hid my face against his chest in the warm roughness of his jersey.

His arms locked me there in a woolly embrace. "Oh, lovey! But you know I have to go—and the time will pass quickly out there for you."

My muffled voice had a thin, childlike tone. "I know. And we need to get Fred's leg looked at. It'll be really good for us all—and there's lots of things I have to do and buy—and on the weekend before we come home we might be able to go and see your mum and dad. . . " I sniffed and blew my nose. "And you'll meet lots of other lighthouse keepers—and maybe you'll be able to get the guys in head office to send Mac out here when Arne and Cis go on leave. . . And that'll be in June. It's only a month away." There! I had even managed to convince myself; there were so many things to look forward to. I threw back my head, took a breath of fresh air and gave a half-pout half-smile, blew my nose again and said, "Sorry, I was silly."

"You're not silly. You're tired."

I sensed the deepness of the night slithering into the room through cracks and doorways while the nor'west wind and rain renewed their attack on the house. I shivered and said, "It's a wild night!"

"Fifty knots this evening. . . It's s'posed to change tomorrow."

"To the south?"

"Yes."

I shivered again; there was only one more day before our departure. "How strong's it going to get?"

"Dunno, but it'll flatten out the sea."

Yes, it would flatten out the sea, at first, then it would bring it in from the other direction—straight onto the landing. Saying nothing, I again sought the comfort of his chest, felt his beard kissing my hair. He said, "You should come to bed, lovey. It's late."

I jumped up and kissed his nose. "No, I've got to finish these pants. You get undressed and try them on. Then you can go to bed. I'll come after I've put the waistband on. . . then all the machining will be finished."

By the following afternoon the weather had, indeed, swung to the south but I was so busy with my preparations for departure that I hardly had time to give it a thought and my mind didn't stop whirring with the last-minute details of leaving home until the morning after that, when I found myself descending the zig-zag above the landing, in procession with Pip, Dave, Peggy and the children. Looking directly down the gully I saw the spindly shape of the crane with the dark, sou'easterly-driven sea heaving toward it. I smelt the salt spray and heard the thunder of water slamming against rock. The new *Enterprise*, not far from the island now, advanced with the swell, climbing down and up all the time. This was nothing like the day I had arrived, with Turi on the *Belfast*. Today I was going to be a real lighthouse keeper's wife, and, now that the time had come, my heart scampered with excitement.

I had taken a 'seasick pill', I had plastic bags in my pocket 'just in case', and, apart from some apprehension on behalf of the children, I felt ready for anything—ready and full of courage—or so I thought, until I came close to the action and saw the great black and white surging ocean, the waiting crane with Arne already on the platform, and the sturdy little boat catching wet rays of wintery sun as she lurched determinedly toward us. Then, to my dismay and bewilderment, I realized that my stomach had begun to churn in sympathy with the scene before me, and that, already, I felt unpleasantly seasick. Seasick on dry land! And disgusted with myself! And puzzled, too.

Nevertheless, before long, with every appearance of serenity, I found myself waiting beside the others on the rocky steps above the block, sheltering Helen against my body and tucking Fred in under my free arm. With the island at our backs we looked east, the sharp wind, the early sun, the smell of the sea assaulting our faces. And, mindful of the wealth of experiences that lay immediately ahead of him, I ignored the sick feeling in my stomach and seized the opportunity to educate our son.

"Just look at that big boat, Freddy!" (She was sixty feet in length and beamy with it). "That's the *Enterprise* and she brings out our mail— our letters—and all our boxes of stores and everything else. . . " (And in much worse weather than this. Every mail day—and the men down here loading and unloading drums and timber and sacks and boxes, all wet with rain and sea water.) "Yes, you can hear its motor now. It sounds like it's singing, doesn't it! Err-err-err, it goes." (Pip had told me proudly that she was powered by a 'big G.M.' and I could see that the new *Enterprise* was worthy of the men's admiration.) "Look, the hull's a nice pale green." (Spruce paintwork lit up by the sun.) "And the deck's brown and it's all wet." (Water was sluicing through the scuppers.) "That must be the captain just going up the ladder. See, he's going to drive the boat from up there." (Up on the flying bridge from where he could see to manoeuvre the vessel towards the rocks.) "And there's Mrs Midtgard looking out the door of the cabin. And that man behind her is coming here to do the work with Mr Midtgard while Daddy's away."

Cis had been out to town and now she was waiting to land with the relieving keeper and his partner who was a friend of hers, but, first, there was a canvas sling loaded with boxes and bags to send up. Arne had swung the boom of the crane around, and a rope sling full of our bags and packs dangled a few feet above the water.

"See, Freddy. Those men at the back of the boat. They're the crew." (Standing on the lively stern in thigh-waders, legs apart, waiting with a giant boathook, as confident in their balance as a circus girl standing on the bare back of a trotting pony). "There, look at that! They've got our bags and now they're going to send up all the other luggage. . . " (This trip was a 'special' and there wasn't much to be landed. The reality of the whole procedure here was as new to me as it was to Fred.)

"There we are! Up it comes! And Daddy's got the landing box ready and soon it'll be our turn to go 'whoosh' down to the boat!"

Yes, soon it would be our turn. I was getting used to the scene, now, though I still felt light-headed with anticipation, and seasick at the sight of the vessel bucking and circling below. But it was obvious to me that feeling sick before I had even got onto the boat was proof that it was 'all in my mind'; and being only in my mind, it could be controlled. (The matter of sea sickness had been discussed at some length during the preceding weeks, so I had primed myself up to be strong.) Now the realization came to me that leaving the island was nothing like embarking in the sheltered waters of a port. For us there wouldn't be the usual time for adjustment as the boat cast off and slowly left harbour. Instead we would begin our journey to the mainland by swinging from the crane and then landing on the deck of a boat that was capering about on the ocean—ready and impatient to carry us across open water towards Cape Jackson and the entrance to the Sounds beyond—two and a half hours distant.

Having landed safely and been assisted over the lurching wet deck by the men, I staggered into the passengers' cabin and floundered about its tiny floorspace, trying to tuck Helen into her carrycot . Then, while Pip sat protectively beside her, I wedged myself in behind the table opposite Peggy and the children, and braced myself for the journey ahead. Fighting the sickness down, I watched anxiously as the small faces around me whitened. Dave had found a red-painted metal bucket with a rope on the handle and, soon, it contained a horrible mixture of half-digested breakfasts. Pip, who never suffered from motion sickness, took it away to empty it and I almost panicked while it was gone, but, sick though I felt, my breakfast co-operated with the sea sickness pill in my stomach and chose to remain there rather than go to the fishes. Then, when Helen began to cry and vomit, I knew that I would never again believe anybody's claims that sea sickness was 'all in the mind'. How could a six-month-old baby have 'talked herself into it'? It was all right for some people. . . some people would have no idea! I stumbled from my seat and Pip moved in beside our wan little son while I attended to Helen.

As the journey continued, Pip and Dave departed from the reeking cabin on many a pretext. Sea water sloshed against the windows. Our whole world was in motion, and I longed for stillness. At last, through the blurry windows, I saw the headland of Cape Jackson to starboard and the lighthouse on the port side. It was a real lighthouse, a lighthouse on a rock lashed by the sea and drowned in spray, but nobody lived there; it was automatic. Pip had taught me a code for telling port from starboard: "port, left, red light—all the short words together; and starboard, right, green light —the long words"; I felt proud to have remembered this little piece of nautical knowledge.

I remembered, too, that, in typical fashion, Pip had claimed that the cure for seasickness was to 'stand under a tree'. A tree! Oh, for a tree at this moment! I began to imagine I was a green lizard up in a tree-top, swaying about in a terrible storm. It wasn't so very unpleasant; in fact the trip hadn't been too bad at all; and I hadn't been frightened. I felt that, really, I had risen to the occasion rather well and that, after this, the voyage from Picton to Wellington on the huge inter-island ferry, the *Aramoana*, would be a dream. I thought about it with sleepy pleasure and my eyes began to close. I was just a lizard in a tree. A lizard in a swaying tree—suddenly overcome by a feeling of immense weariness. Drugged! It was the sea sickness pill. I had said, "I don't believe in pills"—and somebody had said to me, "You mean 'approve'. Pills do exist. You've got to believe in them. They're not like fairies. . . " Yes, I had meant approve. I didn't approve of pills—well, not unless you were dying or something. The children had all been sick in spite of them. But not me. They had worked for me. The packet had warned "can cause drowsiness" and all I wanted to do, now, was sleep. Sleep forever. . .

But the atmosphere in the cabin had quietened. We were now in the lee of Arapawa Island with the long reach of Queen Charlotte Sound ahead of us. One of the crew came in, an older man with a smooth, tanned face and a mild manner. The cabin shrank around his height and strength. I forced my eyes open as we straightened ourselves up around the table and watched as he wiped it clean with a small sponge in a huge hand. He spread a cotton table-cloth over the mahogany-finish formica, then left and came back shortly with plates, buttered bread, knives and forks, a dish of steaming saveloys, tomato sauce, cups of tea. I felt myself responding to his silent, homely demeanour and the proximity of food. Then came his gentle injunction—the murmur of father to child— "Get this into your tummies. It'll soon bring you round." And he was right. The worst of the journey was over.

CHAPTER 13

At My Sister's

The doctor was young, but old enough to inspire confidence. He was my sister Paul's family doctor and 'good with children', and he waited quietly while I removed the dressing from Fred's leg. Fred sat very still in a brave-little-boy way, trying to turn his whimpers into a laugh. It was an apprehensive sound—more like a cry. Only five days before this he had tripped and hurt the wound badly and his cries of pain had set my heart racing with sympathy, worry and guilt. It raced again now—mainly with fear of the doctor's condemnation.

The dressing lifted off easily because Paul had suggested moistening it with an antibacterial cream but the wound looked messy because of it—somehow much worse-looking than usual. I hadn't told the doctor what to expect; had simply said, "I want you to look at my son's leg."

Crouching in front of Fred, he murmured soothingly to him and studied the injury. Then, glancing up at me, he asked, "What is it?"

For a second I felt shocked and confused that the expert didn't know what he was looking at. Then, with a sick feeling, I realized that he probably couldn't imagine how such an injury could have happened. Words tumbled from me. "It's a cut. He sliced it on some iron. There was a big flap of skin and I cut it off. . . with the scissors. I cut too much off. . . " I waited for some reaction, some sort of judgment to descend on me. Nothing. "It was two months ago. It's taking so long to heal." My voice was small and shaking. "I've been really worried about infection. . . "

After a hundred years of silent contemplation the doctor sat back down on his padded chair. "It's coming on all right. There might be a low level of infection but it's well on the way to being completely healed. I'll give you something, a topical cream, to dry it up and harden it off." He pulled open one of the many drawers in his wooden desk and drew out a small jar. "It's one of my own remedies. I'd like to hear how it goes. . . " No reproof. No blame. Just an inquiry, as he dressed the leg, about the lighthouse and our way of life.

So I told him about the island: its isolation, the twice-monthly mail days, the crane at the landing, the tuatara, the sea birds at night. And as he questioned me and listened with a kind of rapt curiosity, I heard my voice grow strong again and felt the worry of the previous two months draining away. Finally he ushered us into the waiting room where Paul sat beside her youngest son with Helen on her knee, a serene island of familiarity among the mothers and children who filled the room.

Paul drove us home from the surgery carefully and with mathematical calculation because she had only recently passed her test and obtained her driver's licence. Although women drivers were often derided and made the butt of feeble jokes by a fair proportion of the male population, more and more women were driving. My sisters and I had grown up in a carless household and the desire to be in control of a steering wheel hadn't come naturally to me, nor to Barb—but Paul was different; and, knowing her energy, ambition and determination, I wasn't surprised to see her in control of a vehicle.

Nor, knowing that energy, ambition and determination, was I surprised that she and her husband were raising their family of four sons to be perfect little geniuses.

I expected nothing less of her because she was the sister who had enriched my own childhood with her particularly lively imagination. She had taught me rhymes while she bathed me; she had made and illustrated my first 'ABC'; she had filled my head with stories before she put me to bed; and, as I grew older, she had taken me birdnesting, had taught me to play hopscotch, had shown me how to gut a fish, and, at times, had teased me and let me know that little sisters, too, have to learn to fight for their rights. She and Barb had been little mothers to me from the day I was brought home from the nursery— passing on to me the values and skills that our mother had earlier instilled into them. They had always been my role models, and I had worshipped in each of them their own special attributes. Even now, as an adult, I was still striving to be as generous and kind as Barb and as innovative and clever as Paul—but both were clever and both were kind. I had grown up believing that no-one else's sisters could be as clever and kind as mine, that no-one else's mother was as wise ours, that our father was the gentlest man that had ever lived. It was a foregone conclusion that I would bring up my own children to be every bit as bright and healthy and well-behaved as my four little nephews.

I hadn't a doubt that Paul was the ideal mother. Only the night before I had awoken Helen, as usual, at ten o'clock to coax her into drinking another part-bottle of milk before going to bed.

And Paul had demanded incredulously, "What are you doing, feeding her at this time of night?"

I had spluttered with embarrassment. It was bad enough to be poking a bottle at the baby's mouth instead of a breast. Already I hadn't lived up to Paul's example. I said, "She doesn't drink nearly enough. The Plunket book says she should have three times as much. . . "

Paul was all for Plunket but not when it got in the way of commonsense. "Yes, but she obviously doesn't want or need it. I wouldn't wake her up to give her a feed at this time of night. Not at her age. She's a happy, healthy baby and she's got plenty of energy."

Straight away I had known she was right, and after that we had sat up late, I pouring into my sister's receptive ears all the worry, thrills and excitement of the past months.

Now, as I emerged from the car in the driveway and followed Paul into her livingroom, I breathed a sigh of relief that my nightmares about Fred's leg were over. No way could I foresee that, from the very next moment, the germ of our next little medical emergency on Stephens Island was about to set out on its path of destruction.

Paul's house was roomy and modern. "It's not flash," she said as she unpacked her carton of groceries, "but it's the best value, and we like the situation with the bush over the bank for the boys to play in. The lawyers are sharks, of course. They screw you every time you buy a house. It's daylight robbery, money for jam for them, but it'll do them no good in the long run. . . We've worked for every penny we've got. Every penny!"

Money! It meant different things to different people and my perception of it was little more than a confusion of ideas from my childhood: the Bible, easier for a camel to go through the eye of a needle than for the rich, young man to enter into the kingdom of heaven;

Dad, on a war pension and proud of it; Mum, always scornful of the 'big bugs' and 'nobs' and saying "We might be poor but at least we're honest." She had made such a success of creating 'something out of nothing' that the feeling had been fostered in me that there was virtue in poverty. And if not virtue, at least challenge. It didn't occur to me that it was the Welfare State that made the challenge of poverty bearable. Mum had always said that good health was the most precious possession of all—good health first, and education a close second—perhaps, with good health and education, we could all become 'big bugs' and 'nobs', those despised yet envied people who had plenty of money! But I didn't envy them, and my sister's talk of lawyers and money made me feel uncomfortable.

It also brought an embarrassing memory fluttering into my mind. It was of the one occasion that Pip and I had required the services of a lawyer. Strangely, it was a memory of the lawyer's magnaminity and of our own foolishness and ignorance. It had happened when we had decided to buy a farmlet. The opportunistic land agent, seeing us for the trusting young babes that we were, had been quick to get our signatures, without even telling us that people generally engaged a lawyer to help them sort out the legal aspects of land deals. Subsequently, when we had realized that the property wasn't what it seemed to be, we had rushed to a lawyer to get us out of the tricky situation—and that lawyer, quite different from those of my sister's experience, had been more than kind to us. Furious at the land agent's unprofessional tactics, he had managed to get the deal annulled. Then, instead of charging us, he had given us a fatherly scolding and told us to be more astute next time. I had felt humbled and grateful, but a cynic would have said that he had simply been lining himself up for future business. I guessed that Paul would say the same thing so I couldn't tell her the story. I knew she would never have got herself into such a situation— she was much too astute.

As well as being astute (and sporty and even good at mathematics) she was 'artistic'. As a teenager, I had grown so tired of hearing the pride in my parents' voices as they proclaimed that Paul had "got her Diploma of Fine Arts—and in only three years, too", and, yet, we had all shared that pride.

In the livingroom, I sat on the couch changing Helen's nappies. I said, "This is a nice big room. . . "

"Yes," Paul answered. "Plenty of room for the boys to horse around without falling over the furniture. Room for my sewing table and the television. We're going to get rid of this wallpaper and replace it with tapa cloth—you know, beaten bark—we brought it with us when we left Fiji. . . Oh, don't put the baby on the carpet! You've no idea what it was like when we moved in. The last people lived like animals."

"She'll be all right," I said. "She's healthy." Hadn't Fred just survived the threat of infection in his leg and wasn't their whole family eating and living here themselves and abounding with good health? The place couldn't be that bad, surely.

"Yes, but you've no idea what it was like. It was overrun with kids. There's a family from further down near the beach—they were in and out of here all the time and they're a moth-eaten lot—just a bunch of scabby little ratbags. The place was a pigsty and you can't clean carpet, not deep down. You shouldn't put her down on it. She'll pick something up, for sure."

"Well, she won't stay on a rug at any rate. She's far too active." There didn't seem to be much else I could do. And I had, long ago, become used to ignoring my sisters when it suited me (though often to my cost). Before long, Helen, with fingers in and out of her mouth as usual, was demonstrating her skill in rolling about on the carpet and getting herself from one side of the room to the other.

A ball shooting overhead diverted Paul's attention to her youngest son. "Dougal, outside if you want to kick that ball." He was only a year older than Fred but Dad had told me, "That boy can already kick a ball like an All Black." And I had felt quite jealous and reminded myself that I should play ball games with Fred so that he, too, could one day have the chance of becoming an All Black.

As the afternoon went on, I brought the washing in from the line and began to fold it. The three little schoolboys arrived home and Fred stood at the far end of the living room, bewildered by their antics. "Ha, ha, ha," he cried, not sure whether to laugh or cry.

"Listen to him!" said Paul, eyeing him speculatively. "What a peculiar laugh. If one of my boys laughed like that, I'd be worried."

If one of her sons laughed like what? How did he laugh? What was wrong with it? "Ha, ha, ha," that's how he laughed. "Ha, ha, ha."

People laughed like that in books. Had I taught him to laugh that way? Trained him up like a parrot to say"Ha, ha, ha"? There seemed to be no end to the pitfalls when you tried to bring up perfect children. But, of course, Paul was thrilled to see my children (neither of them being moth-eaten or scabby). She had taken Helen into her arms straight away, saying, "Look at her, she's brown as a little berry, even in winter!" and she had known exactly how to talk to a travel-weary two-year-old to make him feel important.

Having folded and sorted the clean clothes, I began to iron them, the steam belching out in hissing clouds and hitting my nostrils with the smell of scorch and soap. As I worked I reflected that I was far too sensitive to my sisters' opinions, and that, probably when they were ninety, they would look at me just starting in my eighties and still think of me as a kid.

As I ran the iron over handkerchiefs, underpants, singlets, Paul looked over at me. "Oh, I don't iron all that stuff these days. With the birth of each child I've had to reorganise my time and I iron less and less." That was Paul; always practical and efficient and, with her calm, wide eyes that held you in their direct gaze, she was always totally in control. Her slow and clear way of speaking gave her every sentence the impact of truth and, because I had seen little of her during the previous ten years, I felt I had stepped back into my childhood, feeling all the old emotions of that time and reacting in the same childish ways.

But I wasn't a kid any more and I could handle things differently. I wondered how Pip was getting on at the lighthouse school, what he was learning, whom he was meeting. I hated being parted from him again but it was almost a privilege to have this opportunity to get to know Paul again now that we were both adults.

Leaving the bench where she had been meticulously preparing the evening meal, Paul distributed a piece of raw carrot to each child and one to me as well.

"Thanks," I said cracking my teeth into it. "Just like Mum always did, eh! I always give Fred raw carrot, too."

"Full of vitamin A to make you see in the dark." She answered just as Mum would have done and gave her slow smile that lit me up from the inside. Considering the strength and severity in the set of her mouth and jaw, hers was a particularly delightful smile, aided as it was by the turned-up nose and dimpled cheeks which she had inherited from our father.

Many a time, as a child, I had inspected my own face, hoping to detect some sign of developing dimples and an upward tilt to my nose, not realizing, until I was grown up, that I resembled my mother more than anyone else. Yet I had always thought of myself as 'Dad's girl' while Paul particularly venerated our mother.

I had been surprised to learn, during this visit, to what extent our views of our parents differed. It appeared that, over the years when we had witnessed their differences, we had been silent supporters of opposing sides. Now a strange idea formed in my head: if our separate perceptions of our parents could have been, somehow, extracted from deep in our hearts, (Paul's parents and mine made manifest and placed side by side, supposedly like two sets of identical twins), then these two pairs, although modelled exactly to the dimensions we each had perceived of the one couple, would be unrecognizable to an observer as being anything like the same people.

As I prepared for bed that night I hugged this great insight to myself, mined it for the utmost of its meaning, savoured it for its indication that pools of wisdom might lie untapped in the abyss of my mind.

CHAPTER 14

To and Fro

Don't put her on the carpet." That's what my sister had said. But I had put her on the carpet, and *now* look at her!

In the three days since our homecoming, her face had developed spots. These had turned into blisters which had quickly burst, and, after that, I had almost been able to see them spreading toward each other so that now her face—the whole face of our beautiful baby—had become a mass of running, weeping sores.

We were absolutely aghast, never having seen anything like it before. The infection spread with the speed of summer weed-growth after rain. It ringed her eyes, nose and mouth and spots began to appear on her neck.

Paul's warning came slamming back to me. "Don't put her on the carpet—she'll pick something up for sure," and when she had said "scabby, little ratbags", I hadn't imagined that this was what she had meant.

Before we had left Wellington there had been a little broken blister inside the joint of one of Helen's sucking fingers. It had looked fairly innocuous but we had smeared an ointment on it, a futile exercise because the finger spent as much time in her mouth as out of it. The blister hadn't got much bigger and I had wondered if it was actually the sucking that was making the skin peel off. It certainly hadn't seemed like anything to worry about—but now look at her!

A sou'easterly had brought us home in much the same weather as we had left, except that, this time, we had had a following sea; "up our bum all the way", as Pip had said. After the voyage, as we had walked up the track from the landing, a bedraggled band of refugees, I had sucked in the wild, windy desolation of 'our' island and felt myself coming to life. Once again I had not been seasick, although the constant movement of the *Enterprise* had left me with unsteady legs and the feeling that the earth was swimming beneath my feet—but that was nothing against the fact that we had journeyed 'out to civilisation' and had returned to our stronghold unscathed.

In our absence there had been a birth. Our green gecko (of the barrel tummy and wrinkled elbows) had borne twins while in Cis's care—the sweetest, prettiest little lizards I had ever seen. There had been a death. One of our chooks had died of no apparent cause—Arne was apologetic as if we might think he or the relieving keeper had purposely done it a mischief. And there had been a party. The rest of our chooks had gorged themselves in our precious little garden plot near the house —Arne was even more apologetic. But nothing had mattered because it was so good to be home and together. Pip had brought back a selection of replacement parts for my endlessly broken down, space-age washing machine which threw epileptic fits that neither of us could control, its violent convulsions cracking pipes and fittings with predictable monotony. The tractor had also broken down and the wheelbarrow was being used to transport luggage, stores and equipment about the station.

While Dave had been out of action, nursing a head cold on his first day back home, Pip had worked with Arne. "All day on the tractor's electrics with no luck at all. It's been bloody frustrating."

"Don't swear," I had said. "And look at Helen's face. Those things are getting bigger."

"Well, it *has* been bloody frustrating. But we've got onto the Ministry of Works in Nelson and they're sending a couple of blokes out tomorrow. . . Her face *is* a bit of a mess, isn't it!"

The blokes' arrival couldn't have been more timely. I would be able to leave the island with them, get a ride all the way to Nelson, and get Helen to the doctor. But in two days, my pleasure at arriving home had turned into another round of uncertainty and anxiety. While Pip had worked a long day with Arne, clearing and burning the final remains of the demolished schoolhouse, unloading the maintenance men from the *Belfast* and then fencing all the afternoon—I had worried my way through the hours, handwashing nappies and travel-stained clothing, and preparing for another journey away from home.

As usual, Helen scooted on her tummy over the glossy floor, using her forearms for propulsion, her dark eyes peering out through a faceful of weeping blisters. She wasn't screaming with pain but she was fretful and rubbed her little fists into her face, spreading infection wherever she touched. "Unclean. Unclean." The word moaned through the channels of my mind and seemed to bounce off the walls of the house and echo out into the vast, uninhabited outdoors which on better days could seem so inspiring.

"Unclean! Unclean!" My baby was a leper and nobody seemed to have any answers. *The Ship Captain's Medical Guide* was simply frightening. What we needed was something to fix her up—something from the family doctor who would know exactly what the problem was. We could consult a doctor through the radio but that was always rather hit and miss, and, with the maintenance men going straight to Nelson, the obvious thing to do was to go with them. After contact by radio, the Marine Department office sent a message to my good old dad telling him to expect us. I knew for sure that, however late our arrival, he would be waiting up for me with a warm fire burning.

Pip helped me to pack. He had spent the morning fencing and had killed and dressed two sheep after lunch. He promised to have the washing machine fixed by the time I came back. At the landing he gave me a hug and I was deposited on Turi's boat with the maintenance men. Only three days and six hours had passed since our arrival home on the *Enterprise*. It was Thursday 18 May, bleak and wintery, with a little sun and a lively sea, and, on that same day, Peggy and Dave were thrown into a paroxysm of excitement at receiving a telegram from Head Office, telling them they were to be transferred to Centre Island, in Foveaux Strait. They would have six weeks to prepare for their departure.

In Nelson, although it was my first visit since leaving for the lighthouse, I wanted to hide my baby away from friends and relatives and strangers alike. How could I tell people about our wonderful healthy lifestyle when they could see for themselves that our daughter was oozing—no, overflowing with the sort of old-fashioned germs that one might expect to catch in a slum? I decided to keep a low profile but, in the doctor's driveway, I saw one of my old school teachers advancing with a smile of recognition. After looking helplessly around for some way of escape, I tried to block her view of my daughter's scabby cheeks. "Oh, what nonsense," she scoffed. "She's lovely!" But I couldn't believe she meant it and, even though she then showed more than a passing interest in my new career as a lighthouse keeper's wife, I felt I had lost my one chance of redemption after the abysmal lack of interest I had shown in her class ten years before.

The doctor's rooms were a haven. The same worn, wooden step that I had scrubbed with such energy; the brass bell-plate I had polished; the white-smocked receptionist in the office cubicle that had been mine; the fat old couch that I had tried to keep tidy-looking; the green baize door beyond which patients had carried their problems; the cheery-faced doctor bursting through that door to beckon them in.

And now to beckon me in. One look at Helen's face was enough for the diagnosis. "Impetigo," he said. "Easily cured with the right antibiotic cream. . . " He wrote the prescription in his swinging but copy-book-neat longhand and spent the next ten minutes firing questions at me about the lighthouse service and the island.

I went, then, out to the kitchen at the back of the house to see his wife. Mother of six boys, she was a down-to-earth person who always made me feel welcome. Then I was away, driven by my father in his tiny van, to the corner chemist. He was alone in his shop and greeted me as if I were a traveller returning from a voyage of exploration. I couldn't help but notice that people liked lighthouses and they liked islands, and that they were listening to me with much more attention than in the past. With slight guilt, I felt myself sailing along on a wave of pride and self-importance—but the ugly sight of Helen's pustular sores kept me anchored within reach of reality.

Pustules, blisters and scabs. With the application of the cream they all disappeared as quickly as they had come. It was a miracle cure. The doctor had said it was a common infection and that Helen had quite probably picked it up from the carpet. I looked with sudden distaste at carpets in general. They were everywhere and they were nothing but bug-catchers! I thought with relief of the shiny congoleum in our houses on the light station. And on the Monday after the weekend I went into town and bought myself a floor polisher—triple-headed. I was ready to go home.

And I *could* go home—because the next day was our regular mail day. Dad was delighted to have an excuse to visit the island again, and that afternoon he drove us to Picton. We were both familiar with the routine now: staying overnight in the Federal Hotel on the foreshore; creeping downstairs to the chill kitchen to make tea and toast before the truck rattled to the door to pick us up just before four a.m.; boarding the *Enterprise* at the wharf, our breath puffing out in clouds; and throwing one last look at the sleeping village with the dark sea capturing and fracturing the cold light of its street lamps—it was only eight days since my last journey. I could not foresee that within a month I would be making another.

We settled down in the comparative warmth of the cabin to drowse away the remainder of the night. Ahead of us, in the darkness of the wheelhouse, feet apart at the helm, radar screen flickering beside him, stood a tall man with a wide strong reach. This was Brian Pickering, the skipper, for whom, it seemed, everyone had the greatest respect. Dad had worshipped him right from the start. He had the masculine qualities Dad admired: physical strength, competence and quiet reliability. I think that, not being a leader himself, Dad would have followed such a man to the far side of the earth. And, now that I, too, had travelled on the *Enterprise* with Brian Pickering the master of his ship and so obviously a man of the sea, I was content that everything was in safe hands. Once again, I was happy to be going home.

But was I happy when I got there? Did I settle down to face the bleak midwinter in the true spirit of a lighthouse keeper's wife? Did I live up to my own image of myself as a pioneering woman, warming home and family with the sheer hearty optimism of my indomitable spirit?

How I wished for that envisaged warmth and heartiness, wished I were the sort of bright-natured, cuddlesome woman who brought sunshine into every room. How I wished we were a family given to jokes and easy banter, wished that I could think of even one joke—one sparkling comment that would lighten the atmosphere—that I could be the sort of mother who could make chuckles rumble up from her little son's tummy—that my little son was less serious—and that he would chuckle sometimes instead of saying "ha, ha, ha." I wished I didn't growl at him so often, or smack him. My parents had never smacked. Mum had been a wiser mother than any other—and now she was dead.

I found myself chilled by feelings of dreariness and foreboding and preoccupied with thoughts of illness and death. Tentacle by tentacle the octopus of doom was tightening its grip on me. It had begun as a little octopus when I was a little girl with a sick mother. It had grown with me and I was used to the feel of its clammy arms. Perhaps that was why I didn't recognize it for what it was, and allowed myself to believe, over those two bleak weeks, that the scary inventions of my mind were now a reality.

I could have blamed it on the weather. On the day I came home, a nor'wester of twenty knots had crumpled up the sea, and, the day after that, forty knots had chased cloud and whirlwinds and sheets of spray across the sickly piece of ocean that I could see through our fly-screened, salt-laden windows. For two weeks we saw hardly a ray of sunshine, so I could have felt that the weather was depressing me—but I didn't.

Alternatively I could have blamed it on the changes ahead and the fact that the other wives were immersed in supervising schoolwork and preparations for their separate departures. Dave had already begun hauling boxes out of his storage room in The Palace so they could begin packing their less important items. Cis and Arne were getting ready to go on leave to the Pacific Islands—an exotic eight weeks in the tropics! They would be away when the others left for Centre Island. They would be away for the best part, or the worst, of the winter.

When I had expressed amazement that they saved up their holidays for two years and then went so far away, Cis had said, "But where can you go when you get your leave? You'll find it the same yourselves. You leave the island and have no home and no car. Staying with relatives is all right for a while but it soon wears thin and you feel you're imposing." I could see she was right but Pip and I didn't have to worry about holidays yet. The best thing was that there was still a possibility that Mac would be coming to relieve Arne, but it was only a possibility.

Perhaps, after all, I was just plain lonely after being out in civilisation? Admitting to loneliness would have been tantamount to saying I couldn't cope with isolation, couldn't cope with being a lighthouse keeper's wife; and that was as unthinkable as for a mother to say she didn't want her child. It would be a cardinal sin and I would never be able to face the world again. And, at any rate, I didn't need people. Both Pip and I claimed we didn't even like people much—that the beauty of the natural world was more important to us.

If Pip had been a little more perceptive, a little less believing of my virtues, a little more aware of the workings of my mind. . . But how could he be when I was afraid to show him my true self, and when he himself was so serenely sure of the way things should be? On the occasions that I had succumbed to my night-time fears and worries and had poured them weepily into his sleepy ears, I'd woken up the next day ashamed of my weakness and determined to show that such nocturnal episodes were of no more consequence than bad dreams. And, in the light of day, they seemed embarrassing and were never mentioned.

Perhaps it was my long visit to my sister, coupled with my return to Nelson, that had brought the phantom presence of my mother so strongly into my mind. The litany of her illnessess went back long before I was born; back to her own infancy when her mother had fed her on arrowroot biscuits and milk until she was five because she would 'eat nothing else'.

Mum had blamed this extraordinary feeding for all her later health problems: the constant boils she had suffered as a child, the rheumatic fever and then the rheumatoid arthritis that began to cripple her in her twenties, the toxic goitre that had hospitalised her for months and nearly killed her in her thirties, her debilitation and sickness when she was pregnant with me, the breast cancer that had filled my pre-school years with menace, the stomach rupture, and, finally, cancer again.

Reared on Mum's stories of suffering and illness, of how lucky she was to be alive and how we must all eat up the natural and health-giving food which she and Dad worked so hard to provide us with, I had grown up with a secret terror that one day disease would spring from its hiding place and again ravage my mother, and that, this time, she would die—and how could I ever cope with that? And although, during my schooldays, Mum had experienced a state of relatively good health, I had developed a deep dread of death. It was woven through all the internal turbulence of my childish mind, together with the feeling that my soul was totally alone as it bounced on its way through the caverns of eternity.

Perhaps my fears had bred so prolifically because of my being the youngest in a family ruled by my mother who was ruled by her own poor health. My sisters had always had each other. With only thirteen months between them they had been 'the girls' and I had been the late arrival. "You were a mistake," they used to chorus gleefully—completely negating what they had earlier told me about my being found under a gooseberry bush.

But Mum had said more than once, "The Good Lord must have something planned for you, Jean. The doctor said I would die if I had another baby. He said I should have it taken away—but I wouldn't hear of it. . . I'd already lost one. . . and you can bet your bottom dollar that one would have been a boy. At any rate, as things turned out, I survived and you were another girl, but you were a great joy to me. Those later ones often are. . . "

Fancy that! I was a great joy to her! And because she had saved me, as a foetus, from being 'taken away', there was some kind of destiny awaiting me, and a kind of responsibility on me as well. So I must, (we all must), eat up the good food and grow strong and thrive. And maybe Mum would thrive, too, now that she knew the secret.

But Mum had waited for me to grow up, and then she had died. She had been quite old, of course, fifty-nine, though not really old enough to die. It had been horrible! A horrible year: Pip and I on the orchard living in a horrible house which had the appearance and atmosphere of an airforce lecture hall (which, indeed, it once had been); neither my parents, nor ourselves, having a telephone; and Pip and I visiting Nelson for a few hours on a weekend, never sure how Mum would be, never knowing how to help her.

I had one particularly bad recollection of Mum—thin now that cancer held her in its arms—and unable to keep warm; huddled under a blanket, in a hard little armchair in front of an old two-bar heater, barely able to make herself understood because surgeons had cut away half her tongue. Pip had taken Dad for a drive out into the countryside to give him a break from his constant attendance on Mum in the dolorous atmosphere of that house, and Mum, not understanding, was pathetically agitated that her daughter's husband would go away so selfishly gallivanting. She had always railed against this sort of typically male behaviour and I felt miserable that Pip's good intentions were misunderstood. The house was bleak and dark, its blinds half down, and Mum giving a persistent, dry little cough which I had never heard before.

I had washed up the few dishes and cleaned down the bench in the windowless kitchenette. She stared at the red-hot bars of the heater and coughed again. Then she spoke awkwardly in her terrible, new, slurred way. "What do you think of that cough I've got, Jean?"

Gripped by horror, I shrugged and said lightly, "It's just a cough." At the same time my heart screamed, "It's the cancer, Mum. It's gone to your throat and it's going to kill you. Oh please God, please God, don't let my mother choke to death."

Later my words had echoed back to me many times. "It's just a cough, Mum. Just a cough." And I felt that, somehow, I had failed her. I hadn't even held her hand or put my arm around her because that had not been our custom.

That year Mum's illness had never been far from my mind and at night I had lain awake worrying and praying and hoping there might be a god somewhere who would look after my mother; and maybe there truly was a god because, before the cancer had had a chance to squeeze its fist too tightly about her throat, Mum had slipped away. In hospital for an exploratory operation, she hadn't awoken from the anaesthetic, and Dad, frozen-faced, had told me she would never awaken, that she was in a coma, and that I shouldn't visit her because she wouldn't know me and the medicaments had turned her face a 'ghastly green'. So I hadn't gone to see her; had never seen her again; never seen the ghastly green, although my imagination had painted it in my memory more powerfully, more green, more ghastly than reality ever could. And, again, I had felt that I had failed her. I hadn't wept at her passing. It had all seemed so fruitless. In Fiji, Paul had cried for a week and later said I should have let her know more accurately how sick and close to death Mum had been, but I hadn't known she was about to die. Should I have? Should I have?

Now, on Stephens Island, the day-to-day business continued as usual. Pip uncomplainingly accepted the task of finding interesting things for my father to do and was pleased to see that Helen's face was well on the way to recovery. He was proud that he had had the responsiblity of landing us back on the island. It was the first time he had 'worked the crane for all lifts'. With Arne going away for two months and another keeper soon to be taking Dave's place, Pip would be the only keeper with experience of the way things were done here. He had further chances to practise his crane driving skills later in the week when boats came to the island bringing men: a surveyor to check the safety of winches and crane, and maintenance staff to repair number three generator.

Meanwhile there was no end to the tasks the keepers could do. They shifted coal, built fences, fixed telephone wires, put a new muffler on the crane, rounded up more sheep for meat and killed them, brought Arne's boat up to The Palace, fixed an aerial, painted this and that.

There was the smell of change in the air; but I was largely weatherbound in my little house so separate from the rest of the station, and hardly a whiff of it reached me. I cooked and sewed and mothered my children, and gardened a little when time and weather allowed, but it was as if the rest of the world had disappeared and that, with it, everything I had previously thought of as normality had vanished, too. I was unwary, and unaware that isolation and loneliness can play tricks on the mind. Without even a fight, I allowed random and negative thoughts and anxieties to take possession of me, to take me over. All those childhood terrors, those fears of death and disease, and the ungrieved-over memories of Mum— they swallowed me up in one big, easy bite. And I simply reacted—part of me having believed for years that my life's prescription would be the same as my mother's. Perhaps many women have that feeling at times, until reality proves otherwise.

Pip was so gullible where I was concerned. If I believed I was dying, then he came close to believing it, too. Once again, he helped me to pack, his face reflecting my anxiety. This time I left Fred with him. I left the island on the same day that Cis, Arne and Anthony set out for the exotic South Seas. It was Mac who arrived to relieve them—all our scheming and planning had worked—but I was leaving, too. As I was dropped, again, onto the heaving deck of the *Enterprise* I felt myself swamped by the sensation that I was stepping outside of reality. I was on my way with Helen and my father to Nelson, inexplicably believing that my children would grow up with no memory of their mother, that my husband would have to find a new wife, that my father—oh my poor father!

It would have been a sensible thing to tell the doctor that I was frequently made miserable by swollen glands, headaches and sore throats—and it would have been the truth; but, as a teenager, I had grown accustomed to concealing these persistent symptoms. To be ill in our house had been to be in conflict with our common vision that germs fell down screeching in terror at the mere sight of our impressively healthy bodies—bodies that had been built up with religious ardour by our mother—bodies built up of barrow-loads of fresh vegetables and fortified with brewer's yeast, wheat germ, Maltexo and cod liver oil. So now, in the surgery again, with the doctor saying, "What brings you back so soon?" I simply covered my face with my hands and whispered through the gap between, "I think I've got. . . "

But how could I say the dreaded word for that monstrous thing which leapt out from nowhere and bore people away? I began again, "I think I've got. . . " and, finally, the word twisted from my mouth like an escaping demon. "CANCER."

In the silence that followed, I saw the doctor's penetratingly dark eyes searching me as they had never done before. "Cancer?" In answer to his query I began to tell him, not of the swollen glands, sore throats and headaches that still dogged my life, but of pains in my stomach which, in truth, had not been of particular worry to me until my imagination had magnified them during the previous two weeks on the island. I said that I had these pains. I said that I had had them for years. I said that they had got worse. . .

"Hop up on the couch. . . " he ordered and he prodded my soft abdomen with firm, cool hands—but not a squeak of pain could his questing elicit from me.

Feeling flustered and dishevelled I put my clothing to rights and sat back down on the patients' hard chrome and plastic chair—that same chair which, as a receptionist, I had shoved about as I vacuumed the carpet—that same chair from which my own mother would have received her terrible diagnosis of doom.

The doctor was no fool. He had heard my first statement, "I think I've got cancer", and listened to my unconvincing ramblings that followed. Once again I became aware that his usually cheerful, dark eyes were intent on looking beneath the usually cheerful mask worn by my everyday face. Then he gazed briefly into the middle distance and his bottom lip went up to turn his mouth into a wide straight line. As I waited for his verdict I became aware of the room in which we sat. It was as absolutely the same and familiar as it had been in the past: behind me, the bookcase with the medical encyclopaedias and *The Book of Modern Marriage*; on the mantelshelf, the photo of the doctor's six young sons smiling wholesomely between the two model ships donated by old Mr Talbot; in front of the doctor's plump chair, the oak desk; beside that, the filing cabinet which held hundreds of secrets. . .

The brown eyes flashed back to me. "I don't think you've got cancer." The statement was abrupt but reassuring and he had no intention of making me feel foolish. After that his words flowed past me. . . "It's not that long since your mother. . . You've had to deal with a lot of change—taken your babies away to live in utter isolation. Oh, I know there are other people there but it's not a place you can get away from easily. I'm personally quite sure we'll find you've got nothing to worry about. But I can't let you go back to that island believing you're dying." He reached toward the pigeon-holes of his desk for an x-ray form. "Up to Manuka Street. . . A barium meal. . . You know where to go."

Out in the waiting room I took Helen from Dad's arms and told him ruefully, "I've got to have some x-rays but he thinks I'll live."

The following morning, after a breakfast of something which resembled white liquid shoe-cleaner, I shared the waiting room of the x-ray clinic with a distraught man who sighed heavily and threw himself about in his chair. He said, "I don't know. I don't know what they're going to do with me. They'll have to do something. I can't go on as I am." I began to feel uncomfortable in the face of his distress. It was awful and it was real and it made me feel shamefully well and strong. When a nurse called my name I escaped guiltily, leaving the man alone with his worries.

In a shapeless cotton gown, I stood before the radiologist, Dr Dore, who was ready to begin work in his roomful of machines. He was almost a legend in Nelson, but until now I hadn't met him. I saw he was thin and kind-faced and not young. He glanced again at the notes on the form I had brought with me in a sealed envelope. "If you have had these pains for so many years," he said good-naturedly, "why haven't you done something about them before this?"

"Because—because I thought I was a neurotic."

He shuffled a few papers together and turned his head to look directly at me, eyebrows slightly raised, something almost teasing in the deep creases of his smile. "And *are* you?" he asked gently.

For one wide-eyed moment my gaze was locked into his and then the answer came from me like a breeze from nowhere on a summer day, "Yes. Yes, I probably *am*!" The admission seemed to open up my mind as if someone had pruned back branches that had crowded out the light. Suddenly I could see myself standing there as the eyes of this kindly older man must also be seeing me—young and fit and healthy— and I realised that I really was young and fit and healthy. The little laugh I gave was of astonishment.

After one puzzled, slightly amused look, Dr Dore got on with the business of the x-rays.

I didn't need the results of those x-rays to tell me that everything was normal but I waited for their confirmation before dispatching a telegram to Pip. Not wanting to broadcast my personal problems over the airwaves, I searched for words to convey the message cryptically to him that there was nothing at all to worry about. Pip told me later that he was on duty when the message had arrived after his evening weather report. The Wellington-radio operator had commented slyly, "They must be having funny weather in Nelson for this time of year," and then he had read out my telegram. "Roses are blooming. . . "

Now the most important thing for me was to get home and get on with my life. John Burnand, the man in the Nelson Marine Department office, said there was 'a special' planned to bring Ministry of Works staff off the island. So, once again, Dad drove me and Helen to French Pass. We left long before daylight and on this journey we very nearly did meet with disaster. Distracted by the baby's crying and vomiting, Dad almost failed to take a tight bend on the winding road and, with a roar of wheels in gravel, we slewed onto the brink of a bush-clad ravine. Back on the road again, I thought shakily that it would be a kind of poetic retribution on me if we came to grief before I could get home after this futile expedition.

Turi invited Dad to make the round trip on the *Belfast*. "A bit of fishing on the way home, Jim," he said. When we arrived beneath the crane at midday, with a sou'easterly slopping the sea up the rocks, there seemed to be much less room to land the box on the tiny deck than there had been on the *Enterprise*. Pip was driving the crane. Fred had his little bottom glued to the concrete steps above the block and he didn't move from this position until Dave, Mac and the Ministry of Works men had landed on the *Belfast* ready for an afternoon's fishing. Then our family found ourselves miraculously together and alone with the crane's motor silent and the midday sun bouncing reflections off our smiles.

I was ready to make a fresh start.

CHAPTER 15

Mac and a Paua Expedition

The change had come. Both to the station, which was temporarily under new management, and within myself where the clammy octopus that had haunted me had been mortally wounded. I found myself feeling lighthearted, happy.

Mac had arrived. Arne and his family were far away baking under a tropical sun. Dave and Peggy were letting go of Stephens Island and getting ready to face the bracing climate of Foveaux Strait.

Yes, Mac had arrived and we had agreed that, of course, he should stay in our house instead of living on his own in the relieving keeper's quarters behind the lighthouse. "Kick me out if I'm a pain," he said. Kick him out? I felt honoured. To have his company for another seven weeks would be to share the bond of friendship that had linked Pip and Mac since boyhood, a bond that had always stretched easily to encompass me.

And I had already missed out on nine days of this comradeship of old times. How could I have been so stupid as to have believed I was dying? I would never let that happen to me again. Surprisingly, Pip had accepted my healthy return as if I had been away having a bad tooth fixed, and I found there was no need for explanations to anyone else except myself. Angrily I repeated in my head that, in future, I would know that my silly imagination was a liar and I would just tell it to "shut up". I'd say, "Get thee behind me, Satan," as stern as Jesus had been in the Bible—and I would never again ask to see *The Ship Captain's Medical Guide*. Above all, I would try even harder to be brave and strong so that, with practice, I might improve.

I soon found that our house had become as busy as a bus stop. With Cis away and Peggy in the throes of packing, the men often stopped off for 'a brew' during the morning. They gobbled up my offerings of chocolate cake, chocolate square, chocolate coconut clusters, fruit loaves, peanut cookies and date shortcake with lemon icing—the recipes for which I found within the pages of my trusty little *Edmond's Cookery Book*. Surely there wasn't a housewife in New Zealand without a copy. I also had a book of unusual recipes, vegetarian recipes accompanied by pictures of slender, pretty housewives wearing frilly aprons tied with fly-away strings. From this book I made lunch dishes such as lentil pie and split-pea loaf. I dreamed, as I did so, that I might slightly resemble those virginal, flawless women in the illustrations, but it was difficult to retain such an image as I wrestled with the realities of life: crawling into the coal bunker to fill the coal scuttle, bringing in vegetables covered with dirt from the garden, cutting up great joints of mutton which had to be relieved of pounds of fat before they would fit into the roasting dish.

But now I wasn't the only cook in my kitchen. Mac was as skilled with a wooden spoon as he was with an ice axe, and during my time away he and Pip had taken over my territory with happy efficiency. Apart from leaving Fred with Peggy during working hours, for the remainder of the time they had cared for him together; and I saw, with a pang, that he hadn't really missed me. 'Unca Mac' was his hero now. As always, 'Unca Mac' was everybody's hero, including mine—though I would never let him know it.

At this time we began to board the various maintenance men who came to the island. Although they had been coming and going all year I had hardly been aware of them. Lighthouse wives were paid a reasonable sum to feed these workers, and with an abundance of fresh food available it could be quite a profitable sideline. Our first boarder was an older man, Bill Wellington, who was well known to the others, this being his fourth visit since Christmas. A mechanic, he was based in Wellington and he usually came out to work on the engines in the power house. This time, however, our tractor needed his attention. He arrived with someone called Eric who stayed with Dave and Peggy. Anxious to make an impression, I threw myself into the role of hostess, never dreaming that my poor guest might be too polite to refuse the rich food I served him. Having downed a bottle or two of beer beforehand, he would eat his way valiantly through the evening meal. Then, struggling away from the table with a bellyful of my best efforts (roast meat and vegetables followed by sticky pudding), he would collapse into one of our peculiar armchairs, chuckling affably with faint embarrassment as air farted, with its usual rude gusto, from the red vinyl squabs. I felt I was going to enjoy having boarders.

In my absence a new project had begun. It was a major task that would ensure that the keepers weren't short of a job over the next couple of years. The trolley rails between the Lister and the Ruston sheds were beginning to sag and lean and it had been decided that the old wooden sleepers should be replaced with concrete supports which would be poured in situ. Wooden shutters had arrived on the *Enterprise* and the men had used them to build bins to hold gravel, one beside the Ruston shed and another at Charing Cross. They were twelve feet square and four feet high.

Pip said to Dave, "It looks like you're gonna miss out on all the fun. There'll be a power of gravel to shift over the next few months."

"Dunno how you'll manage without me." Dave popped another piece of chocolate cake into his mouth and grinned.

"Not just gravel," Mac said. "There'll be sand and cement and all the other stuff. Reinforcing. . . "

"How will they send out that much gravel?" I asked.

"Bags," Pip said.

And over the next few months it arrived, one hundred bags at a time, whenever there was room on the *Enterprise*. The men were used to lifting and carrying. The arrival of three or four ton of coal in sacks, or four hundred gallons of fuel in drums, was routine. Their working lives were almost totally physical. Pip was short but the building trade had taught him how to shift heavy weights and had put muscles onto his small frame. As long as he was fueled regularly with plenty of food he seemed to be tireless.

I noticed, now, that his eyes were constantly alight at the revival of his old dreams. Working together most of the time, he and Mac spent their spare moments planning and scheming. They would arrive home wind-tousled and bright-cheeked, the smell of damp woollen jerseys and saddle-tweed trousers creeping indoors with them and mixing with pipe-smoke and the aroma of coffee to fill our kitchen with an intoxicating incense. The house bubbled with ideas and gossip which always simmered down into serious talk about travel, mountaineering, sailing and boat-building. I realized that Pip and Mac had never really given up their dreams of adventuring together.

The idea had always been in Pip that one day he would build a boat—a yacht. Mac, equally enthusiastic, said that trimarans were the coming thing. They were quick, light and safe. "Virtually unsinkable. There are a fair few around overseas now. They're pretty well tried and tested. . . "

Pip agreed that with modern design and construction they'd be almost indestructible. "These good glues you get nowadays leave the old stuff for dead and double diagonal sheathing seems to be the way to go. Thin veneer—glued in the shape of a curve. . ."

"Tremendously strong," Mac said. "It'll stand anything."

"Yeah," Pip said. "They say the wood'll give way before the glue."

They arranged for glue to be sent out on the *Enterprise*. They stuck pieces of wood together with it and left them to soak. They boiled them for hours and then tried to smash them apart. "Amazing stuff," they said.

As they talked, the names of their heroes slipped into their conversations as if they were old friends: Arthur Piver, an American, had developed trimarans that could be built in a backyard; Hedley Nichols, an Australian, championed the double diagonal skin. As I scrubbed carrots, sliced onions, rattled the pots and stirred the gravy, I heard Arthur Piver this and Hedley Nichols that, and although I had nothing to offer during such discussions I felt as if I were included. I began to think it inevitable that one day I would find myself afloat in a trimaran with nothing between me and the dark force of a hurricane but a smear of glue sandwiched between a double diagonal skin. But Pip and Mac would be with me and perhaps I would find that at sea I could be brave. Once more my imagination took flight. On the deck, I would cling to ropes and stays while giant waves smashed down on me and tried to wash me overboard. . .

Actually it did all seem rather scary, and where did lighthouses and children fit into these plans? Mac didn't seem to mind children. He treated them with a kind of distant respect. I'd noticed that sometimes when Helen slithered over the floor on her tummy and made happy, dribbly noises at his feet he'd contemplate her with mild curiosity and say kindly, "What ho, Creeping Thing!" (Creeping Thing!) But would he want to share a boat with her? How long would it take to build a trimaran? Perhaps it would never happen.

Nevertheless the men's companionship and enthusiasm banished the sombre thoughts that had kept me company a month earlier. Our house had come alive. One night a bout of nostalgia led the talk to the good times experienced in tramping club huts and mountain bivies. Before long Pip was demonstrating how to do 'a table traverse'. Our kitchen table creaked and lurched as he slid over the top of it on his belly and then clung, like a sloth, to its underside. Eventually he managed to hug his way up onto the far side so that he was again lying on top of the table—all this without touching the floor. He was an expert at this feat. But Mac wasn't. Having longer limbs and less strength in his arms he hit the floor over and over. When I tried it, I simply slid over the edge into a heap.

Pip then demonstrated that he could flip himself backwards up the edge of a door and end up astride the door itself with his head bumping the ceiling. Mac couldn't do this trick, either. Next they each tried to drink a glass of water while standing on their heads. There was some scientific theory attached to this. My only trick (and neither of them was supple enough to duplicate it) was to climb in and out of a broomhandle without moving my hands. First stepping over it between my arms, then bringing it up over my head and down in front of me so that I could climb through it and untangle myself. These were all strange tricks, and exciting. They stirred a kind of longing in me, perhaps in all three of us. I felt I could go to the end of the earth with these men. I didn't want to simply brush my teeth, say goodnight and go to bed as usual. But of course that was what we did. I lay for a long time, unable to quieten the fever within me—perhaps not even wanting to do so.

For that first month of Mac's stay the enthusiasm and dreaming continued unabated. That we were six hundred feet above sea level with cliffs on all sides was only a tiny obstacle to the idea of building a full-sized yacht. It could be done easily in The Palace. Both agreed that the glueing could be done later. At first everything would be screwed so that it could be dismantled and rebuilt and glued in a more accessible (but unspecified) place.

The way to begin building a boat was to carve a half-model to scale and then cut it up into sections. This would give correct measurements over the entire length. Down in The Palace, Pip worked away at a half-model until its lines were just right. Then, seeming to forget about slicing it up, they painted it white and displayed it on a shelf.

Pip next decided to demonstrate the strength of lightweight trimaran construction by building quite a large model based on a plan found in a magazine. He cut the stringers from a length of tongue and groove which he pirated from the lining of one of the internal walls of The Palace. He then stole a piece of ply from the ceiling of our box room to make the bulkheads. A glance around the interior of The Palace showed that this wasn't the first time it had fallen victim to a desperate lighthouse keeper's search for timber, but the lining of the main room was still intact and, now that it had been cleaned up and turned into a workshop, it was likely to remain unscathed.

Creating this model was almost as time-consuming and technical as planning and building a forty-footer and we all became absorbed in the project. Inevitably I found my mind becoming preoccupied with the basics of boat design, and, with this, came sympathy and an understanding of the homage these men paid to boats. New words slipped into my vocabulary: chine, transom, sheer, and garboard strake.

Two weeks before they were due to leave, Dave's family shifted into the relieving keepers' quarters. Pip and Mac reckoned that most people would do this for only their last couple of nights—after their mattresses and crockery and pots had been packed into boxes and their house made bare; but Dave said it would be better to do the cleaning and packing without the family getting in the way and messing things up. Pip and Mac reckoned Dave couldn't wait to get away from the place— and they were probably right, because they were all sick of one another; perhaps that happened on light-stations.

For several days, Geoffrey, Deane and Alison came to our house to play and give Peggy a chance to get things done. They were quiet children and never a bother. "Mrs Aplin," said Alison politely, "what are these ashtrays doing in the toy cupboard?" and later I muttered to Pip and Mac about how awful it was that a lighthouse child could see pretty paua shells and think of them only as ashtrays. And as for Geoffrey, he was so pale and thin, and always looked cold, and it was so ridiculous to shave the boys' heads right through the winter. Anthony had always had his head shaved, too. That's where the idea had come from. Arne had said a lot of lighthouse people found it the best way of giving a boy a good haircut and it was easy to keep clean and tidy. Tidy? As I saw it, the boys' heads were bald—sunburnt in summer and frozen in winter. Well, I wouldn't be attacking Fred's head with a razor. I'd stick with the dressmaking scissors. . . By this time we were all affected by the waiting and were preparing for the big day—the day of the transfer.

By nine o'clock that morning, all of the outgoing family's boxes would have to be stacked on the landing. There would be about a hundred of them, of different shapes and sizes, and they would have to be handy to the crane so they could be loaded onto the *Enterprise* as soon as the incoming family and *their* gear had swung ashore. Each day, as the boxes were packed and their lids screwed on, they were taken by tractor to the Ruston winch and sent down on the trolley to the storage shed at the Lister turntable. There they would be safe and dry until the morning of the transfer.

So we worked and waited. Now that winter had set in, we had less home-grown produce in our diet. The chooks were moulting and off the lay, all the cows were dry except for Dave's, the garden yielded only carrots, parsnip and silverbeet. Mac had looked into my cupboards glumly and said that other lighthouse keepers' wives had their pantries bulging with food. My cupboards were bare in comparison. He cited the various women he had met while relieving on different stations. So many of them seemed to be superb cooks and their cupboards were like grocers' shops. Chastened, I had sat down at once and made out an enormous order which I sent to the wholesaler on the next boat.

Throughout the country, lighthouse families got their groceries wholesale. I had already done this once, ordering everything by the dozen where possible as was the rule. Later I thought about Mac's criticism. It had hardly been fair; we had plenty of flour and Weetbix and I knew that it was high time I restocked my cupboards. It was just that life had been a bit muddled, lately, with my three trips off the island, and not having things like turmeric and nutmeg didn't put us at starvation level. Our usual standing order of fruit and cheese and extra vegetables came every fortnight and we would always have the richness of mutton and fish and paua—we could rely on that—and paua might look like fried gumboot, but men positively devoured them and begged for more. I usually fried them as steaks in mutton fat, piling their sizzling black bodies onto plates, their green juice soaking into the vegetables beside them. "Vunderbar!" Mac would say theatrically, waving his fork in the air and closing his eyes in ecstasy.

It was a joint decision—the gathering and preparing of paua. "What's for dinner tonight?"

"The tides are right. Shall we get paua?" It had to be done when the tides were at their lowest and not too rough. There was a particular rock platform which was paved with paua, and less than ankle-deep in water on a good day. The quickest route to this place took us past the Ruston shed and on down the extra-green ridge we called 'the airstrip'. This paddock was flat in comparison with the rest of the island but no pilot would have dreamt of landing a plane on it. (Dave had once taken his new mail-order kite there and offered it up to the nor'west wind which had snatched it away and tossed it, like a broken-winged bird, into the mists above the sea.) Where 'the airstrip' met the fence, we would drop into a gully where the ground was powder in summer and sponge in winter and was so riddled with burrows of seabirds that our feet would continually crush through the surface, no matter how careful we were.

Worrying about the poor birds beneath us was one reason I felt badly about going to the paua beach. The other was the final one hundred feet of the journey where I would creep shakily over the crumbly cliff-edge and down an insecure little earth ledge which led diagonally to the sea above a smooth, almost sheer rock slab. Perhaps this was why I suggested to Mac that it would be fun to see if we could get to the paua patch by going around the rocky coastline from the beach south of the landing—and who could tell what we might find on the way?

We set off armed with a flour bag to put the paua in, and a bayonet— Pip's special paua-prising tool. For some time I had thought this to be just a rather heavy sort of knife, rough and rusty with iron rings projecting from the handle. But when my father had spied it he had turned it over and over in his hands with curious reverence. "An old World War One bayonet!" he had murmured, his eyes fixed on a distant place known only to himself. Before this I hadn't even known what a bayonet was but now I knew it was a knife fitted to the end of a soldier's rifle. For us, World War One had been a very long time ago and comfortably far away. Even my mother had been just a child, then, but Dad had been a young man. Mum had told me that parts of the war had been too terrible for my father to talk about, even to her, so I hadn't questioned him about the bayonet. It had now become much more of a treasure to us.

Mac and I quickly realized that this was not going to be a good paua day. As we clambered and slithered down the hill to the beach the overcast sky descended with us and we found ourselves enveloped in fog. The tide wasn't as low as we had hoped and there was a surge. Before long we had rolled our trousers above the knee and were carrying our boots. My feet, wide and flat and still tanned from summer, gripped the wet rocks as we hopped from one to another. My toes were a rosy pink and the salt water caressed my legs. I was once more a child of the seaside. Not so, Mac. His feet looked as if they had spent far too long shut up in boots. I led the way, feeling strong and free and exhilarated at being away from the house. In one hand I carried an orange plastic fishing float we had found among the boulders. Mac had the bayonet, and the white cloth flour bag hung from his pocket. The paua were all safely hidden from us by swirling seaweed and foaming surge.

It was an echoing, rumbling sort of day with wave-sound bouncing off the cliffs and the air heavy with moisture. Sometimes we were down beside the water and sometimes we were clambering through stacks of rocks. The stones and pebbles of the shore were hard and round. Arriving at a huge, smooth boulder which was the only route forward I hung my boots around my neck and passed the orange float to Mac. Then I took a little run at the boulder before the next wave could catch me. From the top I caught the float which Mac threw as if it were a basketball. Not noticing the next big wave welling up behind him, he threw the bayonet—tried to throw it gently because, though blunt, it was still a knife. It clattered against the rock well short of me. Mac stood his ground as the sea foamed up around his thighs. Then, for a second we saw the bayonet, tumbling back with the pebbles in the wash before being swallowed by the sucking sea.

It was gone. Mac floundered around, searching for it but it never reappeared between waves. Although the water wasn't dirty, billions of tiny, swirling air bubbles rendered it ice-blue and opaque. I began to worry that Mac would be lost along with the bayonet. "Leave it," I said. "It's not worth anything."

He scrambled up the rock, wet to his waist. "That was such a stupid thing to do," he said. "I'll come back down here when it's calm and have a look for it."

By the time we reached the paua bed we were drenched with rain and, in spite of our thick woollen shirts, quite cold. Mac was hobbling over the rocks like a lame penguin. I managed to lever half a dozen paua from the platform, using my pocketknife, the water boiling up to my armpits as I groped around for them. At the top of the beach we dragged our socks over our wet feet and jammed them awkwardly into our boots. I looked up at the horrible rock face running with water and the dying annual weeds sagging in the wet earth above it. In my head, I said five words. "Give me courage, please God," and, thus girded, I began the scramble up the slippery bluff.

The kitchen was hot-scone cosy. As I came in with Mac from the dismal outdoors I saw how wonderful it was to arrive home to a house filled with light, and warmth and hot food and family. Pip had steaming cheese scones laid out on a tea towel. He had followed the step-by-step instructions in the *Woman's Weekly* and was proudly and busily wiping down the bench. A ripple of love passed through me.

Fred had made scones, too. Hard little pebbles which had suffered from an excess of kneading. He had flour in his hair and even in his ears. As I picked him up and hugged him the ripple of love gushed back over me as a torrent of joy.

I confessed to only six hard-won paua. Mac confessed to losing the bayonet. With a plateful of hot-buttered scones between us, and their cheesy smell in our nostrils, nothing else could seem too important, but Mac was more deeply contrite at losing the bayonet than we realized. Twice he went back alone to the beach to look for it but returned empty-handed. He was to remember it for the rest of his life—though none of us could know at that time the significance of its eventual replacement or how much shorter than our own lives Mac's was destined to be.

Peggy and Dave had finished packing. Their house was gleamingly empty. I had baked tins of peanut cookies and ginger crunch to fortify them in their tasks; on the evening before the transfer we shared a meal. My cupboards really were beginning to look like Mother

Hubbard's but the big wholesale order would arrive the next day. The weather was rough and wet and rowdy and nobody could see how it could improve by morning but I slept soundly through the wind and rain. For once, it was the men who lay awake worrying.

CHAPTER 16

The Change-Over

Long before daylight we stirred the fire into life and got down to the serious business of drinking coffee and discussing the day ahead—and surely Brian Pickering wouldn't even attempt to come out in a storm like this. Not much could put him off but with the family and all their gear. . . It must be forty-five to fifty knots out there and the sea straight onto the block.

Being in the relieving keeper's quarters, Dave was already in the same building as the office and right beside the radio. But Mac and Pip couldn't bear to leave him to send the weather report and try to contact the *Enterprise* without them. Before six o'clock they shrugged their way into their wet weather gear and launched themselves out into the storm. They wore balaclavas and gumboots. Like both Dave and Arne, Mac often wore the lighthouse-issue heavy oilskin. Pip had worn his only once and abandoned it. He had moaned that he was weighed down by it, he couldn't breathe in it, he would trip over it and it was a danger to shipping. I had turned up the hem ten inches or more and told him that with his sou'wester on his head and his beard poking out between, it made him look like a real lighthouse keeper. He'd said, "Well, I *am* a real lighthouse keeper and I can't work in it. I'd have to stand still all day in that thing and at any rate I can't stand the sou'wester either and I don't like my beard this long." And he'd gone back to wearing the short black parka he had always worn, either with overpants and gumboots or, more usually when he was working in the rain, with leather boots and shorts.

This was not an ordinary day, and with everyone else down in the office sorting out a plan of attack, I couldn't feel happy with my ordinary routine. Reluctantly I began my work, measuring out milk powder and mixing it with boiled water for Helen's first bottle of the day. To have a family leaving and strangers arriving to take their place was the event of the year. The other half of the island's population would change forever and we would be the old hands—at least until Arne and Cis came back. Pip would still be the second assistant because the new people had been in the service longer than we had—longer than Mac, too. He had already met them at their last station, Godley Head. I'd pestered him to tell all that he knew about them. He'd said they had two boys. The younger one would be a good little mate for Fred, perhaps a bit younger. The new keeper was a good bloke and Edna, his wife— well, Mac had said that I'd like her—at least he thought I would, she was a bit different from me, Scottish, and fairly lively but he thought we should get on—though you never knew with women—he never knew—women were a different breed.

Mac was the oldest of three brothers. I was the youngest of three sisters and it seemed we both viewed the opposite sex with doubt and curiosity, laced at times with suspicion, arrogance, fear and hope. Mac was knowledgable and he knew how to *think*. He read books about metaphysics and philosophy. He talked about Jung and Freud. We had some good conversations and I always acted as if I knew what he was talking about. I wished that I, too, could find such books to read but we had only those that arrived on station from the country library service. It was a good service and we had seventy-five books, a mix of fiction and non-fiction, which arrived in cartons every four months, but there wasn't likely to be anything about Freud and Jung, certainly not when you wanted it. We could order books by mail, but on the other hand perhaps it was better to think things out for myself—better than parroting a whole lot of stuff that some bigwig had thought up to impress people.

Mac talked about extroverts and introverts. I decided I was an introvert but he had said, no, I was more likely to be a bit of both. He talked about the ego and the id and repression. Repression was bad. It meant that you shoved thoughts you didn't like into a part of your mind called the unconscious. You didn't know what terrible things lay hidden in your unconscious. We were all screwed up—every one of us. And as for women! Well, for one thing, women suffered from penis envy. Penis envy! Even little girls—it began when they were little girls. How dare he! How dare he say that about innocent little girls! Oh, why did men hate women so much? Wasn't it always men that went to war, that bullied and fought and killed people? But Pip wasn't like that—and neither was Mac, or was he? No, I was as sure of him as I was of my own father—but my father had been to war and what had he done there with his rifle and bayonet? He had been in the trenches in the mud—he had always told me about the mud—and there had been shells and shrapnel which fell all around, and at times he had been a stretcher bearer—and Mum had said that stretcher bearers were the bravest.

I hated war but, sometimes, it must be necessary because of people like Hitler. When I was eleven our headmaster had shown our form 2 class a film that had 'come out of Germany'—a special film that would banish our ignorance and open our eyes, "because it must never be allowed to happen again!" They were still in my memory—those flickering black and white images from the concentration camp—and the horror of one in particular had seemingly left its imprint on my mind for ever. It was live footage of women and children being herded into a pit and buried alive—a tangle of earth and arms and legs, terrified eyes and screaming mouths crumpling beneath a giant bulldozer. Men had done that, had even filmed it. . . men with penises that women were said to envy. Freud must have been a creep. With all his psycho-analysing of people, especially women, he'd been like a peeping Tom.

And yet, could he have been right? I had a secret memory-flash from my childhood of myself, at the age of about eight, trying obsessively and rather unsuccessfully, to pee through a piece of faded pink hose-pipe 'like a boy'. But at that stage I had seen only one penis, (very small), on one very little boy—so how could that have been penis envy? Well, why would any woman want to envy that funny-looking thing? At least Pip couldn't be bothered with such silly ideas. His mind switched off when talk went around to religion or psychology, or the meaning of life.

One day I'd said to Mac, "Pip's not interested in this sort of thing at all."

And he had answered with slow emphasis and in a tone of admiration, "Pip is an extremely *practical* bloke." It had been a finite statement that had left me feeling reproved but proud that Pip's soundness was so thoroughly appreciated. And yet sometimes I did wish. . . oh, but that was silly because I was married to the best man in the world.

The men were certainly taking their time. Having stirred a big pot of porridge on the stove I put it to the far side where it would keep hot. I settled myself on the red vinyl settee with Helen on my left arm slurping contentedly at her bottle, and Fred, lugging his children's encyclopaedia, wriggling up under my right. Behind me the swishing rain and angry wind held the darkness captive against the window. I knew daylight would be slow to arrive. Cool fingers of air slipping off the glass touched my bare neck and made me clutch the little ones closer.

I had the feeling that the day ahead would be long. If the boat didn't come, we would have to find food for Peggy and Dave and the children. We had a forequarter of mutton in the fridge and some neck chops, so we would be all right for the evening meal, and I had enough flour to make bread, scones and biscuits. But poor Peggy would go out of her mind trying to amuse her family down in the relieving keeper's quarters now that everything they possessed had been packed up and taken away.

When Pip and Mac burst into the porch, dropped their wet gear and came inside they were full of energy and hungry for their breakfast. "They're on their way, all right."

"What!"

I felt like an onlooker. I wasn't part of this. They were almost too busy with their plans to explain anything to me. They said Brian was already nearing Cape Jackson. He had the family on board and all their stuff. Brian had said the main thing would be to get the family off first and they'd see what happened after that. Maybe he'd go and hole up somewhere like around the back of D'Urville because this weather wouldn't blow itself out for another couple of days.

I wasn't surprised to hear the boat was on its way. In my experience it had never *not* arrived on schedule and I had heard enough, now, about lighthouse tradition, to know that lighthouse families went wherever and whenever they were told, regardless of the weather or anything else. In the old days, when steamships had serviced the lights, families had been taken off station sometimes with next to no notice at all. The ship would stand off shore while they packed and often the whole family would live on board for weeks, some of them sick as dogs, while the steamer worked its way towards their new station, servicing other lights as it went. I almost felt sick myself at the thought of our new family with two little boys, being tossed about in the violent darkness of the storm outside.

Swallowing their porridge without thought, throwing down one cup of coffee after another, Pip and Mac discussed ways of tackling the morning. If Dave's family couldn't leave they wouldn't want all their boxes to be waiting out in the rain at the landing. It would be best if they were left where they were in the Lister storage shed; but then, if Brian was able to take them off after all, they'd have to be down on the landing ready to go. For the time being, Dave might as well stay with his family, and man the radio a bit longer, until they knew exactly what was happening. Then he could drive the tractor down the hill—but Pip and Mac would go down, now, and get things organised. This had already been worked out before they came home but, with the responsibility for the landing weighing upon their minds, they went over it all again.

Again they clambered into their outdoor clothing and as the door slammed behind them I wished I was able to go with them and be part of the excitement. But it was my job to make bread and scones and pikelets. One way or another, there was no doubt they'd be needed.

Before putting the dirty washing into the machine I turned up the radio and heard the news of the day. Continuing war in Vietnam and gales in Wellington. . . The song of the war, The Green Beret. It was an infectious tune and I liked to whistle it as I went about my work. I wasn't one for catching the words of songs on the radio, but, as it neared its conclusion, they came to me clearly. "Back at home, a young wife waits. . . her man has met his fate. . . da, da, da. . . da, da, da. . . the green beret. Put silver wings on my son's chest, make him one of America's best. . . da, da, da. . . da, da, da, da. . . let him wear the green beret."

Ugh, war! I shuddered and glanced down at Fred who was poised on his haunches contemplating the contents of his toy cupboard and, suddenly, the whole idea of bearing and raising sons seemed unutterably sad. I knew of someone who was away in Vietnam. Mickey had lived in our street and had been in my class at school. After the state houses had been built, our street had become full of kids and we had played cowboys and Indians together on long summer evenings. I had been a hopeless Indian, always dead or tied to a tree by imaginary ropes, and Mickey had hardly deigned to notice me, but I had been glad to be part of the gang. (Now I had that song on my brain. "Silver wings upon his chest. . . da, da, da.") I had met Mickey's dad in Motueka and he had been so proud to tell me that Mickey had joined the army and gone to Vietnam.

"Da, da, da. Proud to wear the green beret. . . da, da, da," I sang as I sorted the clothes and waited for water to run into the washing machine. "Back at home a young wife waits, da, da, da." Why did men always crave action and excitement and leave women at home in the house with the children? I turned on the machine, went to the sink bench and began to scrape out the porridge pot. Sometimes I didn't like being a woman.

Briefly, I wondered how I myself would get on if I were a lighthouse keeper. But I realised I wouldn't even know how to keep the engines running or how to fix them when they needed it, and I'd be terrified of trying to work the crane in rough seas. The thought of such responsibility was too much for me. And earlier I'd thought the crane was certified to carry passengers but now I'd been told that it wasn't. It was simply inspected regularly to ensure it was in good working order. I'd begun asking Pip questions about the crane—not because I was particularly interested but because, during my trips away from the island, other people (always men) had asked me technical questions about it and I'd felt silly not being able to answer them. Now I knew the crane had a Briggs and Stratton motor—seven horse power (or, oh dear, was it nine?) Pip had said that the wire rope was changed every six months and sooner than that if it was damaged. And how could it get damaged? By swinging fore and aft of the boom—that meant towards the land and out. If it swung too far it got caught in the guides and that's what damaged it. Pip had said the only way to stop it from swinging once it had started was to bring it into the rocks, "that's if it's sacks of coal or gravel or something". But what about people? "Well, I dunno. You couldn't do that with people. . ." And what would start the load swinging in the first place? Pip had said it was too easy—if the boom wasn't directly over the boat deck the load would swing. It was worse when the tide was running—which was most times! He had said that the current ran either way, depending on the tides.

When the tide was ebbing in Cook Strait it went east, and as it poured past the end of the island it drew water out past the block and on past the Big Razorback. Sometimes, in rough weather, Brian would wait for the tide to change before working the boat. He would always back the boat into the rocks 'up-current' but, by the time the load was transferred, and especially if they were a bit slow, the boat would have been carried 'down-current', and the load would get a swing on as soon as it left the deck. And, of course, if it were rough and the boat was going up and down, they had to "coincide dropping the load on the deck with the bottom of its travel and lift it off when the boat was rising"—so that the rope was tight when the boat started to drop again.

And once the load was off the deck you had to get it away from the side as quickly as possible so that it didn't endanger the crew or tangle in the rigging. There were three levers on the crane: one for slewing, one for going up and down, and one for releasing when the hook had to go down without a load. . . I found myself standing at the sink and staring into space with the dishcloth in my hand.

Thinking about the crane had filled me with misgivings. Today it would be very rough indeed—as rough as it would ever be for landing. I thought of the new keeper's wife, Edna, and her two little boys, and I pictured Pip out on the crane's skinny, windswept platform, maybe even blinded by spray, trying to bring them safely ashore. I filled a small bowl with warm water, added a teaspoon of sugar and sprinkled yeast on top and then, at last, I heard Dave grinding past the house on the tractor. I leapt to the window and looked out. Yes, he was alone. I turned down the radio, went to the phone, gave three short twists of the handle and waited for Peggy's voice.

After the 'giddays' and 'how-are-yous' I said, "It looks like you're not going anywhere today," and she said that, yes, it looked like that, worse luck. I could hear the kids squabbling in the background. She said the latest news was the same as before. They would try to land the other family and see how they went with the gear, and then the boat would run for shelter. I said that, well, everyone had better come to our place for lunch and we'd cook up the forequarter of mutton during the afternoon and, if the new people managed to get here, we'd all be able to get to know one another. As we talked we wondered if our boxes of supplies would be landed. If they could put the people ashore they should be able to send up the food as well—but you wouldn't know whether they'd even think of it, really.

I said, "Well, if it comes to that, we won't starve. We've still got food but it won't exactly be gourmet eating. I hope you like Weetbix and instant pudding. . ." As I hung the receiver back on its hook my mind raced ahead. If the boat couldn't come for a week the men would have to kill again. I had read, once, about the wreck of the *Dundonald* in the Auckland Islands earlier in the century. The survivors had lived for months on sea birds and seals. If something happened to civilisation—like a really big war or something—we could live forever on Stephens Island on mutton and beef and fish. I often had this fantasy but it always disintegrated when I took it a step further and imagined being condemned to live out a lifetime with Dave and Arne and Cis and Peggy. I was already guiltily pleased that we were to have a new family and even quite happy to have a break from Arne and Cis. At least, in the lighthouse service, we could look forward to a change of faces every year or two. It hadn't taken me long to appreciate the merits of the Marine Department's policy of transferring people from station to station.

Glancing at the clock, I began to fly about the house putting things in order. Then, suddenly remembering that I hadn't yet fed the chooks, I grabbed my plate of scraps and raced out of doors without bothering to put on a coat or hat. The damp wind blew me up the path to get the wheat from the 'dogbox' and shrank the warmth out of me as I dashed back down around the back of the house and up the earth track to the fowlhouse.

"Chook, chook chook." I called them from their shelter and they came tumbling through the little doorway into the mud of the run, the old chooks bedraggled from the moult and the chickens halfgrown and bright-feathered—every one of them developing too much of a little comb on top of its head as if it were going to be a rooster rather than a hen. I left them fighting over the scraps. Back in the house I picked up the empty coal scuttle and ran out to the coal bunker at the gate. Emerging from there with the scuttle piled up with shiny black lumps I straightened up in the wind and surveyed the world.

Grey and white sea writhed along beneath swirling, screaming sheets of spray, the Big Razorback hunched and jagged forming a great bulwark impervious to the wind. I could smell salt. I could taste it. It was the kind of day that made me recall all the salty sea dog stories I had read as a child. The *Enterprise* would be buried in spray. I couldn't imagine how it could remain afloat but I knew that it would. The men revered Brian Pickering's seamanship and had no doubts about the boat itself. If only they could get the people off safely—but of course they would. It was only me who worried and prayed and, in a way, it was all quite deliciously exciting.

By the time I received the phone call from Pip, I was totally organised: the bread rising in tins, scones in the oven, and the clothes and nappies, washed and spun, waiting in the basket for the weather to improve. And the sky outside was lighter although the roaring of wind and sea hadn't eased at all. Pip, clearly in a hurry, was presumably ringing from the phone behind the landing. His voice was scratchy, perhaps even angry, and came through with a rush of wild noises. "The new keeper's wife's on her way up with the kids. Bloody Dave's stuffed the tractor and she'll be walkin' all the way. . . She must be nearly there by now. We'll be a while yet."

Nearly here! Fred was standing on a chair at the kitchen sink, sleeves rolled up, a tea towel pinned to the front of his dungarees. "Kids coming, Freddy," I said. "Different kids for you to play with." I rushed to the window and looked out, but there was no sign of them. "Better stop playing in the water now. Come on, down you get. . ." There was a squawk of protest. "Oh, all right. I'll let the water out and when you've used up that cupful you have to get down." I didn't want three kids playing in the sink. Fred was a methodical and careful child. Even with water-play he didn't make much mess. He continued purposefully pouring his cupful of water from one container to another. I went again to the window and saw people, Mac carrying a small child and shepherding a woman and a boy along the wet road, a sudden ray of sunlight bringing colour to the orange-brown mud and the green hillside.

I dragged Fred away from the sink and tidied him up. We met them at the corner of the house a gust of wind almost sweeping us into a heap. Mac, clearly anxious to get on his way, almost thrust the little boys at me. "Here they are. J'nette, this is Edna. Look after her. She's had a rough time."

The woman mustered the weariest and wannest of smiles and whispered, "Hellaw."

"Hello," I said, my voice sounding disconcertingly cheerful. "It must have been an awful trip for you."

From such an exhausted-looking woman the answer came with surprising strength but her Scottish accent was gentle on the ear. "I'm nivver leavin' this island agin until I gaw awee for guid."

Fred and I took our guests into the house. They eased themselves out of their mud-slimed boots, their coats and hats, and I led them to the spare comfort of the vinyl settee where they sat in a forlorn cluster. When I offered a cup of tea, Edna at first shook her head, then, in a whisper, changed her mind. I took the scones from the oven and flipped them from the tray onto a clean tea towel on the table. I began to split them and spread them with butter and piled them onto a plate beside her. I fetched a jar of my father's raspberry jam and spooned some into a dish. "Help yourself," I urged, again sounding inappropriately cheerful. "You must be starving."

Again, Edna shook her head, "Naw," and I tried not to show the awkwardness I felt at the rejection. The boys, too, accepted nothing but then their mother took a scone, herself, and divided it between them. They began to nibble, the little one still beside his mother, the older one standing in the middle of the tiny room and looking around. They were a pale-faced little family, their brown hair tousled and damp.

I asked if the men had been able to land the stores and again the shake of her head and a whisper, and almost a look of irritation. "I din't knaw."

I gave a self-conscious laugh. "We're a bit short on supplies but we've got enough to get by on."

Fred munched a scone, smearing raspberry jam over his cheeks, and contributed a few of his usual two-syllable comments to the faltering conversation. Hearing Helen awake in her cot, I went into the bedroom and brought her out to meet the company. The boys began to find their appetite and the pile of buttered scones grew slightly smaller. With Helen in my arms I felt more relaxed. I could speak to her and through her without expecting a reply. "See, little girl, new people, a lady and two boys, and they've come a long, long way across the rough, rough sea and I think the poor things have been very, very sick. . . " As she stared around at the new faces, her baby-cheeked smiles warmed the whole room and I fancied they drew us together a little. By the time the others arrived our visitors had begun to look alive.

The men came in on a gust of rugged masculinity, energised as they were by their battle with the south-east gale. There were four of them now, all young, their average age no more than twenty-five. They were still primed for action because, although the new family had arrived, 'the transfer' had hardly begun. Edna's husband, Brian, was lean, perhaps a little shy, but he seemed at home already, and, as the longest serving keeper, he was now, officially, our P.K. until Arne's return.

But—had the stores been landed? It was my most urgent question. I was told that, no, there had been no way. That they had landed only a sling load of the family's boxes and that had been difficult enough and they were bound to contain nothing that was urgently needed. "You'd have no idea what it was like down there. . . " I'd have no idea? I felt faintly insulted.

And how long did they think it would be before the boat could have another go at it? Well, we had all heard the weather forecast, and it didn't look any good for the next day and possibly even the one after that. In my mind I had done an exact stocktaking of our food supply. First and foremost, we had good old dependable Weetbix, the breakfast cereal which I believed could be stored for a century and which I had, therefore, stocked up on in great quantity. For the same reason, we had dozens of sachets of Maggi soup. We also had plenty of milk powder and one cow giving a modest amount of milk. Arne's cow, Milly, had chosen to calve early this morning at the height of the storm, but her milk wouldn't be drinkable for another three days. In smallish amounts we had these supplies: rice, rolled oats, vegetables, potatoes, sugar, and all the bits and pieces such as jam, Marmite, salt and baking powder. We had enough flour for a few more batches of scones, and we had mutton, but—there were fourteen of us.

Like people lost in the bush, we would have to ration everything, not knowing how long the siege would last. In a way our situation didn't seem unfamiliar to me. At the age of about four I had invented a game called Lost, variations of which my young cousin and I had played for years. The beauty of this game had been that it could be played anywhere without any particular toys. We had played it in the dust under the beds, on the sweet-smelling carpet of fallen leaves beneath the lawsoniana hedge, and on the worn and gritty linoleum under our kitchen table. It was a game of 'making do'. It was a game of caring for each other. It was my game.

And this, too, was my game. Neither of the other families had a mouthful of food between them. I could say, "We have this and this and this, so much of this and not much of that." And I could share it out among us. The new people had hardly any personal belongings, no blankets, no pillows, no mattresses, no towels or soap. We could share all of these. The tractor was stuck halfway down the hill where the road turned into the gully above Charing Cross. It had 'thrown one of its tracks' and the men weren't sure how to fix it. This meant they had to distribute the food and bedding by hand or in the wheel barrow. Also, that afternoon, they went between the Ruston shed and number two house carrying to the new family their few bags and boxes that had been landed that morning. Fortunately the wind seemed to have swept the rain away, and, fortunately, each family had a warm house with hot and cold water in the taps. And we all had plenty of Weetbix and Maggi soups.

In our memories the two days that followed would always be synonymous with Weetbix and Maggi soups. It was only two days before the *Enterprise* returned to us but it seemed like three. Always, in my memory, it is three but it was a mere two—and I was thankful it wasn't more. Unlike the little cousin of my childhood, the players in this game were not willing participants. The charm of being 'lost' and having to 'make do' passed them by. They wanted to be getting on with things in the way they had planned. Dave and Peggy didn't want to be still stuck on Stephens Island, waiting in the relieving keeper's quarters, with everything they owned already packed and taken to the Lister storage shed. Edna and Brian wanted to be able to unpack their boxes and make the house their own. Pip and Mac wanted to get on with the transfer and the challenge of landing everything safely. The immobilised tractor was a legacy of frustration that made them want to get rid of Dave before he could touch something else that would fall apart. We were all in limbo.

On the second afternoon I decided to run down to the block to see the conditions for myself. Pip went with me, leaving Mac at home with

Fred and Helen. He was probably as glad to have an hour or two without us as we were to be alone together. I found the disabled tractor a depressing sight. With the south-easterly funnelling past on its way up the gully at about ninety miles an hour it was no place to linger and we beat our way on down the track. Pip said it was a forty-five knot wind, not the worst we had experienced but, from this direction, "pretty hopeless".

The sea crashed relentlessly against the hard base-rock of our island, storming up the landing block and the crane's concrete pillar, snatching up and churning the shattered air into a frenzy of white, blasting a salty wet salute into our faces. How many million billion waves, I thought, to wear away an inch of rock? How many million years to wear an island down to nothing? Wanting to experience what it might be like for the driver of the crane, I crept out onto the platform beside it, my grip on the handrails a measure of the terror that had seized me at simply being there. The black water, the white surge, the feeling of vertigo, made me tremble. Back safely on the landing, I listened as Pip described snatches of the drama of the day before. How he had landed the box on the deck of the *Enterprise* with difficulty, and how big Tom Gullery had emerged from the cabin, sure-footed as ever on the rolling boat, carrying a prostrate Edna in his arms.

Later I learnt that Edna had spent the journey on a bunk in the crew's quarters below deck, endlessly trying to stop the little boys from being thrown about, all of them desperately sick, weak and wishing they could die. After they had been carried, weeping with fear and exhaustion, to the box and had been swung wildly through the air and at last landed, Edna had been dragged upright and directed towards the steps, above which the bleak-looking track zig-zagged over the lichen-covered rocks. Then, sick and shivering, and with nobody to assist her, she had taken the boys by their hands and started to climb. Meanwhile the men had struggled on with the task in hand and it wasn't until Brian Pickering on the boat had thrown up his hands in defeat that Mac had felt free to run up the hill after her.

At eight o'clock on Thursday morning, two days after its first attempt, the *Enterprise* returned to continue with the operation. The 'strong gale' had abated to thirty-five knots—a mere 'gale' in seamen's language—but the sea was almost as bad as it had been for the previous three days, very rough with five-metre waves. Calculations of wave height were based on the average but waves were seldom of uniform height; a tiny lull would always be followed by a comparative increase in size and ferocity. Work at the landing on a rough day would never be dull or predictable, and this day would stretch the men's patience to the limit.

Again I had said goodbye to Dave, Peggy and the children as they passed on their way to the landing. Then, confined to my brightly lit kitchen with the house shuddering and suffering in the gale, I rather glumly surveyed the breakfast debris and tried to picture Arne, Cis and Anthony, basking somewhere in the Pacific Islands, but they were unreal figures with no relation to our present situation. "Get started," I told myself aloud and began to attack the morning's clutter. Soon I found my mind flickering back to Cis with her strong face and ready laugh. Before leaving the island she had lent me a stack of *Burda*, the classy German fashion magazines which she subscribed to and treasured. We both liked to drool over the fantastic clothes they featured, and using the patterns which were included we could turn our hoarded materials into almost anything—into clothes which could take us anywhere.

I found it easy to let my mind slip away from the reality of everyday life and enter the glamorous world that I imagined the young *Burda* models inhabited. And so, two hours later, with Helen bathed and sitting in her high chair mouthing a very hard crust, and Fred once again playing with water at the kitchen bench, I found time to make myself a cup of coffee and sink down into one of our peculiar armchairs—the pile of magazines beside me. While the men, down at the block, fought and struggled to transfer about one hundred and fifty assorted wooden boxes from the storm-washed deck of the *Enterprise* to the landing—and then to deposit another one hundred boxes onto that same elusive and slippery vessel—and then to finally farewell Dave, Peggy, Geoffrey, Alison and Dean, and deposit them. . . I quietly lost myself, for a while, in the glossy world of *Burda* fashion.

But it was only for a while. With a two-year-old and a baby in the house such moments of bliss couldn't last. Before long Fred was squealing outside the door in the back porch and I was saying crossly, "Don't you come back inside until you can stop that noise and be sensible!" With my heart racing I went to the cupboards to look for something to eat and found myself glowering at the almost empty shelves. There was no comfort there for an upset mother, not even a jar of raisins among the Weetbix, Maggi soup and rice. I sighed and Fred crept back indoors with a false smile on his face.

Fred and I often had battles. Sometimes I felt at my wits' end with him and wondered if we were a 'normal' family. With Mac in the house I was embarrassed when our toddler threw a tantrum. Once Mac had said thoughtfully, "I suppose we have to try to see inside his head and work out why he does it. . . "

"He does it because he wants his own way. That's why." I had silenced him hastily, unable to acknowledge, even to myself, that Mac might be able to see something that I couldn't. And what would *he* know about bringing up kids? He'd never had any. It was all very well to read about all these theories but some of them were half-baked. Mac with his talk of things like the Oedipus conflict and his idea that women were masochists—what would he know really. . . ?

"Masochist? What's a masochist?" I had asked him, fascinated, as always, by a new word.

As usual he had sucked away at his pipe before answering. "A masochist actually gets pleasure from pain. . ."

"How could anyone? Pain's pain, isn't it? It's the opposite of pleasure. And why women? I don't enjoy pain and I'm a woman."

"Well, women do actually enjoy making martyrs of themselves. They get pleasure out of subjugating themselves. . . especially to men, and that's the way they get the poor devils on a string. . . "

At this I had felt something jumping guiltily inside me. It was me he was talking about. It must be. But I had said nothing and he had pursued his theme. He'd said he had read a book about it. "In the middle ages," he had said, "the nuns used to suck the pus from the suppurating wounds of soldiers." His eyes had seemed to draw together with a look of incredulity. "*Pus!*" he had repeated again. "I can't think of anything more disgusting!"

Obediently my imagination had shown me what it would be like to suck pus from a suppurating wound: a black and gangrenous wound with foetid odour and my lips sucking on the putrid flesh. It had made me shudder—but, if it would save a life, I would do it, wouldn't I? Wouldn't anyone?

The question came to me again as I looked out the window at the still blustery seascape. Did I enjoy subjugation? Could I bring myself to suck on a suppurating wound? If it were my child, or Pip, or even Mac, surely I would. . . but I wouldn't enjoy it so I wouldn't be a masochist, would I?

I was glad when the men finally bustled in and dumped boxes of stores down on the kitchen floor.

"Did everything go all right?" I asked. "Did Peggy and the kids get off okay?"

"Yeah. They finally made it," Mac said.

And Pip said, "We've tried to sort out which boxes have got the fresh food in them." And though their return was the one thing to which I had looked forward all morning, I felt a twinge of resentment at the sight of their glowing faces and their windswept hair. I envied them the excitement. I envied them their freedom to come and go and throw themselves into the action. For a moment I almost hated them. Deep down, I knew that I wasn't a martyr at all!

They had taken two and a half hours to work the boat—two and a half hours of tension. They had taken the rest of the morning to get the food and stores up to the Ruston shed and then to barrow and carry 'the fresh stuff' to our two houses.

Suddenly I realized that we were all starving. My resentment disappeared as I tore open the damp cartons of 'fresh' food which had been on the boat since Monday. It was now Thursday. We salvaged sausages which looked every bit their age, and eggs, several of which were broken, their slimy albumen oozing through the cardboard containers and onto other packages. Then we got out a pan and fried thick slices of four-day-old bread. We scrambled all the cracked eggs. We fried all the sausages. The latter were always a treat for us, their spiciness a change from the wholesome, home-produced fare which was our norm. We fried them for a very long time and, as we waited and sniffed the air, Mac turned them over and said heartily, "Bangers! Food for kings, oh ahh!"

"Fried bugs!" I said. "How long do you think they'll need to make them safe?"

"Half an hour should be enough. They don't smell half bad, do they!" The spectre of a possible week on a diet of Maggi soups and

Weetbix faded away.

"And what have you got to do this afternoon?" I asked as we savoured the flavour of the food of kings.

"Get Brian's gear off the block and up to the Lister," Pip answered.

Mac added, "I don't suppose we'll get it any further than that. There's a fair mountain of boxes."

"What about the tractor?" I asked. "Do you think you'll be able to get the track back on okay?"

"It'll have to wait for tomorrow. . ."

"It won't be a five-minute job. . ."

"Trust old Dave to leave us with a balls-up."

I helped Fred with the last slippery pieces of egg white that he was chasing around his teddy bear plate. "Yum," I said as he opened his mouth obligingly. He scrambled down from his chair, and Mac, too, stood up and fished in his pocket for pipe and tobacco.

To Pip I said, "Hadn't you better take that calf away from old Milly, today?"

"We'll do that before dark tonight."

"She'll be thinking she's allowed to keep it. She won't want to let you have it."

"Brian's done it all before. He'll give me a hand." Pip began to peel an orange—clumsily, using the same sheath knife with which he slaughtered and dressed our meat. "It looks like Heifer's gettin' closer, too. She's like a barrel. Trust them all to calve just when we're so flat out."

"I can help," I said." I know how to teach a calf to drink from a bucket."

Pip hardly heard me. He cut the mangled orange into bright little pieces, ate them slowly, lost in thought. "Things'd be a lot easier if Dave hadn't slewed that track off."

Nothing was destined to be easy about this transfer and it was to be days before Edna and Brian could finish their unpacking. On Friday the trolley, loaded high with boxes, derailed itself on the steepest part of its journey up from the Lister shed. The sturdy wooden packing cases spilled across the gully. The trolley lay, wheels uppermost, above them. The two keepers who had been attempting to put the tractor back on its track watched in dismay as the third came racing down the line from the Ruston shed. There was no alternative but to carry every trunk and box back down the gully to the Lister storage shed by the turntable. It was a cold, bare, little gully up which the south-east wind still funneled without respite, and the men were fated to spend several days there, both in getting the trolley back up onto the rails and in getting the tractor mobile again. The latter was showing her age and it hadn't been entirely Dave's fault that she had skewed from her track when he had hit a hollow in the road. The men all acknowledged that her tracks were loose and floppy and that she needed careful management—as did the trolley, also, as it travelled up and down the sagging rails which were due for replacement between the two winch sheds.

One at a time, over the following days, the boxes were delivered by wheelbarrow to Edna at her door. Later she was to remember only Mac coming and going and stopping to chat a while, but I was sure Pip and her husband, Brian, had also done their share. When Mac was around other men tended to become almost invisible, such was the force of his magnetic personality. I was jealous. We had had almost sole rights to Mac over the past month and now he was disappearing from our house and spending time at theirs. And Edna—he clearly didn't think she was a masochist or a martyr.

The following week they got the track back onto the little bulldozer.

"How'd you do it?" I asked.

"Brute force and cunning," Pip said.

"Plus a bit of help from Archimedes," Mac added.

"Yeah, Archimedes was a big help—but we could have done with Dave on the end of the pole, really."

"What pole?" I asked.

"The old telephone pole we lugged down from way up the gully."

"It was square in section. We stuck one end of it under the lower side of the tractor. Then we carried down a whole lot of wooden blocks to use as a fulcrum."

"It was just a giant lever. It stuck away out past the side of the road and hung in mid-air over the gully."

"Ohh," I said, "so that's why you're waffling on about Archimedes. You used it like a crowbar to lift the tractor."

Pip grinned. "That's right, how'd ya guess. Mac and Brian, they wriggled right out to the end and lifted it enough for me to manoeuvre the track back into position."

With the trolley back on the rails and the tractor once more wearing both of its tracks, life itself began to run along more smoothly. At home, Pip continued working on his model trimaran until he decided he needed "proper veneer from town" for the double diagonal skin. We were soon milking two cows night and morning and bucket-feeding their calves. Our fridge was stocked again with mutton and milk and cream. Our cupboards were stacked with food which, this time, I had been almost recklessly wholesale in ordering. We had dried herbs enough to stuff a pillow, nutmegs to last a lifetime, enough peanuts and lentils and dried fruit to winter over in Antarctica. We asked the new family to dinner, to coffee, and to afternoon tea.

Edna had a way of telling stories that kept us listening. In her lilting Scots accent she told us about the engaged couple who walked in on their own surprise party without a stitch on. She told us about the time her family had accidentally eaten the ashes of their sadly deceased great-aunt; about the marriage swap at Puysegur Point Lighthouse—and how, when the boat had come to transfer the keeper to his next station, it was the other keeper's wife and children who left with him. It had been a straight-out swap. I had never heard of such goings on! And it had happened on a lightstation between lighthouse families! Being the third family at Puysegur Point at the time, Edna and Brian had been first-hand witnesses to this scandalous affair. Our own stories were tame in comparison.

Two weeks before Arne and Cis were to return, Dad sent out his ten-foot wooden dinghy on the *Enterprise*. It had been stored in his shed ever since he had moved to Nelson ten years before, and, feeling that he would never use it again, he had liked the idea of its having a new home with us. It arrived at the same time as four ton of coal and Pip's younger brother, Bruce, who had recently finished his building apprenticeship. The *Enterprise* was two hours late but by mid-afternoon the men had got the dinghy up to the station without mishap.

They carried it easily into the main room of The Palace with Pip saying excitedly, "She's as light as a feather—her planks are white pine and her ribs are rata."

We stood around her, the men making admiring comments.

"She's tinder-dry but all her seams are still as tight as tight."

"Lovely lines. She's a little beauty."

"Built by a craftsman, all right."

Adding my contribution I said, "I learnt to row in her when I was about eight and she's older than I am." I sensed that this sounded impressively old to all of us and felt encouraged to continue. "Dad bought her, new, for seventeen pounds and we had to wash the sand off our feet before we got into her."

Indeed, for many years this boat had been our family's most prized possession. My mind went back to those early times when we had had no car, no fridge, no washing machine, no vacuum cleaner, no armchairs, not even a handbasin. We had lived in a house so small that my bed had been in the kitchen, only a chair's width away from the table. There had been nowhere else for me to sleep. But in spite of this dearth of material possessions, our family had owned this magnificent dinghy. And now Pip and I were buying it from Dad and it would be ours. It would go with us from station to station and our kids, too, would have to wash their sandy feet before they got into it. We'd look after it as if it were a baby, just as Dad had done. I said, "She was built in Riwaka by an old guy called Val Pollard. He never measured anything—did everything by eye."

The men shook their heads in wonder and I felt sure that they had never seen a vessel like it. Over the next few weeks, whenever Pip had time, he went to The Palace and scraped the old paint from the dinghy, and Mac and Bruce and I shared each discovery with him as he exposed the natural wood and superb craftsmanship— "Each plank's perfectly fitted with not a skerrick of putty or caulking in the whole boat."

But something was happening in our household. It was Mac. He had grown quiet. While, at first, he had entertained us with stories about other stations and had been full of ideas and schemes, he, now, spent his time staring into space and writing up his 'journal'. He enjoyed the discipline of keeping a daily journal. I thought him rather arrogant about it—couldn't he call it a diary? I thought, also, that it would be easier to keep a journal if you were responsible for only yourself. I seemed to be disagreeing with him quite often and I said, one day, "It's a good thing you and I aren't married to each other, isn't it!"

He looked at me steadily. "It would never have happened."

"It could have. . . " I faltered. Somehow, this wasn't what I had meant.

He insisted again. "It could never have happened."

"Ooh.." My answer was a brief mumble. There had been something in his tone (was it challenge, hostility, reproof or all three?) which made me withdraw as a snail withdraws when a child pokes a finger at its questing 'horns'.

Four days before he was due to leave Stephens Island, Mac sat in the peculiar armchair between the door and cupboards in the long narrow room that lay between the sink and the kitchen. He did this every morning between six o'clock and breakfast time. He did it again later in the day. I went back and forth, self-consciously avoiding his legs. Sometimes, now, Pip's brother Bruce's legs were stretched in front of the chair beside the stove and I avoided them, too. On this particular morning, Pip had gone 'to dowse the glim'—a term they used half-jokingly when leaving to turn off the lighthouse light. Bruce would sleep late (the sleep of a young man who felt there was nowhere to go. The sleep of a young man who had thrown in his job after a broken engagement.) Pip and I had been noticing that the feeling in our house was no longer one of harmony. We were disturbed. Mac had always been such a good friend—such good company.

This morning as I traipsed past him for the umpteenth time carrying utensils between stove and sink I felt a need to break down the wall that seemed to encase him. On impulse, I bent down and looked directly into his eyes. I was close, too close, almost near enough to kiss him. I felt the shock of it myself, but I had no intention of kissing him. I said the words that had already formed on my tongue—words that were supposed to be teasing. "Good morning. Some of us aren't very friendly in the morning, are we!" His eyes, brown and distant, looked straight ahead. His gaze leapt the tiny gap between us, passed through my eyes and out through the back of my head as if I were a mosquito on the far wall. I swerved away, knowing I'd done the wrong thing. I had tried to invade his silence and had been deservedly snubbed. I should have treated him as if he weren't there—which was clearly what he wanted.

With hot cheeks I went about my work. It was four days until Arne and Cis's return. Four days before Bruce and Mac would leave. Two months with Mac had been too long for us. I wondered if it spelt the end of a friendship, and, if it did, whether it was my fault. I felt miserable. Poor Mac. He had come from The Brothers Lighthouse to Stephens Island, and soon, after a couple of days in Picton, he would return there. He had quipped lustily about 'the fleshpots of Picton' but I was pretty sure he had been joking. Sleepy little Picton was the place which relieving keepers were glad to see after their six weeks on the rock, but the Federal Hotel with its beer and regulars—was that a fleshpot? Mac had told us that some relieving keepers went quite crazy on The Brothers. They became 'rock-happy' because of the isolation. And when they were rock-happy, some got angry and broke things, some withdrew into their own worlds and others were surly and argumentative. Whatever they did, it was partly excusable because they were rock-happy.

As the day wore on I continued to feel awkward and unsettled and wished Tuesday would come quickly because then the house would be ours again. It was quite literally months since Pip and I and the children had lived alone together, and, while I hadn't minded this while everyone was happy, now I was longing for some uninterrupted family time. Besides this, the task of cooking had become totally my own again and I looked forward to being less of a slave to it.

That afternoon, after Pip and Bruce had gone to The Palace, Mac came into the kitchen. Again I was midway between stove and sink, in one hand carrying chopped onion on a board and, in the other, a pan containing a blob of butter. I stepped over Helen and around Fred, avoiding the toys in my path. I put the pan on the stove and balanced the board and onions on a bowl on the sidedresser among papers and library books.

Mac stood beside the table, lighting his pipe, the smell of smoke blending with that of raw onion. As the butter began to sizzle in the pan, I sensed that he was waiting for my attention but I had been unable to look at him since the early morning incident. He cleared his throat and I glanced his way. It seemed to be an effort for him to speak to me. He said, "I'm rock happy," and, though he looked directly at me, there was no life in his eyes. "If I'm a bastard," he said, "ignore me."

Never able to hold a grudge, I lifted my hands in a carefree gesture, said, "Okay," and turned back to the stove, at the same time knocking the chopped onion and its board flying onto the floor.

He bent dutifully to help pick up the pieces but I said, "Don't worry about them. I'll sweep them up with the brush." I hadn't really believed that Mac, himself, would suffer from rock-happiness or that it could happen on any other island but The Brothers. I began to consider the nature of this malady, and over the following few days I turned it over and over in my mind.

CHAPTER 17

The Way of the Lightservice

A rne and Cis said, "But why? There was food in our cupboards. You could have got into that. . . "

"But we would have felt like thieves. We survived all right on Weetbix and soup. . . If we'd been really starving we would have raided your kitchen." We weren't used to entering anybody's house uninvited and Cis and Arne's was equivalent to the captain's cabin. Only a major earthquake would have sent us scavenging on such hallowed ground. They looked healthy and relaxed after their holiday, and having them back on station was like a family homecoming. So much to tell. So much routine. The old hierarchy reinstated.

Pip and I didn't know when would be our next major change, and, with our house once again entirely our own, we felt free to be silly, or loving or irritable, as the mood might take us. We felt free, and on the whole I felt content. And Pip? He was in love and blissfully happy spending his spare moments caressing and scratching away at the curves of his dinghy—our dinghy.

I wondered if we might never hear from Mac again. His brief last words to me, "Thanks very much and all that," as he'd dashed in to pick up his pack, had been a formality. I couldn't help feeling as if I hadn't measured up, somehow, but I knew that two months of living in the same house together, on an island, would strain almost any relationship. On the mailday following his departure, there arrived from him a package and a length of brass strip for the keel of the dinghy. He had found time to cross the strait to the 'fleshpots' of Wellington before his next period of incarceration on The Brothers, and he had remembered to shop for us. We opened the package and found mahogany veneer for the trimaran, brass screws for the dinghy's keel, a Corning Ware coffee percolator and a bag of ground coffee to put into it. The percolator had been Mac's idea because Pip and I had always drunk instant coffee which had appeared on the market only a few years earlier. We were the first generation to become hooked on it, our parents having been totally tea drinkers, but we had read somewhere that instant coffee might cause cancer. "Good old Mac," Pip said, reading the note he had sent.

Then we read the instructions for the percolator and put it together. We had no idea how to brew real coffee from ground coffee beans. We put in nine cups of water, filled the metal basket with coffee, sat the percolator on the hot stove and waited. Soon dark liquid was spurting up beneath the glass lid. For some days, until the novelty wore off, we drank a lot of coffee. It fostered in me a mild delusion that I was becoming genteel and refined.

Refined and genteel? Such moments of delusion were far apart. As a mother, I sometimes felt myself descending into chaos. One perfectly normal evening when I was about to start the usual toothbrush routine with Fred, he clamped his mouth shut on his little white dots of teeth and wouldn't let the toothbrush inside.

"Come on. Open up your mouth, Freddy." His lips pressed closer together and he turned his face away. "Come on, Freddy. It's not a game." Perhaps it had begun as a game for him but it continued as a battle of wills, he in deadly earnest with his mouth tightly shut and saying not a word.

For me it was the end of a long day in the kitchen with the children— another long day with wind and rain smashing against the house and confining us indoors. My patience was thin. "Look here, if you don't open your mouth this minute you'll have to go to bed with *no story*. . . Right, I warned you, Freddy," and I dragged the silent, pyjama-clad little creature off to his bedroom and tried to tuck him into bed with *no story*.

The bedtime story had already become a ritual. It was the one part of this two-year-old's day during which, wherever we were, he could depend on being totally in harmony with his parents. But tonight. . . oh, how could I have been so cruel as to deprive him of this time of peace and love?

Rather than being tearful and distressed he was absolutely and quite rationally outraged. His mouth previously so tightly closed was now open and indignant. Though his vocabulary was still limited he had enough words to formulate his demand into a chant. "I want 'tory. I want play." I tucked him up firmly and turned out the light. In no time he was back in the kitchen with his chant. "I want 'tory. I want play."

I don't remember how many times we tucked him into bed again but finally we went to bed ourselves and turned out all the lights. With the arrival of their breeding season the dovies were coming in to land each night in increasing numbers. We lay listening to their squawks and gurgles. Together with the constant groaning of the wind, these were the now familiar sounds which would soothe us into sleep. But not tonight! Before long we heard the thud of little feet in the darkness, the sound of a chair being pushed across the kitchen floor, the click of a switch—and light poured through our doorway. Then a little figure at our bedside chanted again, "I want 'tory. I want play."

After trying a thousand times we gave up putting him back into bed, and, up to a point, he gave up on us. We heard him bumping around the house discovering what his toy-cupboard looked like in the deepest part of the night and every so often we heard a weird little wail, "I want 'tory". This continued until morning and when we got out of bed for the last time, at five-thirty, in time for Pip to do his weather observations and turn out the lighthouse light, Fred was still awake. He sat in a chair, now almost a zombie, murmuring every so often, "I want 'tory."

He was so determined! But, of course, I had been equally determined and hadn't given in to him and read a story—and nor had I given in to myself and smacked his bottom. At last his eyes closed. We covered him with a blanket and he slept there in the chair until almost midday while I, exhausted and half out of my mind with worry, wondered what sort of child I was rearing. I knew so little about children, really. But one thing I had learnt from my mother was that once you said, 'No,' you must stick to your word otherwise that child would have you 'twisted around his little finger' for the rest of your life.

After several hours, the changeling of the previous night awoke with a smile on his face and was hungry for his lunch. With relief, we saw that he was again his usual serious and busy little self. Perhaps, after all, he was normal—but the idea lingered in me that I was, perhaps, not a 'proper' mother.

And yet, at the same time, I still believed that I was basically a good mother and that we should have a larger family—that children in a group would be happier and better adjusted than if they were the sole objects of their parents' attention. I had confided this to Mac and his answer had been a question. "What does Pip think of that idea?" I hadn't really wanted to admit to him or to myself that Pip's opinion should have something to do with the matter of how many children he had to provide for. . . but, if they were fostered children, he wouldn't have to pay for them. . . the state would pay. . . and I would care for them. It wouldn't be a burden to him at all. I was glad that Mac wasn't there to witness that long night of no story. On the other hand, always after this, Fred opened his mouth promptly for the toothbrush ritual and, from then on, wherever we were and whatever the time of night, the children's bedtime without a story became as unthinkable to our family as a lighthouse without its light. It was to become the most orderly and peaceful part of every day.

On the hillside behind our house, daffodils were blooming in wind-chewed clusters, the grass was at its greenest, lambs were arriving to complete the spring scene and, again, we were almost bathing in milk. Heifer was giving a bucketful night and morning and, until the middle of August, our little bull calf was drinking half of this. But this calf died suddenly, of 'blackleg', Arne thought, just the same as Dave's calf had done a month earlier. We dug a hole and buried it deep, trying to annihilate the organisms that might have caused the blood poisoning. We had had sheep, too, die with similar symptoms—blood from the nostrils and, after death, a blue tinge in the armpits followed by swift putrefaction. An animal could seem to be thriving one day but be dead the next morning. Death slipped so easily among the animals that I was becoming used to their mortality. Our second cow, Tammy, had disappeared in early winter, and our fine big steer, Red, vanished a week after the death of our calf. Later in September, once the official visit of the lighthouse inspector was safely past, Arne decided to kill his steer, Blackie, before it, too, could fall over a cliff.

The beast was coaxed to stand close to the lighthouse and Arne shot it there. The men dressed and gutted it on the concrete pad and, by evening, the carcase had been hauled up to hang below the balcony.

After hanging from Friday until Tuesday it was lowered to the ground—the task made difficult by a fifty-five-knot nor'wester—and the men spent an entire day in the chill atmosphere inside the lighthouse, slicing and bagging the meat.

Pip, almost stiff with cold, came home that night with a chunk of 'best backsteak' for our dinner. "Arne says just fry it in a good hot pan and not for too long."

I had never eaten prime beefsteak before, (probably because it was so expensive), and I approached it cautiously. Pip wanted his rare. "But that's raw," I squawked. "It's still got blood running out of it." I fried mine until it was brown and crispy on the outside and I averted my eyes from Pip's plate where the pink 'blood' soaked into his mashed parsnip and carrot and boiled cabbage.

Arne had a freezer. It was his own and this was one reason why he ran the generators all and every day. There was no point in us assistants having a freezer at this stage because we would probably be transferred, eventually, to a station where the P.K. was not prepared to flout regulations to the same extent. The meat from an entire cattle beast took up a lot of room in Arne's freezer and he gave us as much beef as we could cope with over the next few days. He promised us more, but it was his beef from his own steer and it was his freezer. He made that clear to us.

Meanwhile big, black Toro, separated again from his ladies, had begun to reassert himself. He trampled fences, sprung gates and his final misdeed was to hurl three forty-four-gallon drums of fuel down the hill from the Ruston shed. Two were recovered by dint of great effort but one seemed to have completely disappeared.

It was Toro's last piece of defiance. Two days later Turi came from D'Urville Island and shot the massive bull as it stood on the road below house number two. He dismembered it and took the four great legs home on the *Belfast*. With the tractor the men pushed the huge and limbless body to the edge of the cliff and over. It was six hundred feet to the beach below, and although it was considered to be great fun to watch large objects leaping and cartwheeling down this steep face, I wasn't there to see it go. Relieved though I was that I would no longer need to fear him, I felt sad that this great and mighty beast should come to such an ignominious and undignified end.

But not all our animal stories were tragedies. Pip brought home a tiny lamb whose dying mother he had had to kill and bury, and we raised it as a pet. Because none of us had had the forethought to have a lamb's rubber teat in stock, we taught it to drink from a bowl, with a finger in its mouth at first, in the same way that we taught calves to drink from a bucket. It was Pip's lamb, (because I had human babies to care for), and it followed him everywhere.

Although it would have been totally imprudent to have had the carcase of Blackie, the steer, swaying from the balcony of the tower on the day of the lighthouse inspector's visit, the arrival of this particular lighthouse inspector was, on the whole, something to look forward to. Billy Kemp's image didn't fit with his title. He was more like a clown than an inspector. First and foremost we all agreed that he was 'a real wag'. Humour tumbled out of him constantly and irrepressibly and he kept us all spellbound with a continuous stream of stories. He was small, bright-eyed, birdlike, even slighter in stature than Pip. And although, at first, I had been wary of him because of his love of beer and his interest in all the masculine pursuits such as rugby and horse racing, I had been quickly drawn in by his warmth.

His expression could change in an instant. Wearing the face of an undertaker he might regale us with a tale of past disaster such as death by drowning or accident on distant lightstations where windswept graves remained as the only reminder. He might finish the story with a solemn shake of his head, "It was a sad business. A sad business." Then, always with perfect timing, after allowing us a moment of silent contemplation, an imp would take over his face, his hand would go to the side of his mouth, and, casting a side-glance that encompassed and captured everyone in the room, he'd say, "Have you heard the one about. . . ?" Like a fiddler, he had us rocking to whatever tune he chose. I couldn't imagine him ever speaking ill of anyone—unless, perhaps, they thoroughly deserved it.

Pip and I had looked forward to his coming because we'd met him twice before. As the lighthouse inspector he had been on the interviewing panel at the Marine Department's head office when we'd applied for the job, and it was he who had slipped us a wink, before we'd departed, and told us we'd be on our way in no time. But we had met him once before this when he, himself, had been a lighthouse keeper—and already something of a legend.

This meeting had taken place a few months before Pip and I were married, when the only ring I sported on my finger was the one worth four new tyres for the Landrover. We had gone for a weekend visit to the light station at Baring Head, the lighthouse which can be seen from the Cook Strait ferry, on the right as it turns to enter Wellington Harbour. We had been invited to come with them by friends of friends of Pip's sister who were friends of friends of some relative of Bill and Kitty Kemp.

Bill and Kitty and their several children, who, at that time, had ranged in age from about three to twelve, had been completely undisturbed by the arrival of enough unexpected guests to play cricket against them on the lawn. I knew I would always remember the green of that lawn, the whiteness of the buildings and the bright red of their roofs—the lighthouse itself adding its romance to the scene, and the ring on my finger a symbol of promise for our future. Later I had gone with Kitty and the younger children to throw scraps to the fowls, and then the whole tribe of grubby-footed children had led us down a cliffside path to visit a gull colony. At home again they had shown us their collection of artifacts and treasures. That night Kitty had fed us all and we had sat around for hours listening to Billy the entertainer. When we left the next day he had told us quite seriously that, after we'd been married a few years, lighthouse keeping would be 'just the job' for us.

Having heard his stories and met his family we couldn't believe otherwise. And yet we had almost forgotten about it for the first two years of our marriage until, one day while picnicking at a wild and remote beach, we had heard gulls mewing and wave-sound echoing upward over rocky bluffs, and then I had remembered and said, "If we were a lighthouse family it would be like this every day!" And after that we had thought of nothing else.

Now I saw that Billy Kemp, the lighthouse inspector, was as funny, as good humoured and as kind to his far-flung flock of lighthouse staff as Billy Kemp, the lighthouse keeper, had been to his tribe of unexpected guests that weekend we had spent at Baring Head. He came to us on Stephens Island on the *Belfast* one Saturday in September. That night we all dined at Number one house, the P.K's house, and sat up so late eating and drinking and listening to stories that we didn't go home but stayed where we were, drifting in and out of sleep for an hour or two before breakfast. I found it odd to be still in Cis and Arne's house at that time of morning but they were gracious hosts as always.

Arne lent Pip his bucket to milk the cow into and, then, after saying goodbye to everyone, we put Helen and Fred into Arne's barrow and wheeled them home feeling strangely exhausted but as happy as if we had spent the night at some sort of pageant.

Bill Kemp was like that. He seemed to bring out the best in people by showing them, with his stories and jokes, that the world was a better place than they had thought. We suspected that, as a lighthouse inspector, he had no trouble in gauging the mood of personnel on a station when he visited. That was his job, of course, to travel around the country making sure the stations were running smoothly. In fact, when he dashed to our door on Monday morning and knocked and said a polite and hasty good-bye, "I'm off now, Janet, good to meet you again. . . " his amazingly bright blue eyes were probably still sizing me up in relation to the job and telling him to which station it would be appropriate to send us next. He was probably already looking for the next family to transfer to Dog Island, that tiny island in Foveaux Strait where they were going to have to do some juggling—perhaps to shift the P.K. and promote the assistant on station. It was a two-man station and it would be best if the newly promoted P.K. could start out with a compatible assistant. We knew nothing about this yet, but those eyes of Bill's, at once so shrewd and humorous and yet so serious, were probably already telling him that the right family for the next transfer to little Dog Island could possibly be us.

During those months of spring, the men's work on station continued as usual. They had gravel and cement to bring up from the landing in preparation for the work on the trolley line. They worked on the road filling in washouts and putting in drainage pipes. Bill Wellington came out again to check all the station's machinery, particularly the generators. The Ministry of Works men came from Nelson with new parts for the tractor which had been out of order again. A new motor was brought out for the crane. A party from the Wildlife Department arrived and Pip spent an evening with them, catching and measuring tuatara and putting identification bands on the legs of dovies.

Cis must have enjoyed having boarders because, still, none of the visitors stayed at our house—and I hardly saw them. I was particularly envious of Pip's getting to know the people studying the wildlife. That same week, ten girls from my old school, Nelson College for Girls, came out for a day and clambered around the perimeter of our yard, searching for tuatara as I stood beneath the clothesline hanging out the day's wash. I looked toward them hopefully with a smile waiting to break out at the first sign of friendliness, but not one of them looked in my direction for more than an instant. Tuatara were much more absorbing for them than the everyday sight of a woman and her washing and as they exclaimed and clustered around their finds I felt more remote from these real flesh and blood young women than I did from the smiling printed models in Cis's *Burda* fashion magazines.

Listening as their chatter and laughter faded away into the distant silence of the fresh spring air, I was swept by a feeling of desolation so complete that I couldn't deny it—would always remember it as an unmistakable feeling of outright loneliness so awful that I wanted to cry—standing there among the hanging sheets and towels with the sun shining more brightly than it had shone for days and Fred beside me happily driving his already rusty pedal car. But there was nothing to cry about because everything was the same as before, and we didn't get lonely on a lighthouse, did we—no, not ever. It was the last thing I could admit to.

With all the comings and goings, Dad had taken the opportunity to visit again. He had made friends with one of the Ministry of Works men, Peter Gorrie, ("a really sound chap"), who kept him in touch with their planned trips from Nelson to the island via French Pass. It was Dad's fifth visit and he stayed almost two weeks. By now he knew the island as well as any of us and was always gathering snippets to tell his neighbours and acquaintances back home. His dear, knotty old face crumpled with pleasure at the sight of his dinghy stripped to the bare boards and ready for undercoating. Pip had unscrewed the brass nameplate and filed off its surface so that the embossed words, 'Val Pollard, Builder, Riwaka', were shiny and bold against a painted background. This little detail was a sure sign to Dad that the dinghy was in good hands. "Aw, you're making a job of her. She'll be like new!" he said. He watched as Pip fitted three ring bolts—one at the bow and two at the stern—so that she could be suspended by rope from the crane during launching. We felt summer approaching and looked forward to the time when our dinghy would carry us around to the beaches and out to catch fish.

Yes, warm weather was just around the corner. We had planted up our garden with peas and beans, lettuce, brussels sprouts and cabbage. As Pip put the finishing touches to the dinghy on 4 October he realised he had been on Stephens Island exactly one year. It was a year since he had left me behind in Nelson, waiting to have the baby. In some ways, in that one year, we had come to feel that this special island belonged to us and that we were bound to have another year ahead of us before it was our turn for a transfer.

We gloated over the glossy curves of our dinghy. "It *is* just like new," I breathed. "Dad'll be so pleased to see it when he comes again." We stood admiring her for a long time—Pip proud of the job he had done on her and I pleased and proud of him for his effort. Only one thing stopped us from launching her. Pip said he would first build her a shed. Just a small one, it would be up near the Lister turntable. Arne kept his boat at the landing behind the place where the trolley came to rest, and there was no room there for another.

Now, after work, Pip spent his time chipping away at the layered rock where his shed was to be. Within a week he had carved out a big enough hole and he sorted through timber and corrugated iron stored in The Palace since the demolition of the old schoolhouse. As he went up and down to the Lister shed he combined his journeys with official station work. On Monday he brought up twenty-five bags of gravel, on Tuesday the concrete mixer, on Wednesday another twenty-five bags of gravel and on Thursday another twenty. Because Edna and Brian had left the station for a two-week break, Arne and Pip were 'working the station two-man'. As this meant they each had to do alternate days of weather duties, Arne was being particularly lenient about working hours. By Saturday evening Pip had finished his little shed. Now let the good weather come!

On Sunday we worked together in the gardens, mowed lawns and burnt rubbish. In the evening we made six pounds of butter. At two shillings and sixpence a pound in the shops that would be a saving of fifteen shillings—except that we must stop thinking in pounds, shillings and pence because, during the winter, the whole country had changed to decimal currency. Next time we went out to town, whenever that might be, everything would be different.

But that trip to town was much closer than we knew, and this was to be our last day of normality for some time. The telegram arrived via the radio as usual. It told us we were to be transferred to Dog Island, a tiny little dot in Foveaux Strait, three miles out from the port of Bluff. We had known from the start that we were all like chess pieces waiting to be moved at the whim of the Department—that this was the way of the lightservice—but our shift had come sooner than we'd expected and for a while we were dizzy with astonishment. We had only four weeks left.

In the ensuing frenzy, Helen's first birthday passed almost unnoticed. Pip brought all our chests and boxes up from The Palace and, by the time Brian and Edna returned from their break, our packing was under way. The whole house had to be scoured. I thought I had kept it clean but now we washed down walls and ceilings and the darkest corners of cupboards. Cis and Edna both helped me by looking after Fred and Helen. During the preceding two months we had begun to paint, first the fire surround and mantelpiece, then the floor of the porch and, latterly, the kitchen cupboards. Then I had begun to rub down the walls and ceiling. Now, although that area looked a mess, it would have to stay that way. Everything had come to a standstill for me except for cleaning and packing.

CHAPTER 18

Looking Back, Moving On

Soon we would be en route to Dog Island. Arne and Cis were the experts and had answered all our questions. It was windswept, tiny— "just a seagull splat on the ocean". Not even thirty feet at its highest point. It was the lowest lighthouse island but it had the tallest tower. At one hundred and seventeen feet, massive! Stephens Island's tower at only fifty feet would look a baby beside it. But Stephens was the highest light above sea level. We were going from the highest island to the lowest. . . Ever since receiving the telegram the everyday thoughts to do with the ongoing routine of our life had given way to speculation about what was ahead, which led, in turn, to a summing up of what lay behind. . .

The mere fact of our leaving the island again set my mind racing and planning. I had once imagined I'd be able to live in this idyllic place without ever wanting to leave, but now I knew better. The purity of my dream about spending my life in splendid isolation had been frequently marred by a dull hankering for the things of the world I had left behind. It was a weakness, of course, which I mustn't allow, yet I had to admit, to myself at least, that living in isolation had brought its own pressures. I would never give in to them. It was simply a case of developing a positive attitude. When the sameness of everything got to me I would sit down and create something. When the lack of stimulation left me feeling dull and dead I'd go for a walk and remind myself how good the world could be. When I felt I would never be able to escape, because raising children was a life-sentence, I would give everything I had and more—and make it my vocation.

And now a new island lay waiting for us. On the one hand I loved it here and had never wanted to leave. We hadn't had nearly long enough to explore and appreciate Stephens Island. Summer would have brought picnics and underwater swimming. . . But on the other hand, after six months without a break, the prospect of leaving brought picture-flashes to me of ferries and buses and cities and people and gardens with flowers and trees, shops where you could just walk in and buy things. . . I'd dress up and go into town and show the children off.

Always ahead of me now I saw the stirring picture of that other island. Its huge lighthouse, the southern seas—cold, inhospitable and beckoning. As a two-man lighthouse it'd have only two keepers, two families, and be perhaps lonelier than Stephens Island. And Dad would have the entire length of the South Island to negotiate before visiting us. I felt badly about going so far from him—but that was the way of the service, and he was in good health (better than he'd ever been), and he enjoyed travelling. He seemed to have gained a new lease on life since he'd been coming to the island.

It was a long way south. For some reason our gear would take at least two weeks to travel by rail, but the waiting period would be a bonus holiday for us. We could hardly believe how lucky we were. We'd have two weeks on the mainland and be paid to do nothing! It wouldn't even be classed as official leave. This job was certainly one of the world's best kept secrets. The Department would even book us into a motel or hotel but we didn't want that. We'd use the time to visit our families. With Invercargill's being so far away we felt we might hardly see them over the next few years. So we'd visit Masterton, and Wellington (where we'd call in at Head Office as was the custom for lighthouse people passing through), then Nelson. But the first stop would be Picton. Dear little Picton!

Picton. I could see it in my mind. It hadn't changed much since I'd first seen it. It had had the 'roll on roll off' ferry for about five years, now, instead of the old *Tamahine* which had done the job for decades. The giant *Aramoana* had made it much easier to move between the North and South Islands. But Picton was still much the same pretty little seaside town surrounded by hills that I'd seen on my first holiday away from the Nelson district—and that had been in 1954 when I'd been not quite eleven years old. Now I was twenty-four.

My thoughts slipped easily back over the Picton I'd seen then. I could see my younger cousin and me on the wharf beside my uncle and aunt. I could smell the mix of salt and fish and diesel oil. I could feel myself right there with my cousin looking up at a huge overseas ship, a wall of red, secured by ropes thicker than my uncle's arms. And further away was the Cook Strait ferry, much smaller and black (or had it been dark green?) waiting to gobble up cars fed to it by crane. Gulls perched on the shiny oval tops of iron bollards and my uncle made the same tired old joke about catching the birds by sprinkling salt on their tails. My aunt said she had a 'head like a pumpkin' and wanted to return to the camping ground. They left us at the roller-skating rink near the foreshore. I sat next to my little cousin. Both of us in tartan skirts, knitted 'jumpers' and socks with sandals. Both with hair-ribbons on each side of our mud-blond heads. We watched the local kids chasing one another around, laughing and teasing. There were two girls my own age, Maori girls with little sisters and brothers in tow. They glided like princesses, metal wheels roaring and grinding over the smooth concrete, bubble gum popping in mini balloons from their pursed lips. I had never seen bubble gum before. Never seen a skating rink.

My uncle came with a newspaper package under his arm and we left the rink to eat fish and chips on the foreshore, feeding the gulls and watching the boats. Later we walked across to the railway yards. We had never seen a train before. Never seen a railway track. My uncle got talking with a driver and soon we found ourselves hoisted up onto an engine which was about to shunt carriages around the yard. The engine was open and everything in it was black. The shunting process involved a lot of rumbling and clanging and bumping. Then, when the engine driver finally handed us down, my uncle said what lucky girls we were. "You'll have to be telling all the kids at school that you rode in the engine of a train," said my uncle. I couldn't think why I'd have to be telling them about such a boring thing.

All this had happened so long ago. A little more than half a lifetime for me, and I thought, now, how strange it was that, of all the memories I had from that holiday, the one which still whipped up my imagination most was something much more fleeting than the romance of the skating rink or the wharves or the shunting engine. It was, in fact, the old woman I had seen for only a few seconds from the window of a train two days later. Thinking about it, now, made me ponder the nature of people's fantasies and dreams and where they might lead them in life. Why should my uncle have imagined that a ride in an engine would be the most exciting thing in the world for a child? And why would my little cousin have been obsessed with bride-dolls and pictures of the royal family while I'd dreamed up a game called 'Lost' and become captivated by the image of the lighthouse heroine, Grace Darling, and later let myself be half haunted by the image of the lone old woman I had seen so briefly from the window of a train?

In my memory it seemed that the train had slowed a little. Perhaps it was negotiating a bend. My aunt was with us on this journey, giving us a 'real' train ride in a carriage in the middle of a snake-line of carriages and I had known we weren't bound for anywhere in particular. My uncle was meeting us at a station further down the line. The journey was 'just for the experience'. First we had looked into people's back yards. Had seen their cats and dogs and children and clotheslines—scenes quite different from those caught when travelling by road. Then we had wound through the countryside.

And that's where I'd glimpsed her. In the middle of nowhere with not a proper house for miles, it seemed. She was an old woman, her grey hair wild, all alone with an armful of firewood and about to enter a hut. It had been a tiny hut. Like a play hut. One room, I was sure. There couldn't have been space in it for more than one person. Perhaps she'd had a cat? But how did she live? I'd shivered then. This surely was the pinnacle of challenge—to live like that—to be alone with yourself, and happy with nobody else for miles. For years this scene had lingered at the back of my mind, prickling me. Perhaps in the same way that Pip and Mac might have been prickled at the sight of the seemingly unreachable peak of a snow-covered mountain. I shivered again now. This time for the sake of the unknown old woman. Perhaps she hadn't been happy? Perhaps she'd been grimly holding on in the face of all odds. . . But still I could see myself, sixty years hence, living in a tiny hut and knowing how to hold on and being happy to 'make do'.

For now, boxes and trunks had taken charge of my life. Because of the risk of damage by water and rough handling, I took great care. First I'd packed books, lining the boxes with plastic then newspaper. They'd have to survive a 'surfboat landing'. Whatever the reality of that, it sounded wet. In my mind I saw white water sweeping an open boat towards a small rocky island. I saw myself gripping the children while strong men tried to steer us to safety. But we'd been told Dog Island had an airstrip of sorts. It wasn't finished but could be used by small planes. Perhaps we wouldn't be in the surfboat at all.

And of course the weather couldn't always be bad. There'd be calm days, even in Foveaux Strait. After we'd settled in we'd be able to launch our beautiful dinghy which we hadn't even time to try out now we were leaving Stephens Island. Arne and Cis said the fishing was great down south. You could catch trumpeter three feet long. They said there were beds of paua around the whole island and they said we could gather pieces of a special little seaweed which washed up during storms. If we dried it on racks, the custard factory would pay us good money for a sackful. We found ourselves looking forward with greater and greater excitement, and at the same time we were letting go of Stephens Island. There couldn't possibly be any cliffs on Dog Island. And, now that we'd heard from the outgoing keeper, we knew there was no cow— so there'd be no bull either. But no cow meant no fresh milk or cream. We'd thought all light stations kept a cow. Still, we might be there only a year, the same as our stay on Stephens. And where might we end up after that?

One day we'd be the P.K.'s family. I couldn't visualise myself ever being as capable as Cis or all those other amazing women that Mac had talked about. Sometimes we'd heard gossip about one or two P.K's wives who 'wore the pants' and were called 'Mrs. P.K.' behind their backs. It was a shameful thing to be Mrs. P.K. with lighthouse folk whispering about you from one end of the country to another. It would be shameful enough to be known as a wife who wore the pants.

As our house became less and less our own I wondered who would live in it next. Its previous tenants had come and gone, leaving no trace of themselves. The others had never mentioned our predecessors and it was almost as if there had been none. Then we heard that the next people had two little girls and a baby so we decided to leave the cot behind for them. Helen had become so agile that she'd be safer in an ordinary bed. Since she'd begun to walk she had changed from a baby into a little girl. A bandy-legged little thing covered in bruises who climbed up and over anything in her path. Now she was always either falling headfirst into an empty box or climbing up on a full one and tumbling off. "If she survives," I joked proudly to anyone who'd listen, "she'll be climbing mountains by her fifth birthday."

Fred 'helped' me to pack, too. To him every box was a boat. Boats brought stuff to us. They carried us hither and thither. It was natural that a small lighthouse boy would become boat-crazy. Much as I believed that the differences between the sexes were largely induced by society I couldn't help but see that Fred had a natural aptitude for things that were considered 'masculine'. Each day he 'helped' screw the lids down onto boxes and I was reminded of my mother's amazement when, aged only nine months, he had screwed plastic nuts to plastic bolts as easily as would a two-year-old. His serious nature stood him in good stead. He'd watch quietly and intently, his long-lashed, brown-green eyes absorbing everything. I wanted to tell everyone how clever and beautiful my children were, but that wasn't the thing to do. Besides, I'd heard that the Chinese would never boast about their children lest malevolent spirits were listening. It sounded like a wise precaution.

At the beginning of our last week we left Fred and Helen with Edna and went for a walk. It was mid-afternoon, the sun already gaining its summer heat, grass and vines moving at our approach as brown skinks flicked out of sight. I hadn't seen much sun lately and I wondered if maybe there hadn't been much to see. With the pace of our cleaning and packing and last-minute gardening about to become frantic, this walk would be our last on the island. On the top ridge I spread my arms out. "Goodbye Island," I sang. "Goodbye, tuataras. Goodbye frogs that I've never even seen." A little breeze carried my voice away over the western side.

I leaned further back and looked up at big soft clouds chasing each other overhead and felt a stillness stealing over me. "I'll be glad when the week's over," I said. "All this scrubbing and packing-up's a bit of a picnic. At least we know it'll all be finished by boat day, whatever happens."

"We probably *are* going overboard a bit with the cleaning," Pip ventured.

"We have to. Remember those people we were told about. It's a wonder their light shades didn't fall down and kill someone, they were that thick with dust? Stories like that follow you around for years in this job." Pip was silent and I carried on. "At any rate I'd like to leave everything right for the next people. We'd want someone to do the same for us."

Ahead of us a hawk flew up. Quite close. Yellow feet dangling, brown feathers whitened by age.

"He knew a nice sheltered spot to sit," Pip said. "Shall we make use of it ourselves?" We flopped down into the springy cushion of muehlenbeckia vines—mingi mingi, we called it.

Unable to lie quiet I propped myself up on one elbow and looked down past the old radar station toward the lighthouse. "I wonder if we'll ever come back here." We both stared out towards the horizon, thinking our own thoughts, but suddenly my eyes focused on something close to me. Something red and glistening about the size of a pea. It was scarlet against the green of a leaf and it was moving. "What on earth is that?"

We bent towards it, watching the slow throbbing of this tiny thing, all alone on its leaf. "There's blood." Pip pointed to two little splashes on nearby leaves.

"And a foot!" I whispered, pointing to the lifeless foot and lower-leg of a skink which lay, with its scaly toes curled, a few inches away. Now I recognised that little red glistening palpitating plum. "It's a heart. That hawk! How long can a heart beat like that all by itself?"

We stared at this bizarre last dance. "The heart," I whispered. "It must be designed to keep on beating, no matter what."

We watched it slow and die, this already dead thing, and in no time its surface had begun to glaze in the heat of the sun.

I became conscious of two dark-gold eyes, and, from only an arm's length away, I saw, facing me, a middle-sized female tuatara, chin in the air above puffed up gullet pouch, a front foot either side below. Expressionless, motionless in a cavity where the vines met the earth.

I pointed. "See that little toot watching us."

Pip said soberly, "Soon there'll be no more toots for us."

"They have them on some of the lightstations up north."

"Not like here, though. This is their stronghold."

"I wonder," I said. "This is an amazing place but I wonder sometimes. I wonder if it's going to be okay. It's been wrecked, really, by the lighthouse keepers over the years. I wonder if it's a bit like that heart. Still beating. Still trying to keep going when its soul's been ripped apart. . ."

"I reckon you're getting a bit carried away there." Pip was laughing at me. "The tuataras are all right. There are thousands of them. There's plenty of lizards and things. You wonder too much."

"I know I do," I said. "But only to you."

He rolled over in the mingi mingi away from the tiny pathetic remains of the hawk's meal. I stood up and looked down at him. "Kids'd love this stuff," he said, joyfully somersaulting backwards on the tangle of vines.

I dived after him. "It's like a great big springy bed!" He grabbed me and I lay with my head on his arm, the cleaning and packing and everything else seeming as though it were a million miles away.

A couple of days before our departure, Pip took our dinghy to the landing and tied it down on the block. "It's as secure as I can make it. I don't like it being there with the weather getting worse but I can't do much else, really."

That night there was a terrible storm, coupled with a high tide. We lay awake listening to the screeching wind, and, at daylight, Pip fled to the landing.

On his return I knew as soon as I looked into his eyes. And those eyes cried real tears as he told me. The sea, a massive tide with wind and enormous waves, had swept the block and thrashed the shiny little dinghy half to pieces. "It's wrecked! Its ribs are broken. Its planks have been wracked and twisted. There's a big chunk ripped right out of the stern."

Standing in the derelict-looking kitchen, surrounded by packed boxes waiting for their lids to be fully screwed down, I hugged him close. "Will you be able to fix it?"

"No, it's ruined. I'll be able to patch it up but it'll never be the same." His voice quivered into nothing.

Staring past his bent head, I thought about how we had worried that the fresh, new paint might suffer at the mercy of the railways on its long journey south to Dog Island, and my eyes cried, too. Not only for the precious little dinghy which had been so much a part of my childhood, but for Dad who had been so happy that it was in good hands, and for Pip whose hands had so willingly taken responsibility for it. My tears were for them both, my best loved men. . . for their disappointment and their smashed-up dream.

But on we went with the last of the packing. Mattresses folded over, wrapped in sheets of black plastic, taped, then sewn inside sacking bags. Everything even better sealed and packed than the year before, because a surfboat sounded even more threatening than landing by crane.

"I don't really want to go out to dinner, tonight," I muttered tiredly. But of course we must because this would be the time of saying goodbye to the others. My hands were dry from my ardour with Ajax. The floor polisher had been run over the floor for the last time and now was packed away in its box. There wasn't a speck of dust in the house. We were ready to walk out and shut the door and nobody would ever say that my lightshades might fall down and kill someone. I felt like a cleaning rag myself, all worn out and falling into holes.

I don't know why I should have been so surprised and overwhelmed by the dinner party that followed. Cis and Edna had decided it should be at number two house. Everyone had joined forces to fête us on our way and after the rigours of the past week something melted inside me. I felt surrounded: Cis and Arne, Edna and Brian, and the children: Anthony, Ken and Gavin—all so warm and cheerful and the adults so openly sorry that we were leaving. What had we done to deserve such a send-off? Surely we'd never again be with such good people.

I looked fondly at Edna. With her, for the first time, I'd been able to relax and share with another woman some of the realities of bringing up children. "And you know," she'd said to me, "I'd try to make that poor little boy pick up and put away every one of his blocks, and he was barely two years old. . . " And hearing her say that I'd felt able to tell about the time I'd tried to force Fred to pick up every clothes peg and put it back into the bucket he'd overturned. He hadn't even been much more than one year old and I'd kept putting the pegs into his hand and smacking it when he'd dropped them. It hadn't worked, of course, and I'd ended up picking up the pegs myself and hating myself for trying to force him. That night Fred had had a nightmare. And I was sure that the demon that frightened him must have been his mother. Every time he had a nightmare after that I seemed to be able to trace it to some altercation we'd had. To know that Edna, too, had sometimes fallen short of being the perfect mother had made me think that one day she and I might become real friends. But there was no chance of that now. None at all.

And Cis, too. In some ways, looking back, it was surprising how little we'd really seen of each other in a year. I remembered a few shared morning teas, occasional picnics, and two or three dinners together. Earlier in the year, once (and only once) I'd asked Cis and Arne to dinner, had spent all day preparing it. But Arne had rung at the last minute (less than an hour before we'd expected to be sitting down to a meal together with them), and said would we mind very much if they didn't come. Not come? After all my work and planning and anticipation? And with everything extra-special in their honour? I had said I wouldn't mind at all.

But I had minded very much indeed. Pip and I could have fed a dozen orphans in our kitchen that evening as we'd waded through the menu alone. In the absence of any explanation from Cis or Arne, I'd wondered if I'd done something wrong—or whether, in fact, they simply didn't like us enough to want to dine at our place. We hadn't dared to invite them to dinner again. That they'd subsequently never mentioned the matter or felt it necessary to offer us any reassurance had made it clear to me that there were social boundaries that couldn't be breached.

But tonight I could see that everybody was genuinely sorry to see us go. They piled our plates with food and said we all must keep in touch and that we'd been the very best of people to be on station with. We felt loved and appreciated, and, blinking away tears at the thought of leaving, I wished we'd been able to be this open with each other all along. But I saw that somehow we'd had to maintain a little bit of reserve and dignity as a form of protection in case things had turned sour. I suspected that, up to a point, this would have to be the way things always were on a lightstation—unless, of course, you could believe in yourself enough to be totally open with everyone.

When the evening was over we wrapped our children in blankets and carried them to the relieving keepers' quarters next to the lighthouse. There we laid them, still sleeping, in unfamiliar beds, and before long zipped ourselves into our sleeping bags in the same room. For the first time (but not the last), we could see, from our bedroom window, the light from the lighthouse wheeling like the arms of God across the world of night outside.

Through half-open eyes and with thoughts drifting I watched the great lens assembly turning in the tower, saw the splashes of light which were flying dovies, felt the regular passage of those guiding beams like the beating of a heart within me. We were keepers of the light. The light kept us. This was where a real lighthouse family should live—somewhere within sight of the tower.

"Are you awake?" I whispered to Pip.

He gave a small grunt.

"On Dog Island we'll live close to the lighthouse."

An even smaller grunt.

"It would be fun to live right inside the lighthouse, wouldn't it."

But by this time the lighthouse keeper's wife was the only person left awake.